Hands-On Cloud-Native Microservices with Jakarta EE

Build scalable and reactive microservices with Docker, Kubernetes, and OpenShift

Luigi Fugaro
Mauro Vocale

BIRMINGHAM - MUMBAI

Hands-On Cloud-Native Microservices with Jakarta EE

Commissioning Editor: Aaron Lazar
Acquisition Editor: Alok Dhuri
Content Development Editor: Zeeyan Pinheiro
Technical Editor: Sabaah Navlekar
Copy Editor: Safis Editing
Project Coordinator: Vaidehi Sawant
Proofreader: Safis Editing
Indexer: Rekha Nair
Graphics: Alishon Mendonsa
Production Coordinator: Aparna Bhagat

First published: January 2019

Production reference: 1310119

Published by Packt Publishing Ltd.
Livery Place
35 Livery Street
Birmingham
B3 2PB, UK.

ISBN 978-1-78883-786-6

www.packtpub.com

Contributors

About the authors

Luigi Fugaro's first encounter with computers was in the early 80s when he was a kid. He started with a Commodore Vic-20, passing through a Sinclair, a Commodore 64, and an Atari ST 1040, where he spent days and nights giving breath mints to Otis. In 1998, he started his career as a webmaster doing HTML, JavaScript, Applets, and some graphics with Paint Shop Pro. He then switched to Delphi, Visual Basic, and then started working on Java projects. He has been developing all kinds of web applications, dealing with backend and frontend frameworks. In 2012, he started working for Red Hat and is now an architect in the EMEA Middleware team.

He has authored *WildFly Cookbook* and *Mastering JBoss Enterprise Application Platform 7* by Packt Publishing.

Mauro Vocale was born on March 25, 1980 in Venaria Reale, Italy. He started to work in Java and Linux OS in 2001. He is a passionate open source developer, and he is excited to be working for a company like Red Hat as a middleware consultant since November 2015. He is a Certified Oracle Master Java SE 6 Developer, Oracle EJB, and Web Component Developer for JEE 6 and JBoss EAP 7 administration.

As a consultant, he has the opportunity to implement enterprise applications in many different scenarios and, like many IT people, he takes big enterprise companies through the journey of digital transformation and microservices adoption.
He was the official reviewer of *Mastering JBoss Enterprise Application Platform 7*, published by Packt Publishing.

About the reviewer

Sebastian Daschner is a Java freelancer working as a consultant and trainer, and is enthusiastic about programming and Java (EE). He participates in the JCP, helping to form future Java EE standards, serving in the JSR 370 and 374 Expert Groups, and collaborating on various open source projects. For his contributions to the Java community and ecosystem, he was recognized with the titles Java Champion and Oracle Developer Champion.

Sebastian is a regular speaker at international IT conferences, such as JavaLand, JavaOne, and Jfokus. He won the JavaOne Rockstar award at JavaOne 2016. Together with Java community manager, Steve Chin, he has traveled to dozens of conferences and Java User Groups on his motorbike. Steve and Sebastian have launched JOnsen, a Java conference held at a hot spring in the countryside of Japan.

Packt is searching for authors like you

If you're interested in becoming an author for Packt, please visit `authors.packtpub.com` and apply today. We have worked with thousands of developers and tech professionals, just like you, to help them share their insight with the global tech community. You can make a general application, apply for a specific hot topic that we are recruiting an author for, or submit your own idea.

`mapt.io`

Mapt is an online digital library that gives you full access to over 5,000 books and videos, as well as industry leading tools to help you plan your personal development and advance your career. For more information, please visit our website.

Why subscribe?

- Spend less time learning and more time coding with practical eBooks and videos from over 4,000 industry professionals

- Improve your learning with Skill Plans built especially for you

- Get a free eBook or video every month

- Mapt is fully searchable

- Copy and paste, print, and bookmark content

Packt.com

Did you know that Packt offers eBook versions of every book published, with PDF and ePub files available? You can upgrade to the eBook version at `www.packt.com` and as a print book customer, you are entitled to a discount on the eBook copy. Get in touch with us at `customercare@packtpub.com` for more details.

At `www.packt.com`, you can also read a collection of free technical articles, sign up for a range of free newsletters, and receive exclusive discounts and offers on Packt books and eBooks.

Table of Contents

Preface

Businesses today are evolving rapidly, and developers now face the challenge of building applications that are resilient, flexible, and native to the cloud. To achieve this, you'll need to be aware of the environment, tools, and resources that you're coding against. This beginner's guide will help you take your first steps toward building cloud-native architectures in Jakarta EE.

This book will begin by introducing you to cloud-native architecture and simplifying the major concepts. You'll learn how to build microservices in Jakarta EE using MicroProfile with Thorntail and Narayana **Long Running Actions** (**LRAs**). You'll then delve into cloud-native application X-rays, and we'll explore the MicroProfile specification and the implementation and testing of microservices. As you progress further, you'll focus on continuous integration and continuous delivery, in addition to learning how to Dockerize your services. The concluding chapters will help you grasp how to deploy microservices to different target environments using Docker and how to get ready for the cloud. You'll also cover concepts and techniques related to security, monitoring, and troubleshooting problems that might occur with applications after you've written them.

By the end of this book, you will be equipped with the skills you need to build highly resilient applications using a cloud-native microservice architecture.

Who this book is for

This book is for developers with basic knowledge of Java EE and HTTP-based application principles who want to learn how to build, test, and scale Java EE microservices. No prior experience of writing microservices in Java EE is required.

What this book covers

Chapter 1, *Jakarta EE – the New Open Source Life of Java EE*, describes the evolution of the Java SE and Java EE platforms in order to help you to quickly become useful in the new cloud ecosystem. We will discuss Jakarta EE (the new Java EE) and the possible future of Java EE.

Chapter 2, *Microservices and Reactive Architecture*, describes what a microservice is and explains its basic principles. We will describe the differences between a monolithic application and a microservice application. In this chapter, we will also become familiar with the principles and API of the MicroProfile initiative.

Chapter 3, *Cloud-Native Applications*, describes the concepts and the paradigm of writing an application that's ready for the cloud. We will describe the meaning of a cloud-native application, microservices, and the Twelve-Factor App methodology. We will focus on the design and the implications for both software and architectures.

Chapter 4, *Building Microservices Using Thorntail*, discusses how to create a distributed microservice architecture using the Jakarta EE and MicroProfile specifications, along with with Thorntail. It covers a basic example of a microservice architecture built on top of Thorntail, an implementation of the MicroProfile and Java EE specifications.

Chapter 5, *Eclipse MicroProfile and Transaction – Narayana LRA*, explains how to implement and handle transactions in a microservice architecture, in particular regarding the aspects related to **atomicity, consistency, isolation, durability (ACID)**, **Extended Architecture (XA)** transaction, application compensations, and the saga pattern. We will implement an example of handling transactions using Narayana.

Chapter 6, *Linux Containers*, discusses the concept of Linux containers, using the Docker image format. We will learn how to implement a Docker file, and how to build and run a Docker image.

Chapter 7, *Platform as a Service*, describes the main use of the OpenShift **Platform as a Service (PaaS)**. We will also describe how PaaS can get the best out of technologies such as Docker and Kubernetes. We will also describe how to move your microservice architecture onto the cloud.

Chapter 8, *Microservices Patterns*, won't describe the complete lists of patterns to use with the microservices approach, but we will concentrate on the most commonly used ones to get you started and interested in the topic of patterns.

`Chapter 9`, *Deployment*, explains how to decompose an application and let our microservice architecture take shape from it. We will implement patterns with a testing application.

`Chapter 10`, *Monitoring*, explains how to monitor your microservice architecture, benefiting from our PaaS. We will also describe and use Grafana to provide an additional monitoring system.

`Chapter 11`, *Building Microservices Using Spring Boot 2*, explains how to create, through Spring Boot, the same microservices that were developed in the previous chapters.

`Chapter 12`, *Building Microservices Using Vert.X*, explains how to realize, through Vert.x, the same microservices developed in the previous chapters.

To get the most out of this book

Readers are required to have some knowledge of Java EE and HTTP-based application principles.

Specific installation instructions are given in the respective chapter's README file in their respective folders on GitHub.

Download the example code files

You can download the example code files for this book from your account at `www.packt.com`. If you purchased this book elsewhere, you can visit `www.packt.com/support` and register to have the files emailed directly to you.

You can download the code files by following these steps:

1. Log in or register at `www.packt.com`.
2. Select the **SUPPORT** tab.
3. Click on **Code Downloads & Errata**.
4. Enter the name of the book in the **Search** box and follow the onscreen instructions.

Once the file is downloaded, please make sure that you unzip or extract the folder using the latest version of:

- WinRAR/7-Zip for Windows
- Zipeg/iZip/UnRarX for Mac
- 7-Zip/PeaZip for Linux

The code bundle for the book is also hosted on GitHub at `https://github.com/PacktPublishing/Hands-On-Cloud-Native-Microservices-with-Jakarta-EE`. In case there's an update to the code, it will be updated on the existing GitHub repository.

We also have other code bundles from our rich catalog of books and videos available at `https://github.com/PacktPublishing/`. Check them out!

This book uses open source components. You can find the source code of their open source projects along with license information at: `https://github.com/jlprat/reactive-jee/blob/master/LICENSE`

We acknowledge and are grateful to these developers for their contributions to open source.

Download the color images

We also provide a PDF file that has color images of the screenshots/diagrams used in this book. You can download it here: `https://www.packtpub.com/sites/default/files/downloads/9781788837866_ColorImages.pdf`.

Conventions used

There are a number of text conventions used throughout this book.

`CodeInText`: Indicates code words in text, database table names, folder names, filenames, file extensions, pathnames, dummy URLs, user input, and Twitter handles. Here is an example: "Every time a new item is published by the observable, the `onNext()` method is called on each subscriber until the observable finishes its data flow."

A block of code is set as follows:

```
<!--https://mvnrepository.com/artifact/io.reactivex.rxjava2/rxjava -->
<dependency>
        <groupId>io.reactivex.rxjava2</groupId>
        <artifactId>rxjava</artifactId>
        <version>2.1.14</version>
</dependency>
```

When we wish to draw your attention to a particular part of a code block, the relevant lines or items are set in bold:

```
public interface FootballPlayerRepository extends
CrudRepository<FootballPlayer, Integer> {

}
```

Any command-line input or output is written as follows:

```
$ java -listmods
```

Bold: Indicates a new term, an important word, or words that you see onscreen. For example, words in menus or dialog boxes appear in the text like this. Here is an example: "Click the **Generate Project** button to download a scaffold of a Maven project."

Warnings or important notes appear like this.

Tips and tricks appear like this.

Get in touch

Feedback from our readers is always welcome.

General feedback: If you have questions about any aspect of this book, mention the book title in the subject of your message and email us at customercare@packtpub.com.

Errata: Although we have taken every care to ensure the accuracy of our content, mistakes do happen. If you have found a mistake in this book, we would be grateful if you would report this to us. Please visit www.packt.com/submit-errata, selecting your book, clicking on the Errata Submission Form link, and entering the details.

Piracy: If you come across any illegal copies of our works in any form on the Internet, we would be grateful if you would provide us with the location address or website name. Please contact us at `copyright@packt.com` with a link to the material.

If you are interested in becoming an author: If there is a topic that you have expertise in and you are interested in either writing or contributing to a book, please visit `authors.packtpub.com`.

Reviews

Please leave a review. Once you have read and used this book, why not leave a review on the site that you purchased it from? Potential readers can then see and use your unbiased opinion to make purchase decisions, we at Packt can understand what you think about our products, and our authors can see your feedback on their book. Thank you!

For more information about Packt, please visit `packt.com`.

1
Jakarta EE - the New Open Source Life of Java EE

We are living in a new era of information technology. All people like me, who started work at the beginning of the 2000s, have gone through a constant but gradual evolution of languages, frameworks, and architectures. The last year has marked a great change in the way we approach a software release.

The great competition that drives the global market has changed the cultural approach of companies, which now have a milestone target—the reduction of time to market. The need to release a new business service as soon as possible is the main target of a company, regardless of their business area.

From an information technology point of view, this need has been translated into a complete review of development platforms and their updating and evolution processes.

From an enterprise point of view, this change, defined as digital disruption, is leading to the need to review company structures with regard to the organization of roles and skills, as well as to the policies of continuously updating to keep up with market needs. The community side of developers has led to a conceptualization of ideas as has not been seen for some time.

The best way to comprehend all the ideas that are being born around these concepts is through the open source model.

In this chapter, we will cover the following topics:

- Open source
- The Java programming language
- OpenJDK 9 and 10
- Java EE – MicroProfile.io – Jakarta EE

Open source

First of all, we start with a definition of open source—it is a way of thinking about the development of software that encourages the sharing of ideas and code. All sections of a product—documentation, source code, and so on—should be made publicly available. Using this model, you can build a product that will be able to benefit from the continuous improvement boosts given by the community in terms of standards, security, and technology evolution.

Sometimes, people confuse open source with the concept of no cost, which means we can use the technology for free. Using a technology only on the basis of its cost (cheap versus expensive) can expose your project to very high risks, including the failure of the objectives set. This way of perceiving open source is extremely reductive and dangerous.

Open source is much more. It is a model, like a philosophy, that encourages open collaboration and the sharing of ideas. An idea becomes stronger and more useful if more people collaborate to identify the weaknesses in order to improve them and find the right solutions. The intent is to promote these ideas in order to create an ecosystem based on solid rules for building the architecture of the future and to make all ideas freely available.

In this way, a community is created that cannot only develop the ideas that have emerged, but also continues the work of improvement, evolution, and dissemination. We can therefore state that, as in all other sectors, even in information technology, unity is strength.

Once the standards on which the technologies are based have been identified, it is possible to move on to their realization. In this stage as well, open source represents the best approach.

All stacks of software can grow in a better way if implemented under the open source model. Imagine having a community spread around the world that could test, evaluate, update, and fix your code in many different scenarios; a team composed of people, of different cultures and different skills, linked by a common goal—to create and consolidate a development framework. What company has such a special team?

If we think about the most common tools and framework used in information technology, we could immediately have an idea of how much open source communities are involved in our work life:

- **Software foundations:**
    - **Eclipse Foundation**: http://www.eclipse.org/
    - **Linux Foundation**: https://www.linuxfoundation.org/
    - **Python Software Foundation**: https://www.python.org/psf/

- **OpenJDK**: http://openjdk.java.net/
- **Operating systems**:
    - **Fedora**: https://getfedora.org/
    - **Linux kernel**: https://www.kernel.org/
    - **CentOS**: https://www.centos.org/
- **Containers**:
    - **Docker**: https://www.docker.com/
    - **Kubernetes**: https://kubernetes.io/
- **Middleware**:
    - **Apache Software Foundation**: http://apache.org/
    - **WildFly**: http://www.wildfly.org/
    - **Jakarta EE**: https://jakarta.ee/
- **Operations**:
    - **Ansible**: https://www.ansible.com/community
    - **KVM**: http://www.linux-kvm.org/page/Main_Page
    - **OpenShift**: https://www.openshift.com/
    - **OpenStack**: https://www.openstack.org/
- **Storage**:
    - **Ceph**: https://ceph.com/
    - **Gluster**: https://www.gluster.org/

This is only a fraction of the great number of open source communities involved in just a few critical areas. Do you still continue to think that open source means only free of cost?

One of the key points of the open source model is participation. Collaboration between people in the community is fundamental and solves one big question that companies often have—should they build a solution from scratch, or buy a solution that implements their requirements?

It's difficult to have all the skills needed to build an entire development framework. Buying a product from a vendor may solve the problem and reduce the effort of implementation, but leaves you unable to know the limit of your solution and the margins for improvement.

Using an open source-based solution gives you the opportunity to know exactly what you're using, letting you know whether your solution will be able to adapt to the future evolutions of information technology.

You should choose your open source community and project based on your needs.

Now you are ready to build your environment using open source products, frameworks, languages, and so on, and do the following:

- Share your knowledge through blogs, social networks, and all free channels that give you the opportunity to disseminate knowledge and encourage the exchange of ideas.
- Create your source code and donate it to the community, using one of the open source licenses and standards (`https://opensource.org/licenses`).
- Fork, star, watch, and create issues on open source repositories, such as GitHub, in order to promote good principles and ideas.
- Take part in the source life cycle of the open source project, and submit code that is able to solve issues that you may encounter during your experience.
- Help with documentation, in order to allow an increasingly clear and simple use of open source code.
- Help to test features; this could help the community to increase the strength of code, and gives an easy-to-understand example of usage of code.

In other words, you can become part of the community and make your contribution according to your skills, and the time you can dedicate.

From the application development perspective, open sourcing has provided a great contribution over the years. One of the most popular programming languages that has grown (thanks to the help of open source communities—this is one that will be the leading actor in our microservice journey) is Java.

The Java programming language

Java is a full-featured and general-purpose programming language that was initiated in 1991 by a team led by James Gosling and Patrick Naughton at Sun Microsystems. Let's take a look at the evolution of Java in the hands of its developers.

Sun Microsystems

Sun Microsystems released the first Java public implementation, version 1.0, in 1996. The concept of *write once run anywhere,* with the promise of great portability of software and ease of learning and use from the developers (in particular for automatic memory management and object-oriented paradigms) have all facilitated the rapid spread of Java in the information technology ecosystem.

The evolution and spread of the language was fast and continuous. After the two releases JDK 1.1 (February, 1997) and **Java Standard Edition (JSE)** 1.2 (December, 1998), Sun Microsystems released **Java Platform, Enterprise Edition (Java EE** (which was formerly known as **Java 2 Platform, Enterprise Edition (J2EE)).**

This was intended as a set of specifications, based on **Java Platform, Standard Edition (Java SE)**, dedicated to enterprise applications that were rapidly moving from a desktop's local environment to a web browser environment.

At the end of 2006, Sun decided to donate the major part of the core code of the **Java Virtual Machine (JVM)**, Standard and Enterprise Edition, as open source software under the terms of the **General Public License (GPL)**. At the beginning of 2007, Sun completed the process, making all of its JVM's code available under free software and open source distribution terms. The final result of this process is the creation of OpenJDK, which became the open source implementation of the Java SE.

The work Sun did during these 10 years, from the first public release of 1996 to the birth of OpenJDK and the open source release of the JVM core and JSE platform in 2007, ideally made its role with regard to Java seem like that of an *evangelist*.

Oracle Corporation

After this great period, Oracle Corporation acquired Sun Microsystems in 2009-2010.

At the beginning of this new era, Oracle declared that it will continue supporting and investing in Java for customers. You can take a look at the declaration on the following site: `https://web.archive.org/web/20100131091008/http://www.oracle.com/us/technologies/java/index.html`

Despite this declaration; the resignation from Oracle of James Gosling, the father of Java, in 2010; and the lawsuit against Google in 2012 related to the use of Java in the Android SDK; changed the perception of the community about the future of the Java language.

Oracle tried to give new impulse to Java and, after almost five years, released a new Java SE version (JDK 7 - July, 2011) and a new Java Enterprise Release (Java EE 7 - June, 2013). Furthermore, OpenJDK became a reference implementation of Java SE since version 7.

The rapid evolution of business requirements and the slowdown of the Java source life cycle convinced Oracle to change the strategy about the Java platform with a clear bet on the open source model.

OpenJDK binaries are the reference implementation of the JSE platform. OpenJDK is an incubator of the latest new features and has defined time-based releases that will be delivered every year in March and September. The version numbers follow the schema of year-month (YY.M). Unlike the previous release approach, this one will not be delayed to await a major feature to be completed and stabilized—an example was the delay of JDK 8 due to Jigsaw project issues, which was then retargeted into JDK 9.

With the new model, the new features will not be merged all together into a release source control repository until they are complete. If they are not ready to be included in a new release, they will be retargeted for the next release or later. The intention of this model is to avoid problems with a feature that, if not ready, could delay an entire release that could contain other features useful for developers.

Those enterprises and organizations that don't necessarily want or need to upgrade at a rapid pace will be free to choose a vendor to have support for a specific Java version, depending on market reaction. The same choice was also made for Java EE.

During the years, the platform became very big. The need to maintain backward compatibility and the delay of new Java SE releases, on which it depends, have made the platform very difficult to manage, delaying its evolution and making it unattractive for environments, such as cloud and microservices, in continuous evolution.

Eclipse Foundation

At the end of 2017, Oracle announced the donation of Java EE to the Eclipse Foundation. Initially, the project was named **Eclipse Enterprise for Java (EE4J)**. After a survey taken by the community, the name of Java EE was changed, in order to avoid legal problems due to the fact that Oracle owns the trademark for the name Java, to **Jakarta Enterprise Edition (Jakarta EE)**—the entry point for the new platform is Java EE 8.

Under the umbrella of the Eclipse Foundation community, and with the commitment of the major vendors, the Enterprise Edition platform could start a new life in order to accelerate the adoption for the implementation of business applications for a cloud-native world.

The migration of all source code to Jakarta EE is proceeding quickly but, in the meantime, the evolution of the cloud environment and microservices require immediate answers in terms of standards and implementation models.

For this reason, Eclipse MicroProfile was created, as it's meant to optimize Enterprise Java for a microservice architecture. MicroProfile is aimed at spurring innovation that may result in future as a standard, but at the moment requires a faster rate of change than the intentionally measured pace of a standard process.

The expectation is that the existing Eclipse MicroProfile community and other open source communities should continue leading the way. Jakarta EE will incorporate Java innovations from these projects and communities into new versions in order to have complete and strong standards.

The following screenshot shows the history of Java EE releases, in terms of versions and the time duration between each of them, in months:

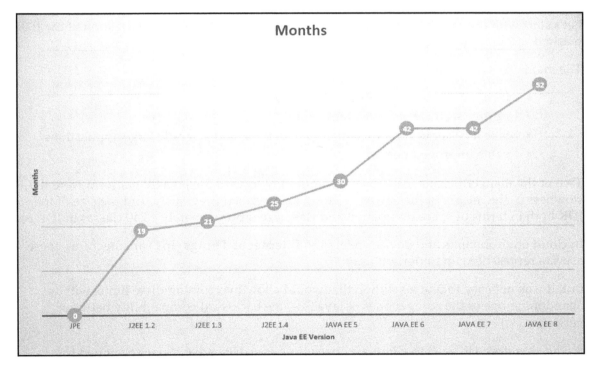

As you can see, the intervals between releases keep getting longer, and the last release version, which is Java EE 8, came out after 52 months!

In the next section, we will analyze the details of the latest OpenJDK versions, 9 and 10, and the Java EE 8 platform. These represent the base on which Eclipse MicroProfile is found, which is the Java Enterprise proposal for the realization of microservice architectures in cloud environments.

OpenJDK 9 and 10 – key features for cloud environments

Java SE 9 and 10 introduce some important new features and improvements.

A detailed analysis of the new features is out of the scope of this book. We will look at the main innovations that have brought added value to the use of Java within cloud platforms and microservices.

JDK 9

Let's start with Java SE 9, the revolutionary element entailing the modularization of the JDK reached through the Jigsaw project (http://openjdk.java.net/projects/jigsaw/).

The main goals of this new feature are as follows:

- Make Java SE more flexible and scalable
- Improve security and maintainability
- Make it easier to construct, maintain, deploy, and upgrade large applications
- Enable improved performance

Two of the main criticisms made by the community toward the Java SE platform were the slowness in the release of the newer versions, as described previously, and the size of the JDK both in terms of space occupation and class size (approximately 4,240 classes in JDK 8).

In cloud environments and devices related to **Internet of Things** (**IoT**) architectures, these aspects represented an important limit.

But, it was not easy to find a solution that would allow overcoming these limits without abandoning one of the cornerstones of Java SE—the backward compatibility between versions.

It was, therefore, difficult to eliminate obsolete classes or remove classes designed for internal use but used intensively, especially by the framework, via Java reflection. The most famous example is the one put up by Sun Microsystems, which is related to the com.sun.misc.Unsafe class. It specified that: sun.* packages are not part of the supported, public Java interface. If you want to see the actual release, you can visit this link: https://www.oracle.com/technetwork/java/faq-sun-packages-142232.html

Through the Jigsaw project, it was not only possible to modularize the JDK in its core code but also to provide a tool for the realization of applications able to significantly decouple the interfaces of exposure of its services with respect to the actual implementation.

For JDK core code, it is possible to encapsulate JDK APIs, as described in JEP 260 (`http://openjdk.java.net/jeps/260`), using the following approach:

- Encapsulate, by default, all internal APIs that are considered non-critical.
- Encapsulate all internal APIs, that are considered critical, for which exist, in JDK 8, supported replacements.
- Do not encapsulate critical internal APIs, but implement the following steps:
    - Deprecate them in JDK 9
    - Define a plan to remove these APIs in JDK 10
    - Implement a workaround solution via a command-line parameter
    - Remove, from the JDK distribution, a limited number of supported **Java Community Process** (**JCP**) standard APIs
    - Remove the extension mechanisms and the endorsed standards override

- Java EE modules, due to the Jigsaw project, are not resolved by default.

In this way, you can easily obtain a small bootable Java runtime that contains only the features, in terms of classes and interfaces that you really need, avoiding the presence of useless code and that can have only negative side effects in terms of footprint and space allocation.

You could easily analyze this using the following command:

```
$ java -listmods
```

As mentioned before, both the JDK and the application can benefit from modular development. Decoupling the components present in the applications is essential in microservice architectures, which need a very agile software life cycle to reduce time to market.

Using a modularity approach, you could easily achieve the following:

- Loose coupling between components
- Clear contracts and dependencies between components
- Hidden implementation using strong encapsulation

The main element in your implementation is the module.

Developers can organize their code into a modular structure, within which are declared dependencies inside their respective module definition files.

The properties of a module are defined into a file named `module-info.java` that contains the following attributes:

- The module name
- The module's packages that you want to make available publicly
- The dependencies, direct or transitive, that the module depends on
- The list of the services that the module consumes
- All possible implementation of the service that the module provides

The following are the main keywords used to set the main features of a module through the `module-info.java` file:

- `module`: The module definition file starts with this keyword followed by its name and definition.
- `provides ... with ...`: The `provides` keyword is used to indicate that the module provides implementations for a defined service interface. The service interface is expressed using the `with` keyword.
- `requires`: This keyword is used to indicate the dependencies of the modules. A module name has to be specified after this keyword and the list of dependencies are set through multiple required directives.
- `transitive`: This keyword is set after the `requires` keyword; with this feature, you are declaring that any module that depends on the module defining `requires transitive <modulename>` gets an implicit dependence on the `<modulename>`.
- `uses`: This keyword is used to indicate the service interface that this module is using; a type name, complete with fully qualified class or interface name, has to be specified after this keyword.
- `opens`: This keyword is used to indicate the packages that are accessible only at runtime; you can also use them for introspection, using Reflection APIs. This is quite important for libraries and frameworks that use reflection APIs in order to be as abstract as possible; the `opens` directive can also be set at module level—in this case, all packages of the module are accessible at runtime.
- `exports`: This keyword is used to indicate the packages of the module that are publicly available; a package name has to be specified after this keyword.

But the two approaches, Java Jigsaw module and **Open Service Gateway Initiative (OSGi)**, have some differences.

OSGi's adoption is largely due to its support for dynamic component control. In this case, plugins or components are loaded dynamically and then activated, deactivated, and even updated or removed as needed. Presently, this dynamic module life cycle is not available with Java modules.

Additionally, compared with Java modules, OSGi supports improved versioning. Other OSGi advantages are related to isolation; for example, bundle changes require only the direct dependencies to be recompiled, whereas a Java module's entire layer, along with all child layers, need to be recompiled if just one module changes.

The downside is that OSGi bundles still suffer from class path issues, such as runtime exceptions for missing dependencies, or arbitrary class loading for packages with the same name.

Additionally, OSGi requires a class loader per module, which can affect some libraries that expect only a single class loader. Java modules don't allow split packages which is considered a big improvement in Java overall, and don't have similar class loader requirements or restrictions. One big advantage Java modules have over OSGi is compiler support.

I think we can get the most out of the modularization of the application components in a microservice architecture, combining the best of both technologies. The overall strategy is to use Java modules to modularize libraries (either imported or exported) and the JVM itself, and use OSGi on top to handle application modularity and dynamic life cycle control.

JDK 10

JDK 10 introduced some new features. As mentioned earlier, we will concentrate on the most important features related to cloud environments and microservice architecture.

The first one is Docker awareness, which is supported for Linux only. With this feature, you can extract container-specific information about the number of CPUs (automatically) and allocated memory (automatically).

The following new JVM configuration parameters have been introduced:

- `-XX:UseContainerSupport`: The JVM has been updated in order to be aware that it is running in a Docker container. In this way it will extract container specific configuration information and it will not query the operating system. The more important information that it will be extract is the total memory that have been allocated to the container and the amount of CPUs. The value of CPUs available to the Java process is calculated from any specified CPU shares, CPU quotas or CPU sets.
- `-XX:ActiveProcessorCount`: This value overrides any other logic of CPU detection implemented automatically by the JVM.
- `-XX:InitialRAMPercentage/-XX:MaxRAMPercentage/-XX:MinRAMPercentage`: This parameters allows users that run the JVM into Docker containers to have more control over the amount of system memory that will be used for the Java Heap allocation.

A great performance improvement is achieved with the Parallel Full GC for G1, as described in JEP 307 (`http://openjdk.java.net/jeps/307`). With this feature, full GC occurs on parallel threads with great benefits, such as the following:

- Low latency
- High throughput
- No/fewer **stop-of-world** (**STW**) pauses
- Improved G1 worst-case latencies

In order to obtain better performance, it has also introduced the application **class-data sharing** (**CDS**) with JEP 310 (`http://openjdk.java.net/jeps/310`). This feature reduces resource footprint when multiple JVMs are running on the same physical machine, and improves the startup time of applications.

Furthermore, processes and applications can share common class metadata (class data), from a shared archive (the CDS archive); prior to Java SE 10, the use of CDS had been restricted to the bootstrap class loader only.

Another important element in an environment such as the cloud that must be as responsive as possible is the Thread-Local Handshakes feature, defined in JEP 312 (`http://openjdk.java.net/jeps/312`). It's a new way to execute a `callback` on threads that reduces the impact of acquiring a stack trace sample, for example, for profiling operations. It makes it possible to cheap-stop individual threads, reduce stops of STW pauses, and give better GC performance. With the Thread-Local Handshakes feature, it is possible to stop single threads and not just all threads or none—in this way, you don't need to make a global JVM safe point, giving a great performance improvement.

Last but not least, JDK 10 makes it possible to perform heap allocation on alternative devices, as described in JEP 316 (`http://openjdk.java.net/jeps/316`).

This great feature, realized with the contribution of Intel, allows the JVM to allocate the heap needed to store Java objects on a different memory device specified by the user, for example, a **Non-Volatile Dual In-line Memory Module** (**NVDIMM**).

This aspect could be extremely important in a multi-JVM environment, where you will instruct the processes with lower priority to use the NVDIMM memory while instructing the higher priority processes to use **dynamic random access memory** (**DRAM**).

I have described only a small set of the new features released in JDK 9 and 10 that demonstrate the great effort done to improve the Java language and make it a good choice for microservice implementation in cloud environments.

In September 2018, JDK 11 was released with some new great features, such as Epsilon—a no-op garbage collector.

Do you still have doubts about the use of Java for new microservice architectures?

Java EE – MicroProfile.io – Jakarta EE

The Java EE platform is one of the main tools for creating enterprise applications, thanks to a series of standards and specifications whose implementations have allowed us to manage crucial aspects such as transactions, security, scalability, concurrency, and management of the components it is deploying.

Together with Spring and Pivotal technology, Java EE represents the implementation model for modern Java-based enterprise applications on any kind of deployment platform.

As previously stated, the delay in the evolution of the platform and, consequently, in the release of new versions able to meet the new requirements related to the implementation of microservices in cloud environments have generated in the community a sense of distrust in its use.

I don't want to start some sort of *religion war* on which technology among Java EE, Spring, or others is regarded as the best to implement modern applications. Java EE 7, the latest stable and supported version, was released in 2013, and it received very positive feedback from the community.

Java EE 7's relevance in the ecosystem of enterprise applications has been very
important, as evidenced by the following survey—Developers Affirm Strong Support for Java EE 7 in DZone Survey

Spring's influence on Java EE was clear and helped to improve the platform by making it significantly less complex for example, through the following:

- The arrival of Spring and Hibernate has provided new ideas and approaches to development, which has given birth to EJB 3 and JPA 1, which represent the two major innovations introduced in Java EE 5.
- Spring Dependency Injection was the base on which **Context and Dependency Injection (CDI)** was built.
- Spring Batch has merged into JBatch specification (JSR 352 https://www.jcp.org/en/jsr/detail?id=352).

Since its creation, Spring has become popular among developers, thanks to the ease-of-use approach and a speedy time to market that allow us to quickly adopt technological innovations, such as microservices and cloud native applications.

Java EE, instead, and in particular after version 5, has a slower time to market; the reasons are related to the length of time needed to write specifications, and the implementation and certification time. Usually, several months are needed for a specification release to be supported and certified by the application servers.

Recently, this gap has widened:

- Spring Boot has increased its ease of use through the convention-over-configuration principle.
- Spring Cloud is becoming the major platform used in cloud-native developments by leveraging open source components from Netflix, which creates modules that implement important cloud concepts such as service registry, service discovery, load balancing, monitoring, and so on.

Now the question could be—is Java EE still a good choice to make microservices and cloud-native applications?

In my opinion, the answer is yes.

First of all, Java EE, in particular version 8, introduced or has consolidated a great number of specifications that are extremely useful for microservices implementation, such as the following:

- CDI 2.0
- **Java API for JSON Processing (JSONP) 1.1**
- **Java API for JSON Binding (JSON-B) 1.0**
- **Java API for RESTful Web Services (JAX-RS) 2.1**
- Java Servlet 4.0

CDI 2.0 defines the behavior of CDI outside of a Java EE container, allowing the use of patterns such as inversion of control even in contexts such as third-party utility libraries.

The specification is split in three parts—core CDI, CDI for Java SE, and CDI for Java EE. This split makes CDI more modular in order to help other Java EE specifications better integrate with it.

The de facto standard for API communications in microservices environments is the JSON format. Java EE has two great specifications, JSON-B and JSONP that can help developers to easily produce and process a JSON payload.

JSONP has great support, with utilities such as JSON Pointer, JSON Patch, JSON Merge Patch, and so on, for meeting the **Internet Engineering Task Force (IETF)** standards (https://www.ietf.org/standards/). It has also added editing operations to JSONObject and JSONArray, and introduced helper classes and methods to better utilize Java SE 8 Stream operations.

JSON-B set a JAXB-like API to easily marshal or unmarshal Java objects to/from JSON. It created a default mapping between classes and JSON, and a standard support to handle the `application/JSON` media type for JAX-RS. It's a natural follow-on to JSONP specifications, and closes the JSON support gap.

JAX-RS 2.1 standardized some features most used in microservices development, as follows:

- Server-sent events
- Non-blocking I/O in providers (filters, interceptors, and so on)
- Reactive programming paradigms to improve JAX-RS asynchronous clients
- Hypermedia API enhancements

In this way, it has facilitated integration with other JSRs and frameworks.

Servlet 4.0 introduced support for HTTP/2 protocol and the use of request/response multiplexing, server push notifications, and so on. It's also aligned with the latest HTTP 1.1 RFCs.

All the specifications and features described previously are certainly useful, but not sufficient to make Java EE suitable to meet the needs of cloud-native applications and microservices.

Now, the main targets are as follows:

- Deploy the applications onto the cloud
- Build microservices in an easy manner
- Enable more rapid evolution of applications

The community, through the Java EE guardians (`https://javaee-guardians.io/`) and the **Java User Groups** (**JUG**), pushed for modernizing Java EE for cloud and microservices environments. The target is to extend the Java EE platform in order to make it able to build microservice architecture, while still maintaining backwards compatibility with previous Java EE versions. Furthermore, the community wanted a migration path to evolve the consolidated applications into cloud-ready applications that could take advantage of new cloud development and deployment models.

In detail, the request was to obtain functionalities as follows:

- Client-side circuit breakers in order to make remote REST invocations fault-tolerant
- A standard way of health checking Java apps
- A secret vault to shadow sensitive data
- Multitenancy support to accommodate the needs of complex applications
- OAuth and OpenID support technologies have rapidly emerged as a de facto standard in security context implementation
- An externalized configuration store to make it an easy process to promote applications across environments

The answers to these requests were essentially two, as follows:

- The creation of the MicroProfile.io project, in the middle of 2016
- The new life on Java EE with the Jakarta EE community project at the end of April 2018

MicroProfile

MicroProfile.io is an open source community specification for Enterprise Java microservices, and it aims at optimizing Enterprise Java for a microservice architecture.

The delay in the release of the new version of Java EE, and the rapid change of the technological scenario (which is increasingly oriented toward cloud platforms and microservice architectures), have pushed a community of individuals, organizations, and vendors collaborating within an open source (Eclipse) project to bring microservice features to the Enterprise Java community.

Some of the major players in the history of the Java EE platform are involved in this project, such as Payara, Fujitsu, Tomitribe, IBM, Red Hat, Hammock, SmartBear, Hazelcast, and Oracle to name a few.

The project is based on the idea of extending the main features of the Java EE with new specifications essential to meeting the requirements of the new technological context.

At the time of writing this book, the project is at version 1.3, and is composed of the specifications shown below:

New Implementations	Updated Implementations	Unchanged implementations
OpenTracing 1.0	Metrics 1.1	Fault tolerance 1.0
OpenAPI 1.0	Config 1.2	JWT propagation 1.0
REST client 1.0		Health check 1.0
		CDI 1.2
		JSONP 1.0
		JAX-RS 2.0

As mentioned previously, in addition to the specifications relating to CDI, JSONP, and JAX-RS used to expose the API via RESTful web services in JSON format, there are a number of new specifications such as configuration, fault tolerance, **JSON Web Tokens (JWTs)**, metrics, health checks, JWT propagation, OpenTracing, OpenAPI, and the REST client that are able to allow the realization of microservices in cloud environments.

In the following chapters, we will analyze in detail these specifications, with examples of code that will allow us to understand their purposes well. For now, let's have a quick introduction to the objectives of each of these new specifications, based on the descriptions that are given in their GitHub repositories:

- **Config**: A common feature, not strictly related to cloud or microservice architecture, is the ability of the applications to be configured based on the running environment. Usually they use properties files in different formats, but the request is to have the opportunity to update the configuration properties without the need to rebuild and repackage the application. Also, the changed values should be retrieved by the client without the need to redeploy and restart the application. This requirement is extremely important for microservices running in a cloud environment. The MicroProfile Config specification defines the way to implement this concept.
- **REST client**: This specification defines how to invoke RESTful services over the HTTP protocol. The REST client implementation outlines a continuity with Java EE/Jakarta EE, suggesting the use of JAX-RS 2.0 specifications in order to give the ability to reuse code written in tradition Java EE applications.

- **Fault tolerance**: One of the most important features required in cloud and microservice environments is resiliency to failure. This specification defines a way to provide different strategies to drive the execution and the result of computation implemented by the code; for example, providing fall backs and an alternative result when code execution fails due to unexpected exceptions. Retry strategies, bulkheads, and circuit breakers are enterprise integration patterns that you should implement to adhere to this specification.
- **Metrics**: In a distributed environment such as a **Platform as a Service** (**PaaS**), it is essential to retrieve metrics related to the execution environment. Usually, companies use agents that shadow the complexity to retrieve this information. In the past, the **Java Management Extension** (**JMX**) was implemented for this purpose. This specification extends JMX and defines another two main aspects, as follows:
    - A standard way for MicroProfile servers to expose monitoring data to management agents
    - A standard Java API that applications should use to expose their telemetry data to operations teams
- **OpenAPI**: The main goal of this specification is to define a standard Java API that implements the OpenAPI version 3 specification defined here: `https://github.com/OAI/OpenAPI-Specification/blob/master/versions/3.0.0.md`. The applications should adhere to this specification to expose their API documentation.
- **JWT propagation**: The most used technology in microservice architecture is the RESTful web service as compared to the HTTP protocol, and so the security of the APIs exposed must be guaranteed. The RESTful architecture services should be stateless—this means that any security state associated with a client is sent to the requested service every time a new request is performed. The security context is always recreated and the systems must perform both authentication and authorization validation on every request. The principal security protocols are based on security tokens—OAuth2, WS-Federation, OpenID Connect, WS-Trust, and **Security Assertion Markup Language** (**SAML**) are the main ones. The target technologies of JWT propagation specification are based on standards defined by OAuth2, JWT, and OpenID Connect.
- **OpenTracing**: The microservice usually runs in distributed system environments, so it's extremely important to trace requests in order to rebuild the execution flow of the code. This specification defines APIs that describe how incoming and outgoing requests should be traced by an OpenTracing-compliant Tracer Object. They also set the way to access a configured Tracer Object.

- **Health check**: The monitoring of the production infrastructure is a key point of the operation teams—it's important to always know the state of a node in order to react quickly if there are issues. These APIs describe the rules for determining the state of a node. In a PaaS health check specifications could be used to determine whether a node needs to be discarded and replaced by another instance using automatic mechanisms, reducing the out-of-service time.

One of the main goals of these specifications is the compatibility with the well-known cloud platforms, such as, Kubernetes.

It is expected that MicroProfile 2.0 will align all APIs to Java EE 8 in order to obtain a set of features, as shown below:

New Implementations	Updated Implementations	Unchanged implementations
JSON-B 1.0	CDI 2.0	OpenTracing 1.0
	JSONP 1.1	OpenAPI 1.0
	JAX-RS 2.1	REST client 1.0
		Fault tolerance 1.0
		Metrics 1.1
		JWT propgation 1.0
		Health check 1.0
		Config 1.2

At this moment, there are some products that have already passed the **Technology Compatibility Kit** (**TCK**) tests of the JSRs described before, or that are in the **in progress** state.

The main products are as follows:

- Open Liberty (https://openliberty.io/)
- WebSphere Liberty (https://developer.ibm.com/wasdev/websphere-liberty/)
- Thorntail (https://thorntail.io/)
- Payara (https://www.payara.fish/upstream_builds)

You can find the updated list of the MicroProfile implementation at the Eclipse MicroProfile Wiki (https://wiki.eclipse.org/MicroProfile/Implementation).

So, now we have a great community, that of MicroProfile.io that is building a Java EE on steroids. But, how will Java EE evolve, and how will the new features made available by MicroProfile be included in it?

The evolution of Java EE is Jakarta EE.

Jakarta EE

Last September, Oracle announced, with the support of IBM and Red Hat that Java EE was going to move to the Eclipse Foundation. Since then, some other important companies have joined the initiative with strategic or participating-level commitments.

Following are the members involved in the Jakarta EE project:

- **Strategic members**:
  - Fujitsu
  - IBM
  - Oracle
  - Payara
  - Red Hat
  - Tomitribe

- **Participating members**:
  - CloudBees
  - DocDoku
  - Genuitec
  - IncQuery Labs
  - Lightbend
  - Microsoft
  - Mizuho
  - Pivotal
  - RCP Vision
  - SAP
  - UseOpen
  - Vaadin
  - Webtide

The community requires that the Jakarta EE platform evolve faster than Java EE—to continue to be a reference platform for cloud architectures and microservices, which evolve rapidly, it is necessary to quickly incorporate into new versions of the platform the new features coming from open source communities, such as Eclipse MicroProfile.

Jakarta EE should make developers able to build cloud-native and mission-critical applications using the decades of developer experience built that Java EE was built upon.

The migration process from Java EE to Jakarta EE is complex, but, despite everything, it is proceeding relatively quickly.

After dealing with all the legal aspects related to the use of the name *Java* and *javax* within the specifications, it started the phase of migration of projects, specifications, and reference implementations to the Eclipse Foundation repositories.

This process requires a lot of effort because there are approximately 110 repositories to transfer. You can find the complete list with the project statuses here `https://dmitrykornilov.net/2018/05/09/jakarta-ee-projects-summary/`.

The community is performing the following activities:

- Internal license checking in order to make sure licenses are correct.
- Internal third-party analysis in order to identify what dependencies should be replaced with their latest versions to fix major bugs and security issues.
- Renaming the original projects with the following scheme:
    - *Eclipse Project for XXX* for API projects
    - *Eclipse XXX* for implementation projects
- Issuing transfers in order to preserve issue numbers and history without losing the previous job.
- Building environments in order to create the infrastructure needed to compile and run, in an agile continuous-integration way, the projects that make up the Jakarta EE platform.
- Aligning the previous projects' repositories in order to set a message that communicates that the project has been transferred to the Eclipse Foundation.

The base version for the final first release of Jakarta EE is Java EE 8.

At the end of the process, we will have a platform that will make all actors (vendors, Java communities, individuals, and so on) able to interact as peers with no one vendor holding, as in the spirit of the open source model.

So, with the power of the open source model, expressed in Jakarta EE and MicroProfile, do you think Java can still be a major player in the cloud and microservice world?

In my opinion, the answer is yes, and throughout the rest of the book, we will see together how to maximize the potential of Java and of the PaaS to create microservices in distributed environments.

Summary

In this chapter, we covered the fundamentals of the open source model and the origins of Java. We walked through the evolution of the Java SE and Java EE platforms in order to understand the causes of the birth of Jakarta EE and MicroProfile entities.

In the next chapter, we will speak about the new architecture approaches that have revolutionized enterprise applications—microservices and reactive architectures.

Microservices and Reactive Architecture

2

The global market is rapidly evolving and with it the business models that have led the main companies, both in the IT field and beyond, in the last decades.

The need to be the first to market their products has become the *mantra* of companies. In a phase like this, where social media, and the internet in general, allow you to quickly spread your brand and quickly influence the market, being quick to release proposals that intercept the needs of society is the key to success.

Numerous market analyses have been presented in this regard, which depicts a state of deep transformation. Here are some examples:

- By 2020, more than 75% of the S&P 500 will be companies that we have not heard of yet
- By 2020, every business will become a digital predator or digital prey
- Among surveyed executives, 87% believe digital technologies will disrupt their industries and yet only 44% indicated their organizations were taking appropriate measures to avert disruption

    To refer to the source of this data, please visit:

- `https://www.innosight.com/insight/creative-destruction/`
- `https://www.cisco.com/c/dam/r/en/us/internet-of-everything-ioe/assets/files/Digital_Predator_Or_Digital_Prey.pdf`
- `http://marketing.mitsmr.com/PDF/MITSMR-Deloitte-Digital-Infographic-2016.pdf?src=report`

It almost seems like an apocalyptic scenario, doesn't it? Fortunately, this isn't the case. What is expected is a scenario that requires an ever-faster need for innovation to satisfy a market that is evolving at speeds that we are not used to.

The answer to this need is **digital transformation**. What is it? It's a transformation of business by revamping all the main assets of the companies—the business strategy, marketing approach models, products, targets, and so on, by adopting digital technologies. In this way, companies will be able to accelerate the sales and growth of the business.

This process requires a restructuring of the corporate structures, through the adoption of agile methodologies and DevOps, which are needed to make the corporate structures more rapid and efficient so that they can design and release efficient, scalable, and therefore a high-performance architecture—in a nutshell, **microservices**.

In this chapter, we will cover the following topics:

- MicroProfile and the principles of **microservice architecture** (MSA)
- **Service-oriented architecture (SOA)** versus MSA
- From monolith to microservices
- Reactive systems and reactive programming

MicroProfile and the principles of MSA

In this section, we will describe the basic principles of microservices and their features, and present the benefits and the drawbacks of this new way of designing and building applications.

What are microservices?

Microservice architecture is based on the concept that an application should contain a collection of loosely coupled, independent, and atomic services, which implement business capabilities. Using this approach, it's easy to build software that splits a big enterprise application, also known as a monolith, into smaller and consistent contexts, known as microservices.

It also enables the fast evolution of a company's technology stack, thanks to the building of autonomous and independent DevOps teams. Microservices are usually created and managed by small teams that must have enough autonomy to change the microservices' internal implementation details with or without a small impact on the rest of the architecture.

MSA, thanks to its modular structure, enables a short and quick release of complex and large applications using approaches such as continuous delivery/deployment. A microservice must be able to be invoked by any client, regardless of the technology with which it was implemented; so it must be language, platform, and operating system agnostic.

And to be consumed, it should expose APIs for third parties that represent a sort of contract between them.

Benefits of microservices

Deploying an MSA provides some important benefits:

- **Single responsibility**: Each microservice should cover a well-defined business domain—the **domain-driven design (DDD)** approach can help developers build software that adheres to this concept to obtain an autonomous and atomic system.
- **Explicitly published interface**: A producer service publishes an interface that is used by a consumer service. This is one of the most important points because the published interface represents the contract between the producer and the consumer—once the interface has been published, the API should not be modified. A new version of a contract must be followed by a new version of the interface to avoid unpredictable impacts to the service consumers.
- **Independent deploy, update, replace, and scale (DURS)**: A business domain could be made by a different set of microservices. To guarantee the continuity of business services, both in the case of issues or a new release version of one of the microservices that make up the suite, each service should be independently deployed, updated, replaced, and scaled.
- **Isolation**: This is a prerequisite for resilience and elasticity. A microservice should share nothing with other microservices. In this way, it's easier to scale each service as well as allowing each of them to be monitored, debugged, and tested independently. It could also enable fault isolation to avoid issues with the entire business channel if only one microservice is affected by a problem. An issue, for example, an unclosed database connection or a memory leak, must impact only the faulty service and not the entire application. Using this strategy, you will be able to isolate the fault to a single service, avoiding propagating it to the rest of the suite.

- **Diversified technology**: As I described earlier, MSA divides a complex domain into smaller contexts that are followed by dedicated teams. These teams are completely independent of each other and, for this reason, are able to choose the best technology to implement the microservice based on their skills, the business requirements, the strategic choices made by the company, and so on.
- **Smart endpoints and dumb pipes**: Each microservice owns its domain logic but it should not cover a big context. The domain must be atomic but small and well-defined. Also, the communication protocol must be simple—at the moment, the de facto standard is represented by RESTful over HTTP.

- **Independent scaling**: Each microservice can scale independently with different strategies—horizontal scaling and vertical scaling—based on what is needed. This is a different approach than that in monolithic applications, which may have different requirements and must be deployed as a single unit (e.g., **Enterprise Application Archive** (**EAR**) and **Web Application Archive** (**WAR**)).
- **Improved communication across the team**: A microservice is typically built by a full-stack team that has all the necessary skills. All members work as a single team, with the same objectives, significantly improving the quality of what they build. They remain wholly responsible for a project, even in the production environment, ensuring quality in the project life cycle both in terms of technological evolution and monitoring.
- **Independent upgrades**: Each service should be deployed independently from other services. In this way, a developer can decide to revisit the underlying implementation of the system without the risk of impacting other parts of the suite of services. The use of **continuous integration** (**CI**)/**continuous delivery** (**CD**) can help automate the process of checking code quality and releasing new software versions with confidence.

After listing all of these positive aspects, can we say that microservices are the ideal solution in any scenario? The honest answer is no.

Microservices are not the magic potion that will solve all the architectural problems in your applications. They also require significant investment in terms of resources and skill acquisition.

In the next section, we will summarize the drawbacks so that we have all the elements to make the right choice for our project.

Drawbacks of microservices

It's not very easy to build an MSA. First of all, you need to invest in people skills. In addition, you must adopt methodologies such as Agile and DevOps to create a full-stack team that is able to obtain the following:

- **Service replication**: One of the benefits of MSA is that it is easy to scale up. But to do this, you need an infrastructure that enables this feature using a standard mechanism based on, for example, metadata. **Platform as a Service** (**PaaS**) is the ideal environment but to use it, your teams should have or obtain competencies in this area and your applications must be cloud ready or cloud-native. Therefore, you need to heavily invest in people and resources.

- **Service discovery**: In a microservice ecosystem, services are distributed to guarantee load balancing and failover into immutable infrastructure provided by, for example, containers in a PaaS or immutable VM images using the major virtualization providers. Services scale up and down based on certain predefined metrics. In this scenario, it is difficult to know the exact address of a service until it is deployed and ready to be used. The exact service endpoint address is usually mapped by service registration and service discovery. Developers and operational people need to write code and maintain infrastructure that makes it easy to do so. The architectural design phase is different from the past. Therefore, you need to refactor the existing applications or design new ones in a different manner using these new actors.

- **Service monitoring**: In a distributed environment, it is essential to monitor services and log information. This enables you to take proactive action if, for example, a service is consuming unexpected resources (such as CPU, memory, or threads) or has some issues (such as resource leak, memory leak, or a database connection leak). It's extremely important to create a system that is able to aggregate logs from different microservices, visualizing them in an easy way for operation teams, developers, and business users. If you don't build this infrastructure, you could encounter some difficulties in the production environment since you will not able to debug the application and react to an issue in an effective way.

- **Resiliency**: Usually, a full business workflow is built by the invocation of multiple services being distributed in different environments—for this reason, it is easy to predict that one of these services could fail, independent of the hard work made by the development team to test it. For this reason, developers should try to avoid the failure by automatically implementing corrective actions to guarantee that the system's workflow continues to operate properly. It's not very easy to predict failure, so your team must contain highly skilled senior staff that can help design this type of software.

- **DevOps**: There is no microservice without automation. CI/CD are essential for microservice-based applications to succeed. You need to identify bad software quality, performance issues, runtime execution exceptions, and so on, at the earliest opportunity via well-automated unit testing, performance testing, static code analysis, and deployment pipelines. It's extremely hard to build and maintain this type of automation in a source and infrastructure life cycle.

- **Resource and network overhead**: A full suite, which is needed to implement a complex business domain, is built by multiple microservices. This means that a great number of applications require more resources to run than traditional monolith applications. You need to build this type of infrastructure or learn to use a cloud-native platform in all core development areas—**Infrastructure as a Service (IaaS)**, **PaaS**, **Software as a Service (SaaS)**, and so on. Do you have all of the necessary skills to choose, develop, and maintain these platforms?

Another important consideration is the *as-is* infrastructure. Maybe, in your organization, there are great monoliths or SOA applications that work great. Should you abandon them or completely rewrite them? If neither, how can you migrate them to a cloud-oriented infrastructure?

Another aspect that is difficult to manage is the consistency of the data—how can you preserve it in a system that is distributed and heterogeneous in terms of the implementation of technologies?

So, after the collection of all points, positive and negative, the challenge is deciding when it makes sense to use an MSA.

For those who have built enterprise applications over the past 10-15 years, concepts such as services, isolation, and data ownership bring to mind another architectural model that has been the foundation of enterprise applications—SOA.

So what are the differences between MSA and SOA? Let's take a look at them in the next section.

SOA versus MSA

Service-oriented architecture is a way to design software where the business services communicate through a standard communication protocol, usually **Simple Object Access Protocol (SOAP)**, over a network. The main target of an SOA is to be independent of vendors, products, and technologies. The principal unit of an SOA is the service—a small unit of functionality that can be accessed remotely, and acted upon and updated independently.

The communication between services happens via direct exchange of data or it could involve two or more services that are coordinated by an orchestrator, **Enterprise Service Bus (ESB)** that is responsible for managing the execution flow.

There are two main roles in an SOA—a service provider and a service consumer. The first one is the service that's defined within the SOA while the second one is the point where consumers interact with the SOA. In addition, the data storage is shared within all services in an SOA.

The problem, however, is that an SOA is usually associated with an ESB, which is used to integrate monolithic applications—it is identified as a complex architecture, difficult to scale, and extremely coupled with proprietary vendor solutions. So it's sometimes difficult to think about SOAs in a positive manner.

After massive dissemination and utilization of SOA platforms at the beginning of the 2000s, there was a slow and progressive decline of this architecture due to the reasons we described earlier.

However, MSAs can be seen as an evolution of SOAs—many of the techniques defined in microservice specifications were born and consolidated from the experiences of developers who used them in large enterprise organizations using service-oriented architecture and patterns. For this reason, MSAs are receiving increasingly positive feedback from the community and their use is rapidly expanding among enterprise companies.

Differences between MSAs and SOAs

As I mentioned earlier, there are some common points between MSAs and SOAs, so much so that you can define MSAs as an evolution of SOAs. But what differentiated these two architectural designs and where did SOA fail?

Let's try to summarize their different features and concepts:

MSA	SOA
It's based on team collaboration using Agile and DevOps methodology. It sponsors freedom of choice regarding the implementation technologies, with no shared resources or governance models.	It's based on shared common governance and is implemented using ESBs and a standard communication protocol.
A fundamental principle is that each microservice must own the data so it must have independent data storage.	It allows services to share the database.
One of the key points is the automatic scalability that is a native benefit of containers. MSA could be defined as a cloud-native architecture.	It was born before the arrival of the container—scalability policies don't fit very well in cloud environments.
The execution environment is not based only on application servers—it's possible to use a slim web server, such as Tomcat, Undertow, Jetty, and so on, in a classic way (deploying the application on top of it) or with the Uber JAR feature. It's also possible to use a Javascript engine, such as Node.JS, a reactive system, such as Vert.x, a Scala ecosystem, and so on. It's a polyglot architecture.	It's based on a common platform, usually a traditional Java EE application server, for all services deployed to it.
It prefers lightweight protocols such as HTTP, REST, and so on to make the environments as performant as possible.	It supports multiple message protocols but the major one that's used is the SOAP.
Communication between services is based on less elaborate and simple messaging systems—HTTP verbs using JSON objects or an asynchronous messaging pattern (**Java Message Service (JMS)**, **Advanced Message Queuing Protocol (AMQP)**, **Message Queuing Telemetry Transport (MQTT)**, **Server-Sent Event (SSE)**, Push Events, and so on).	Communication between services is based on XML messages using SOAP protocol, often orchestrated by a single ESB.
It has a strict concept of bounded context.	It's focused on business functionality reuse so full isolation is not guaranteed.
DevOps, CI, CD, and Agile methodologies are mainstream in MSA architecture.	CI is used and sponsored in an SOA environment. The other ones listed in the MSA column have been introduced in recent years but don't represent the base philosophy of the design.
One of the main concepts is the immutability of the software and of the infrastructure. A code change should cause a new application release while an infrastructure modification should cause a release of new container images. MSA is often related to a cloud environment.	A code change requires the update of the monolith while an infrastructure update should be obtained with a modification of the properties' configuration settings.
It's focused on decoupling, even at the cost of violating the **don't repeat yourself** (**DRY**) pattern.	It maximizes application service reusability in terms of code and business implementation.

Finally, we can't say that one architecture is absolutely great while the other one is totally wrong. There are some positive aspects in SOAs. Maybe, the points which led to its decline are:

- Strong coupling between services due to protocol communication and code sharing that increases the time to release a new version and make it difficult
- Vendor lock-in due to the presence of ESB proprietary implementation
- Limit of the scalability due to the technologies used

We can think about MSA as SOA on steroids—it reuses the benefits and overcomes the limitations with a new way of thinking and designs focal points using the great new features of cloud environments.

The most common approach to evaluate MSA is to refactor a classic Java EE monolith application. In this way, people can examine whether the key features are present in the new design and how they can implement them. After that, they will start to think about building a microservice cloud-native application from scratch.

From monolith to microservices

Usually, large organizations have already invested a large number of resources in existing monolith applications that represent the core of their business.

According to Gartner research (*Kurt Potter, Sanil Solanki, and Ken McGee, Run, Grow, and Transform the Business IT Spending: Approaches to Categorization and Interpretation, Gartner G00308477, June 27, 2016*):

> "The CIO of a company invests 70% of his budget to maintain the current portfolio, 19% to evolve the existing applications and only 11% to build new applications."

Besides, there are also some examples, such as the one described in *The Majestic Monolith* (`https://m.signalvnoise.com/the-majestic-monolith-29166d022228`), that demonstrate that a monolith application is not the devil like someone has said.

So, why tear down the monolith?

The response is always the same. In most cases, the monolith has shown its limits in terms of reduction of time to market, having limited agility, making technology evolution difficult, being an obstacle to CD, and increasing technical debt, among other things.

What is a monolith?

In terms of Java EE, a monolith or a monolithic application is one that is usually distributed as a single unit, such as a WAR or an EAR archive. All the functionalities are packaged into this unit and divided into multiple layers that are responsible for implementing a specific area of the application:

- User experience in a frontend layer is implemented using the **Model-View-Controller** (**MVC**) or Model View/View Model patterns
- A business layer responsible for exposing business services to the frontend layer or third-party consumers
- A data layer that interacts with the database to manage the standard **create**, **read**, **update**, **delete** (**CRUD**) functions

This is only a minimal description of a monolith structure—the more complex the application, the more patterns and layers are used to implement it.

You can use the Java EE monolith example at `https://developers.redhat.com/ticket-monster/` to better understand the structure of this type of application design.

Migration path

Consider that the migration process will allow you to create a microservice-based, cloud-ready application and not a microservice cloud-native application.

Some restrictions derive from the nature of old Java EE specifications that are not microservice-oriented; the main one is certainly the database.

Remember that each microservice must own the data, so it must be associated with a single database instance. It's hard to split a single database instance, designed for a monolith application, into multiple instances associated with new bounded contexts that are implemented by microservices.

Concepts such as foreign keys, data integrity, and database transactions, intended to guarantee validity even in the event of errors using the **atomicity**, **consistency**, **isolation**, **durability** (**ACID**) paradigm, are difficult to maintain through multiple database instances that are managed by distributed and heterogeneous applications.

To refactor a monolith into microservices, you could evaluate and implement the following steps:

1. **Divide the frontend layer from the backend layer**: The separation should not only be from the code point of view (e.g., creating two Maven projects) but also from the distribution unit point of view (e.g., creating two WAR files, one for the frontend and the other for the backend). These two macro areas of the project have usually different release life cycles and need different skills. Having two teams that develop these areas will give you the opportunity to best implement these actions.

2. **Split the backend layer into multiple microservices**: You should analyze your complex domain and divide it into multiple simpler domains that must be fully consistent. Remember that to be a real microservice, you should also create a dedicated database for each of the new microservices. You could decide to postpone this process to a second phase. In this way, you could benefit from all of the positive aspects of an MSA in terms of ease of development, isolation, resiliency of code, and ease of deployment. But without the full ownership of the data and continuing to use a shared data store, your multiple distribution units continue to form a monolith.

3. **Change the way to expose your data**: Replace obsolete communication protocols, such as **Enterprise Java Bean** (**EJB**) remote, or complex methods such as SOAP web services, with a light communication model such as HTTP RESTful.

4. **Change the data transfer protocol**: Remove strong coupling modes, such as Java objects, for example, using Java serialization, or using heavy and complex structures, such as XML payload, in favor of loose coupling, and an easy and light structure such as JSON objects.

5. **Remove heavy orchestrator actors**: If your monolith runs in an SOA, replace ESB objects with the use of **Enterprise Integration Pattern** (**EIP**) to orchestrate the workflow process inside a coarse-grained service.

These are the basic and fundamental steps that you should implement to migrate from a monolith structure to an MSA. Consider that it's not mandatory to perform the steps we have described, and the respective points described in each step, all at one go.

You could proceed to disassemble the monolith gradually in order to evaluate the consequences of the updates to your application, team workflow process, and company structure. As suggested in the Agile methodology, splitting the work into little sprints could help you evaluate the real impact of your job and react faster to potential failures.

Reactive systems and reactive programming

The term *reactive* is widely used in the definition of MSAs.

But what is a reactive architecture based on? The definition of reactive is *to give an answer after a stimulus*. Reactive software is, therefore, able to adapt its behavior and react to receive stimuli.

To build a reactive architecture for microservices, the following models must be combined:

- **Reactive programming**: A development model based on the observation of streams of data, which provides a way to react to their changes and propagate them toward other actors
- **Reactive system**: An architectural model that is used to build robust and highly reactive distributed systems based on asynchronous communication using messages

The definition of a reactive system was formalized, in version 2.0, in September 2014 through the reactive manifesto (`https://www.reactivemanifesto.org/`). The key concepts of the reactive system are as follows:

- **Responsive**: The system must respond in a timely manner.
- **Resilient**: The system must remain reactive and functional even in case of failure of some of its components.
- **Elastic**: The system must remain reactive uniformly, regardless of the workload to which it is subjected.
- **Message-driven**: The reactive systems must communicate with each other through asynchronous messages to favor their decoupling and isolation.

We can, therefore, think of a reactive system as an architectural design to build distributed systems, whereas reactive programming is the implementation of the principles defined in the reactive system that must adhere to the reactive manifesto.

Reactive systems

A reactive system is a definition of a set of principles that are needed to maintain the responsiveness of and build systems that are able to respond to requests even with failures or under heavy load.

To build such a system, a reactive system chooses a message-driven model that is considered reliable and performant. All the components interact with each other using messages that are sent and received asynchronously. To decouple senders and receivers, components send and receive messages using virtual addresses.

But what's a virtual address? It's a destination identifier that's usually expressed as a URL. The delivery semantic depends on the technology used in the reactive programming frameworks to implement them.

In this design, there is no block during the execution of the flow—senders do not wait for a response; they may receive a response later and in the meantime, they can continue to do their job of sending other messages.

So the main core of a reactive system is an asynchronous messaging design that should be able to guarantee the following properties:

- **Elasticity**: The ability to scale horizontally that comes from the decoupling provided by message interactions. A load balance strategy is used by consumers of the messages, which are sent to a virtual address to distribute the load and guarantee high performance.
- **Resilience**: The ability to handle failure and to recover messages that comes from the ability to handle failure without blocking the execution of the services workflow. Thanks to the asynchronous aspect, components don't wait for responses and a potential failure of one component would not impact others. Furthermore, when a node that is consuming a message fails in the operation, the message can be processed by another node registered on the same address.

With the possession of these two characteristics, a system could be considered responsive.

This set of principles is very important when you intend to build microservice systems that are distributed and that are beyond the control of the caller.

Reactive programming

Reactive programming can be considered as the implementation of the guidelines that are defined in reactive systems. It is a programming model based on asynchronous data streams, oriented around the flows and propagation of data.

In reactive programming, the software must react to external stimuli, which are events that could be anything—variables, data structures, user inputs, caches, properties, and so on. These stimuli are called **streams**.

The names that are used to call the actors into reactive programming are related to the framework used to implement it.

In this chapter, we will try to quickly analyze the main Java frameworks that are able to implement a reactive system:

- RxJava
- Spring reactor
- Vert.x

For each framework, we will implement a simple example based on the Maven software project management tool. To try these examples, you need to have an IDE that enables Maven builds or have Maven installed in your workstation—follow the instructions described at `https://maven.apache.org/install.html` to do it.

Finally, we will quickly address how to make a Java EE monolith reactive, without rewriting the application through one of the frameworks we listed previously, but taking advantage of the latest asynchronous and messaging features made available by Java EE.

RxJava

RxJava is a Java framework that implements the specifications that are described in Reactive Extensions (ReactiveX `http://reactivex.io/`) about APIs for asynchronous programming with observable streams. Using RxJava framework, developers can easily create event-based and asynchronous applications through observable sequences.

This framework is built on top of the observer pattern to create sequences of events—it also exposes classes and methods that allow developers to compose these sequences. It also makes it easy to handle features that are hard to implement but absolutely necessary in reactive systems, such as threading, synchronization, thread safety, concurrent data structures, and so on.

In this section, we will use version 2 of the framework, since version 1 reached its end of life as of March 31, 2018. It is published under the Apache 2.0 license and is open source.

The main elements of RxJava are as follows:

- **Observables**: They are the sources for the data and begin to provide data once a subscriber listens on them. An observable source may emit nothing or any number of items and it can finish successfully or with an error. Sources may never terminate and can potentially produce an infinite stream of events. This feature is the same as the ones that are provided by the stream class that was introduced in Java 8.
- **Subscribers**: An observable can have multiple subscribers. Every time a new item is published by the observable, the onNext() method is called on each subscriber until the observable finishes its data flow. If the outcome is successful, then the onComplete() method will be called on each subscriber; otherwise, the onError() method will be called on each subscriber. In every situation, the flow must be processed and an action must be taken to react on the stimuli received by the system and represented by the data stream.

To use the RxJava2 framework, you must add it on the dependencies declaration of your project. If you're using Maven, you can do it simply by adding RxJava via the following snippet:

```
<!--https://mvnrepository.com/artifact/io.reactivex.rxjava2/rxjava -->
<dependency>
    <groupId>io.reactivex.rxjava2</groupId>
    <artifactId>rxjava</artifactId>
    <version>2.1.14</version>
</dependency>
```

Now, we are ready to write our simple first class:

```
package com.reactive.examples;

import io.reactivex.*;

public class RxJavaSimpleTest {
    public static void main(String ... args) {
    Disposable subscribe = Flowable.just("Welcome on RxJava2 World")
        .subscribe(System.out::println);
        subscribe.dispose();
    }
}
```

In this class I used a Flowable class that, as described in the Javadoc (http://reactivex.io/RxJava/2.x/javadoc/io/reactivex/Flowable.html), implements the Reactive Streams pattern. It exposes intermediate operators, factory methods, and the features that make your application able to consume reactive dataflow.

The `Flowable` object creates a data flow based on the string `"Welcome on RxJava2 World"`. After that, it signals the given String to the subscriber (in my example, the `System.out::println` method) and, finally, it completes. After running the class, you will see the following output on the console—`"Welcome on RxJava2 World"`.

RxJava2 provides base classes that enable you to process different types of data streams and perform different operations against them.

The following is another simple use example of RxJava2 base classes:

```java
package com.reactive.examples;

import io.reactivex.Completable;
import io.reactivex.Flowable;
import io.reactivex.Maybe;
import io.reactivex.Single;
import io.reactivex.functions.Consumer;
public class RxJavaBaseClassesTest {

    public static void main(String... args) {
        // A flow of exactly 1 item or an error
        Single.just(1)
            .map(i -> i * 5)
            .map(Object::toString)
            .subscribe(System.out::println);

        // A flow with exactly one item.
        Maybe.just("May be I will do
something...").subscribe(System.out::println);

        // Never sends any items or notifications to a MaybeObserver
        Maybe.never().subscribe(o -> System.out.println("Something is
here...never happened"));

        // A flow without items but only a completion or error signal
        Completable.complete().subscribe(() ->
System.out.println("Completed"));

        // Example of simple data flow processing
        Flowable.just("mauro", "luigi", "marco")
            .filter(s -> s.startsWith("m"))
            .map(String::toUpperCase)
            .subscribe(System.out::println);
    }
}
```

If you execute this class, you should see the following output:

```
5
May be I will do something...
Completed
MAURO
MARCO
```

The output reflects the description of the components' behavior that I made in the Java class. I obtained the following:

- The exact computation in the first line: `1 * 5` result
- The output that confirms the execution of a `Maybe` condition
- The output that confirms the end of the execution process
- The result of a simple filter and `map` operation

RxJava contains a list of modules that enable interaction with other important frameworks that are used to implement the main patterns that are used in MSA, as follows:

- **Hystrix**: A latency and fault tolerance library that's used to prevent the cascading failure, which is derived from service outage third-party remote systems
- **Camel-rx**: A library that simplifies the use of Camel components to implement a Reactive Extension
- **Vert.x RxJava**: A module that provides easy integration with Vert.x toolkit, which we will examine later
- **RxJava-jdbc**: A library that enables you to change the way you interact with the database, usually in synchronous and blocking mode, using the stream API to process result sets and do functional composition of statements

The impact of this framework in a Java SE environment is very important. This experience gave birth to reactive systems initiative that aims to define a standard protocol for asynchronous streams running on **Java Virtual Machine** (**JVM**).

The RxJava team was part of this initiative that led to the definition, in Java SE 9, of a set of interfaces, `java.util.concurrent.Flow.*`, dedicated to the implementation of the concepts defined by the Reactive Streams—actually, the interfaces available in JDK 9 are equivalent to their respective Reactive Streams counterparts.

Although the examples that are presented are very simple, they still make it clear how different the design of applications in reactive architectures is. The classic request/reply model, with a consequent block waiting for the reply, is replaced by a completely asynchronous, non-blocking model, such as the publish/subscribe model. For Java EE developers, this is a known and widely used model in the **Java Message Service** (**JMS**) specification.

Frameworks such as RxJava expand these concepts, allowing their use even in scenarios of exposure and the use of APIs, typically of MSAs. Javascript developers, or in general those more used to working in client-side contexts with new technologies, who are HTML 5 oriented, know about these paradigms very well, which are the basis of their implementation model.

You can find more details about RxJava by visiting the GitHub repository of the library: `https://github.com/ReactiveX/RxJava/`.

Spring WebFlux and reactive stacks

We can consider RxJava as a low-level framework, containing specific implementations of reactive concepts. But how do architectural frameworks, such as Spring, think about reactive structure in enterprise environments?

The traditional web framework developed in Spring Suite, Spring Web MVC, was built on top of the Servlet API and servlet containers, mainly Tomcat. The reactive implementation, named Spring WebFlux, was introduced in Spring 5.0. It fully supports Reactive Streams, non-blocking, and runs on different server types:

- Traditional, such as a Servlet 3.1+ container (Tomcat)
- A new performant web server based on Java NIO, such as Undertow
- Asynchronous event-driven network servers, such as Netty

Historically, Spring has represented the framework that allowed us to overcome the limits present in the Java EE platform. As described in `Chapter 1`, *Jakarta EE – the New Open Source Life of JEE*, it is not appropriate to say that Spring has represented the evolutionary push that has allowed for continuous and constant improvement of the Java EE ecosystem.

Also, in the case of reactive architectures, Spring presented solutions that are capable of implementing what was requested by the Reactive Streams and not easily obtained with previous versions of Java EE.

In reactive architecture, but also in cloud environments and microservice systems, there is a need for non-blocking APIs to handle high concurrency of requests with a small number of threads to easily scale the infrastructure with fewer hardware resources.

Java EE 7 and Servlet 3.1 did provide an API for non-blocking I/O, but some of the core APIs are synchronous, such as Filter, or blocking, such as those for the `getParameter` and `getPart` methods of the Servlet API.

This was the reason that drove Spring to build a new common API that could be used inside any non-blocking runtime. Netty based its core around these concepts and, for that reason, was chosen as the runtime execution environment for Spring WebFlux.

Spring WebFlux is the new Spring implementation of Reactive Stream's specifications. The main target is to create a new set of functional and richer APIs that can enable developers to compose `async` logic, which is the basis of reactive programming. The core library of Spring WebFlux is Reactor (`https://github.com/reactor/reactor`); it provides two main APIs: Mono and Flux. Thanks to these new APIs, it is easy to work on data sequences of *0..1* and *0..n* through a rich set of methods and implementations.

So to build a reactive stack in Spring, should I leave Spring MVC and use only Spring WebFlux?

The answer is no. The two modules can coexist and are designed for consistency with each other. In particular, in an MSA, you are free to use a polyglot microservice, either in terms of programming languages or in features implemented by the chosen framework.

In the case of Spring, you can use Spring MVC, Spring WebFlux controllers, or, with Spring WebFlux, functional endpoints. The difference is strictly related to the programming model, which could be annotated controllers or functional endpoints.

Let's try to realize a simple example of exposure of a service via an HTTP protocol through Spring WebFlux.

We can use Spring Initializr to quickly bootstrap our application. You should connect to `https://start.spring.io/` and then perform the following steps:

1. Set `com.microservice.webflux` as the project's **Group**.
2. Set `demo` as the **Artifact** name.
3. Set `reactor` in the **Search for dependencies** field and select **Reactive Web** from the drop-down menu.
4. Click the **Generate Project** button to download a scaffold of a Maven project.

This is a snapshot of what you have done so far:

Once downloaded, unzip the project's file into a directory and open your Maven project with your favorite IDE to create the classes that are needed to build the service.

Please ensure you have set the Spring repositories into the Maven `settings.xml` file. Otherwise, you need to do so by choosing from the following, based on your preference:

- Spring Snapshots repository: `https://repo.spring.io/snapshot`
- Spring Milestones repository: `https://repo.spring.io/milestone`

The first class to create is the handler that will be responsible for handling the requests and creating the responses:

```
package com.microservice.webflux.demo;
import org.springframework.http.MediaType;
import org.springframework.stereotype.Component;
import org.springframework.web.reactive.function.BodyInserters;
import org.springframework.web.reactive.function.server.ServerRequest;
import org.springframework.web.reactive.function.server.ServerResponse;
import reactor.core.publisher.Mono;
@Component
public class DemoHandler {
    public Mono<ServerResponse> hello(ServerRequest request) {
        return ServerResponse.ok().contentType(MediaType.TEXT_PLAIN)
            .body(BodyInserters.fromObject("Welcome on Spring WebFlux world!"));
    }
}
```

This `handler` class has a static behavior and always returns the string `"Welcome on Spring WebFlux world!"`. In a real scenario, it could return a stream of items, derived from a database query or that were generated by calculations. The `handler` method returns a Mono object, the Reactive equivalent of Java 8's `CompletableFuture`, which holds a `ServerResponse` body.

After creating the `handler`, we need to build a `router` class that intercepts the requests directed to a specific path, in our case `/welcome`, and returns as a response the result of the invocation of the `handler` method:

```
package com.microservice.webflux.demo;

import org.springframework.context.annotation.Bean;
import org.springframework.context.annotation.Configuration;
import org.springframework.http.MediaType;
import org.springframework.web.reactive.function.server.RequestPredicates;
import org.springframework.web.reactive.function.server.RouterFunction;
import org.springframework.web.reactive.function.server.RouterFunctions;
import org.springframework.web.reactive.function.server.ServerResponse;
@Configuration
public class DemoRouter {
    @Bean
    public RouterFunction<ServerResponse> route(DemoHandler demoHandler) {
        return RouterFunctions.route(RequestPredicates.GET("/welcome")
            .and(RequestPredicates.accept(MediaType.TEXT_PLAIN)),
demoHandler::welcome);
    }
}
```

Now that we have the `handler` and the `router`, it's time to construct the `WebClient` class, which is needed to hold the content of the invocation and exchange it into a specific return value type, in our case, a string:

```
package com.microservice.webflux.demo;

import org.springframework.http.MediaType;
import org.springframework.web.reactive.function.client.ClientResponse;
import org.springframework.web.reactive.function.client.WebClient;
import reactor.core.publisher.Mono;
public class DemoWebClient {

    // Externalize the URL in a configuration file
    private final WebClient client =
WebClient.create("http://localhost:8080");
    private final Mono<ClientResponse> result =
        client.get().uri("/welcome").accept(MediaType.TEXT_PLAIN)
```

```
        .exchange();
    public String getResult() {
        return ">> result = " + result.flatMap(res ->
res.bodyToMono(String.class)).block();
    }
}
```

This is a classic example where Spring WebFlux introduces an important change compared to the traditional Spring MVC RESTTemplate. The WebClient implementation of Spring MVC is blocking while Spring WebFlux is non-blocking, following the reactive philosophy.

Finally, we need to make our simple application executable. Reactive Spring WebFlux supports an embedding Netty server as the HTTP runtime that will host the application and expose the service via the HTTP protocol:

```
package com.microservice.webflux.demo;

import org.springframework.boot.SpringApplication;
import org.springframework.boot.autoconfigure.SpringBootApplication;
@SpringBootApplicationpublic class DemoApplication {

    public static void main(String[] args) {
        SpringApplication.run(DemoApplication.class, args);
        DemoWebClient demoWebClient = new DemoWebClient();
        System.out.println(demoWebClient.getResult());
    }
}
```

The `main()` method of my class uses Spring Boot's `SpringApplication.run()` method to start the application. Now, compile the application using Maven, via the `mvn clean package` command, or through your favorite IDE, in order to obtain the executable JAR file that will be created inside the `$PROJECT_HOME/target` directory that is the location where you unzipped the scaffold project that was created by Spring Initializr.

Finally, it's time to run our application via the `java -jar target/demo-0.0.1-SNAPSHOT.jar` command (ensure you are in the `$PROJECT_HOME` directory).

You will obtain an output like this:

As you will notice, at the end of the output there is the string, `Welcome on Spring WebFlux world!`, that is the result of the method defined in the `DemoHandler` class. You can also test the method invocation using a browser and setting the URL to `http://localhost:8080/welcome`. You will obtain the same result:

If you prefer to follow **test-driven development (TDD)**, you can build your JUnit test to verify that the service's output is what you expected:

```
package com.microservice.webflux.demo;

import org.junit.Test;
import org.junit.runner.RunWith;
import org.springframework.beans.factory.annotation.Autowired;
import org.springframework.boot.test.context.SpringBootTest;
import org.springframework.http.MediaType;
import org.springframework.test.context.junit4.SpringRunner;
import org.springframework.test.web.reactive.server.WebTestClient;

@RunWith(SpringRunner.class)
@SpringBootTest(webEnvironment = SpringBootTest.WebEnvironment.RANDOM_PORT)
public class DemoRouterTests {

    @Autowired
```

```
        private WebTestClient webTestClient;

        @Test
        public void testWelcome() {
            webTestClient.get().uri("/welcome").accept(MediaType.TEXT_PLAIN)
                .exchange().expectStatus().isOk()
                .expectBody(String.class).isEqualTo("Welcome on Spring WebFlux
    world!");
        }
    }
```

By launching the `mvn test` command, you will be able to verify that the output is what you expected.

In sum, we just implemented an easy scenario that shows you how you can implement, expose, and consume an API in a reactive way using Spring Reactor and Spring WebFlux.

Vert.x

Vert.x is an open source Eclipse toolkit that's used to build distributed and reactive systems.

Eclipse Vert.x provides a flexible way to write applications that are lightweight and responsive due to its implementation of Reactive Stream principles.

It is designed to be cloud-native—it allows many processes to run with very few resources (threads, CPU, etc.). In this way, Vert.x applications can better use their CPU quotas in cloud environments. There isn't any unnecessary overhead caused by the creation of a great number of new threads.

It defines an asynchronous and non-blocking development model based on an event loop that handles the requests and avoids long waiting on the client side while the server side is stressed by a high number of invocations.

Since it's a toolkit and not a framework, Vert.x can be used as a typical third-party library and you are free to choose the component that is needed for you to target.

It does not provide an all-in-one solution, but it gives you the scaffolds that you can assemble to build your own architecture. You can decide to use a Vert.x component inside your existing application, for example, a Spring application, maybe refactoring a particular section to be reactive and better respond to a heavy load. It's also a good choice for implementing HTTP REST microservices thanks to its high volume event processing.

Vert.x runs on top of JVM but it doesn't work in Java alone. You can use all the programming language ecosystem around JVM. You can also use Vert.x with Groovy, Ceylon, JavaScript (maybe using a Java-provided JavaScript engine such as Nashorn) and JRuby.

A diagram having a list of Vert.x modules can be seen here: `https://www.eclipse.org/community/eclipse_newsletter/2016/october/article4.php`. As you can see, there are some components that can help you build a reactive microservice.

The main component of Vert.x is the **verticle**. The verticle is the programmable unit where you implement the business logic of your application. Although it's optional in the Vert.x toolkit, it's highly recommended to use it to obtain a clear separation of duty in your architecture. It provides an actor-like deployment and concurrency model, similar to what you can obtain using Akka—a toolkit for building resilient message-driven applications—and it's always executed on the same thread.

A single thread may execute several verticles, using the event loop mechanism, and a single verticle instance usually starts one thread/event loop per core.

A Vert.x application can be composed of multiple verticles; each one implements a specific section of the domain business logic to follow the principles of single responsibility and the separation of duties. Each verticle should communicate to the others in a loosely coupled way—for this purpose, Vert.x uses an event bus, that is, lightweight distributed messaging. When a verticle wants to listen for messages from the event bus, it listens on a certain virtual address, as defined in Reactive Stream specifications.

Now, it's time to create our first simple microservice application. As I mentioned earlier, for Spring Boot and Spring WebFlux, as well as for Vert.x, there is a project generator utility that helps you create a scaffold for the project. The generator is available at `http://start.vertx.io/`.

Set the fields with the following suggested values (feel free to substitute them with whatever you want):

- **Version**: 3.5.0
- **Language**: Java
- **Build**: Maven
- **GroupId**: `com.microservice.vertx`
- **ArtifactId**: `demoVertx`
- **Selected dependencies**: **Vert.x Web**

The following is a simple screenshot of what I described previously:

Once the ZIP file is downloaded, unzip the context into a directory, open the project with your favorite IDE and, finally, launch the first build from your IDE or by using the following Maven command:

```
$ mvn clean compile
```

In this way, you have created a simple runnable Vert.x application.

You will notice that there is a simple verticle class, MainVerticle.java, in the com.microservice.vertx.demoVertx package that creates an HTTP server, listening on port 8080, and returns a simple plain text message, "Hello from Vert.x!":

```
package com.microservice.vertx.demoVertx;

import io.vertx.core.AbstractVerticle;

public class MainVerticle extends AbstractVerticle {

    @Override
    public void start() throws Exception {
        vertx.createHttpServer().requestHandler(req -> {
```

```
        req.response().putHeader("content-type",
"text/plain").end("Hello from Vert.x!");
        }).listen(8080);
        System.out.println("HTTP server started on port 8080");
    }
}
```

To run the application, you can do the following:

- Launch the `$ mvn compile exec:java` command
- Build a fat JAR, with the `$ mvn package` command, and then launch the executable JAR with the `java -jar target/demoVertx-1.0.0-SNAPSHOT-fat.jar` command

The final result will be the same—an up-and-running HTTP server:

```
. . . .
HTTP server started on port 8080
Jun 20, 2018 11:09:16 AM
io.vertx.core.impl.launcher.commands.VertxIsolatedDeployer
INFO: Succeeded in deploying verticle
. . . .
```

You will also have a service exposed via HTTP that you can invoke at the URL `http://localhost:8080`:

Now, we are ready to update our source code so that we can implement a simple microservice.

First of all, we create the classes that are needed for the RESTful web service. We must build an easy Java **Plain Old Java Object** (**POJO**) to store the author's information:

```java
package com.microservice.vertx.demoVertx;

import java.util.concurrent.atomic.AtomicInteger;

public class Author {

    private static final AtomicInteger COUNTER = new AtomicInteger();
    private final int id;
    private final String name;
    private final String surname;

    public Author(String name, String surname) {
        this.id = COUNTER.getAndIncrement();
        this.name = name;
        this.surname = surname;
    }

    public String getName() {
        return name;
    }

    public String getSurname() {
        return surname;
    }

    public int getId() {
        return id;
    }
}
```

Then, we make the `AuthorVerticle`, which has the purpose of exposing the data; in our example, the list of the book's authors. There is a static initialization of the data, as well as the usual creation of the `Router` and of the HTTP server to serve the requests:

```java
package com.microservice.vertx.demoVertx;

import io.vertx.core.AbstractVerticle;
import io.vertx.core.Future;
import io.vertx.core.json.Json;
import io.vertx.ext.web.Router;
import io.vertx.ext.web.RoutingContext;
import java.util.LinkedHashMap;
import java.util.Map;

public class AuthorVerticle extends AbstractVerticle {
```

```
    private final Map<Integer, Author> authors = new LinkedHashMap<>();

    private void populateAuthorsData() {
        Author mauro = new Author("Mauro", "Vocale");
        authors.put(mauro.getId(), mauro);
        Author luigi = new Author("Luigi", "Fugaro");
        authors.put(luigi.getId(), luigi);
    }

    private void getAuthors(RoutingContext routingContext) {
        routingContext.response().putHeader("content-type",
"application/json; charset=utf-8")
            .end(Json.encodePrettily(authors.values()));
    }

    @Override
    public void start(Future<Void> future) {
        populateAuthorsData();
        Router router = Router.router(vertx);
        router.get("/authors").handler(this::getAuthors);
vertx.createHttpServer().requestHandler(router::accept).listen(8080,
            result -> {
                if (result.succeeded()) {
                    future.complete();
                } else {
                    future.fail(result.cause());
                }
            });
    }
}
```

Finally, we refactor the `MainVerticle` class, which will be responsible for deploying the verticle we created previously:

```
package com.microservice.vertx.demoVertx;

import io.vertx.core.AbstractVerticle;
import io.vertx.core.Future;

public class MainVerticle extends AbstractVerticle {

    @Override
    public void start(Future<Void> future) throws Exception {
vertx.deployVerticle("com.microservice.vertx.demoVertx.AuthorVerticle", res
-> {
            if (res.succeeded()) {
                System.out.println("Deployment id is: " + res.result());
            } else {
```

```
                  System.out.println("Deployment failed!");
              }
          });
      }
  }
```

Now, we can launch the application:

```
$ mvn compile exec:java
```

Then, we can invoke the RESTful service using the URL
`http://localhost:8080/authors`. You will obtain the following result:

```
 JSON      Dati non elaborati      Header

 Salva   Copia                              ▽ Filtra JSON

▼ 0:
      id:        0
      name:      "Mauro"
      surname:   "Vocale"
▼ 1:
      id:        1
      name:      "Luigi"
      surname:   "Fugaro"
```

You can test your service, following TDD, and also implement a JUnit test:

```
package com.microservice.vertx.demoVertx;

import io.vertx.core.Vertx;
import io.vertx.ext.unit.Async;
import io.vertx.ext.unit.TestContext;
import io.vertx.ext.unit.junit.VertxUnitRunner;
import org.junit.After;
import org.junit.Before;
import org.junit.Test;
import org.junit.runner.RunWith;

@RunWith(VertxUnitRunner.class)
public class AuthorVerticleTest {

    private Vertx vertx;
```

```
        public AuthorVerticleTest() {
        }

        @Before
        public void setUp(TestContext context) {
            vertx = Vertx.vertx();
            vertx.deployVerticle(AuthorVerticle.class.getName(),
    context.asyncAssertSuccess());
        }
        @After
        public void tearDown(TestContext context) {
            if (vertx != null) {
                vertx.close(context.asyncAssertSuccess());
            }
        }

        /**
         * Test of start method, of class AuthorVerticle.
         * @param context
         */
        @Test
        public void testStart(TestContext context) {
            final Async async = context.async();
            vertx.createHttpClient().getNow(8080, "localhost", "/authors",
    response -> {
                response.handler(body -> {
                    context.assertTrue(body.toString().contains(""name" :
    "Mauro""));
                    async.complete();
                });
            });
        }
    }
```

Check the result by running the $ mvn test command.

Here, again, we implemented an easy example that shows you how to use Vert.x to build reactive microservices. You can find more details in the Vert.x documentation at https:// vertx.io/docs/.

Reactive Java EE monolith

Java EE doesn't include reactive paradigms in its specifications. The reason is simple—it was born before the ability to design architecture in this way was developed. For this reason, it's not very easy to make Java EE reactive.

Despite this, the latest Java EE releases introduced, and subsequently improved, one of the key features of the Reactive Stream specifications—asynchronicity.

So if you don't want to rewrite your application using one of the frameworks we described earlier, or other options such as Akka, you could try revisiting your Java EE classic implementation to make it reactive-oriented.

Java EE has the following two main aspects that could be useful for this topic:

- The ability to process requests in asynchronously
- The ability to decouple communications between its components via messages

Let's examine these features in more detail.

Asynchronous processing

There are common scenarios in enterprise applications that are usually synchronous and blocking, for example, database or remote server calls. In those cases, the call at these methods takes some time to return, usually with a client thread that is blocked waiting for the answer. Let's consider a simple example—a Java EE servlet that queries a database, using a service, and prints the list of the records, in our case a list of authors (yes, I know, I'm a little bit egocentric):

```java
@WebServlet(urlPatterns = "/authors")
public class AuthorServlet extends HttpServlet {
    ...
    @Override
    protected void doGet(HttpServletRequest req, HttpServletResponse resp)
throws
        ServletException, IOException {
        final List<Author> authors = authorService.getAuthors();
        final ServletOutputStream out = resp.getOutputStream();
        for (Author author : authors) {
            out.println(user.toString());
        }
    }
}
```

You must wait for the invocation of the database query, implemented in `authorService.getAuthors()`, to be completed to get the response. Therefore, the client stays blocked until the request is processed.

Let's try to make the servlet asynchronous:

```
@WebServlet(urlPatterns = "/authors", asyncSuppported = true)
public class AuthorServlet extends HttpServlet {
    ...
    @Override
    protected void doGet(HttpServletRequest req, HttpServletResponse resp) throws
        ServletException, IOException {
        final AsyncContext asyncCtx = req.startAsync();
        asyncCtx.start(() -> {
            final List<Author> authors = authorService.getAuthors();
            printAuthors(authors,
asyncCtx.getResponse().getOutputStream());
            asyncCtx.complete();
        });
    }
    private void printAuthors (List<Author> authors, ServletOutputStream
out) {
        for (Author author : authors) {
            out.println(author.toString());
        }
    }
}
```

With a simple update, we made our servlet asynchronous, freeing our client to perform other operations while waiting to receive the answer to the request that was made.

Well, you could argue that nobody writes servlets nowadays. But, are you sure about that?

In an MSA, the standard communication is based on a RESTful web service that, in the Java EE world, is implemented by JAX-RS—these specifications are built on top of servlet specifications.

Then, we can revisit our simple servlet in a RESTful way:

```
@Path("/authors")
public class AuthorResource {
    ...
    @GET
    @Produces(MediaType.APPLICATION_JSON)
    public Response getAuthors() {
        final List<Author> authors = authorService.getAuthors();
        return Response.ok(authors).build();
    }
}
```

Now, we can make it asynchronous:

```
@Path("/authors")
public class AuthorResource {

    ...
    @GET
    @Produces(MediaType.APPLICATION_JSON)
    @Asynchronous
    public void getAuthors(@Suspended AsyncResponse response) {
        final List<Author> authors = authorService.getAuthors();
        response.resume(Response.ok(authors).build());
    }
}
```

An annotation, @Asynchronous, and a **Context Dependency Injection (CDI)** method parameter, @Suspended AsyncResponse response, are used to make it asynchronous. A quick win!

But remember, never wait forever and never couple your application with the issues of other services. Therefore, always set a timeout to abort the invocation in case of an unrecoverable issue.

This is the final version of our easy example:

```
@Path("/authors")
public class AuthorResource {
    ...

    @GET
    @Produces(MediaType.APPLICATION_JSON)
    @Asynchronous
    public void getAuthors(@Suspended AsyncResponse response) {
        response.setTimeout(2, TimeUnit.SECONDS);
        response.setTimeoutHandler(resp ->
```

```
        resp.resume(Response.status(Status.REQUEST_TIMEOUT).build()));
        final List<Author> authors = authorService.getAuthors();
        response.resume(Response.ok(authors).build());
    }
}
```

This approach is very useful if your application contains a mix of heavy- and soft-loaded queries. In this way, you can obtain a higher throughput and have the opportunity to fine-tune your application server.

We have spoken about how to expose our API asynchronously. But what should you do to obtain the same results in the business logic layer?

We can implement it using EJBs. Some people consider EJBs to be the devil: I disagree.

This negative impression was born due to the complex and poor performance implementations related to version 2.1. The new ones, from version 3.0 to version 3.2, simplify the use and the configuration, and enrich the platform with a great number of new features.

I consider exposing your service using EJB remote as deprecating. You should never communicate via EJB remote, as it is a strong coupling and poor performance way to do this. However, the EJB local can be used outside of a Java EE container because they are only POJO, simplify some core topics such as the handling of thread safety, the concurrency, the transaction life cycle, and so on. I think that an improvement in Jakarta EE that can be implemented in the next feature would be the deletion of EJB remote from the specifications.

Now, let's get back to our business layer implementation.

This is the classic synchronous implementation:

```
@Stateless
public class AuthorService {

    public Author createAuthor(final String name, final String surname) {
        final Author author = new Author(UUID.randomUUID(), name, surname);
        em.persist(author);
        return author;
    }
}
```

Let's make it asynchronous:

```
@Stateless
public class AuthorService {

    @Asynchronous
    public Future<Author> createAuthor(final String name, final String
surname) {
        final Author author = new Author(UUID.randomUUID(), name, surname);
        em.persist(author);
        return new AsyncResult<>(author);
    }
}
```

This is easy—tell the container to make the invocation asynchronous, using the
@Asynchronous annotation, and change the return type from classic POJO to Future<T>,
which is implemented by AsyncResult.

After doing that, we can implement our RESTful class to use the new feature:

```
@Path("/authors")
public class AuthorResource {
    @POST
    @Consumes(MediaType.APPLICATION_FORM_URLENCODED)
    @Produces(MediaType.APPLICATION_JSON)
    public Response createAuthor(@FormParam("name") final String name,
@FormParam("surname")
        final String surname) {
        final Future<Author> authorFuture =
authorService.createAuthor(name, surname);
        try {
            final Author author = authorFuture.get(2, TimeUnit.SECONDS);
            return Response.ok(author).build();
        } catch (InterruptedException | ExecutionException |
TimeoutException e) {
            return Response.serverError().build();
        }
    }
}
```

However, we can do this in a better way by using the CompletableFuture class, which
was introduced in Java SE 8:

```
@Stateless
public class AuthorService {

    @Asynchronous
    public void createAuthor(final String name, final String surname, final
```

```
        CompletableFuture<Author> promise) {
        final Author author = new Author(UUID.randomUUID(), name, surname);
        em.persist(author);
        promise.complete(author);
    }
}
```

Instead of returning a `Future`, we made our method `void` and told the Java EE container to inject a `CompletableFuture` that will be responsible for notifying the end of the operation.

Now, we can revisit the RESTful implementation:

```
@Path("/authors")
public class AuthorResource {
    @POST
    @Consumes(MediaType.APPLICATION_FORM_URLENCODED)
    @Produces(MediaType.APPLICATION_JSON)
    @Asynchronous
    public void createAuthor(@FormParam("name") final String name,
@FormParam("surname") final
        String surname, @Suspended AsyncResponse response) {
        CompletableFuture<Author> promise = new CompletableFuture<>();
        authorService.createAuthor(name, surname, promise);
        promise.thenApply(response::resume);
    }
}
```

I prefer this approach instead of the use of `Future`. `Future` is, at the moment, the only solution to implement asynchronicity in Java EE, but it has some limitations compared to `CompletableFuture`; for example, it is not able to build and use the new `lambdas` feature.

Messaging communications

Java EE offers the ability to implement loosely coupled services that can communicate with each other, maintaining a guarantee of delivery and fault tolerance. This feature is implemented through the JMS that was introduced in Java EE since the beginning of the platform. The purpose of this specification is to decouple services and process messages, producing and consuming them asynchronously.

The new version of the specification, JMS 2.0, which was introduced in Java EE 7, simplifies the use of this specification and reduces the boilerplate that's needed to implement the message producers and consumers.

The following is an easy example of a message producer:

```java
public class AuthorProducer {
    @Inject
    private JMSContext jmsContext;
    @Resource(lookup = "jms/authorQueue")
    private Destination queue;
    /**
     * Send Message.
     */
    @Override
    public void sendMessage(String message) {
        /*
         * createProducer: Creates a new JMSProducer object that will be
used to
         * configure and send messages.
         */
        jmsContext.createProducer().send(queue, message);
    }
}
```

Now, it's time to implement the consumer:

```java
@MessageDriven(activationConfig = {
@ActivationConfigProperty(propertyName = "destinationType", propertyValue =
"javax.jms.Queue"),
@ActivationConfigProperty(propertyName = "destinationLookup", propertyValue
= "jms/authorQueue")})
public class AuthorMDB implements MessageListener {
    /**
     * @see MessageListener#onMessage(Message)
     */
    public void onMessage(Message rcvMessage) {
        TextMessage msg = null;
        try {
            if (rcvMessage instanceof TextMessage) {
                msg = (TextMessage) rcvMessage;
                System.out.println("Received Message from queue: " +
msg.getText());
            } else {
                System.out.println("Message of wrong type: " +
rcvMessage.getClass().getName());
            }
        } catch (JMSException e) {
            throw new RuntimeException(e);
        }
    }
}
```

It's easy to implement decoupling messaging services in Java EE.

Obviously, this is not enough to declare that the traditional Java EE approach is reactive-friendly.

But the approach we described above can help you update your traditional monolith to be less synchronous and less I/O blocking to better serve the new way to design enterprise and cloud-native architecture.

Summary

In this chapter, we discussed microservices, MSAs and reactive architectures, as well as the principles of SOAs. We learned how to modernize an application, thus transforming a monolith into an MSA. We also reviewed how the main opensource frameworks, like Spring and Vert.x, have implemented reactive principles in order to help developers build cloud-oriented applications that are scalable, reliable, and cost-effective. Finally, we learned how you can update your traditional JEE applications in order to implement an asynchronous and non-blocking system as the first step toward building your own MSA.

In the next chapter, we will look at cloud-native applications and microservices so that we can understand how to design and implement them.

Cloud-Native Applications

3

In recent years, we've been hearing a lot about the cloud, but without real meaning. It was just a buzzword, and everybody was rushing to get some Amazon EC2 instances and put some services on it, just to spread the word—*It's in the cloud; I put it in the cloud; we're in the cloud.*

Embracing the cloud is much more than deploying something on it. Behind the word *cloud*, there's an entire world that isn't about a new technology or innovation or migration (even worse, transformation); it's about a revolution.

It's a revolution in terms of infrastructure, and development, deployment. Revolution in terms of teams.

The key point for the infrastructure is automation. Everything needs to be automated—provisioning servers, disk space, memory, networks, and resources—everything.
The key point for development is *keep it small*—small pieces of software independent of each other; small development teams focused on a few tasks that need to communicate excessively and receive feedback from failing software as fast as possible. The latter is possible only with automation—build automation, test automation, and deploy automation. The new infrastructure is built on the concept of automation. If you don't automate, you can't be elastic, flexible, resilient, and fault tolerant.

Getting into the cloud means changing your work habit, changing a company to organize and structure its IT department.

How do you start with cloud-native applications? First of all, a deep assessment of the actual infrastructure is mandatory. Integration boundaries, security, legacy systems, appliance components, processes, and business and operational requirements—all of these aspects need to be checked to find weaknesses and strengths. The assessment can lead to training people and creating new teams.

A cloud-native application is an application that takes into account all of the characteristics of the cloud architecture. Only then can you start the most beautiful game—building your cloud-native application.

One of the most used approaches to build a cloud-native application is microservices. The difference between a microservice and a cloud-native application is that the former can be provided by any infrastructure and the latter is the same but it takes into account all of the aspects of the nature of the cloud, and distributed environments, where a single place can't be considered.

Going back to the cloud architecture, the advantages of having microservices in addition to automation is efficiency:

- **Auto-provisioning**: Infrastructure as code
- **Auto-redundancy**: Cloud-native applications are inherently resilient to failure
- **Auto-scaling**: By constantly measuring your microservices, you can decide when it's appropriate to add more nodes (scale out)

A common way to deliver microservices is through Linux containers. Microservice architecture and Linux containers brought a lot to each other. Every microservice has to be a self-contained unit—dedicated resources, CPUs, memory, and disk space. Imagine delivering such services on a single **virtual machine** (**VM**) or tens or hundreds of VMs. The process would take quite a long time, the infrastructure would start lacking resources quickly, and in the short term, your infrastructure wouldn't be enough anymore—this would be a waste of money, a waste of time, and a waste of resources.

Containers fit the self-contained unit approach of microservices very well, from an infrastructure point of view. Containers are lightweight, isolated, and provisioned in seconds—actually in milliseconds.

In this chapter, we'll cover the following topics:

- Twelve-factor applications
- Microservices
- Runtime environments

Twelve-factor applications

Despite the characteristics of the cloud, there several factors that make an application a cloud-native application, and these can be found in the *The Twelve-Factor App* manifesto, available at `https://12factor.net/`

Let's analyze these twelve factors one by one.

Code base

The first factor is related to the source code, where it is kept, and how it should be kept. Every change in the code must be saved and tracked into the source code repository. Nowadays, there are plenty of choices: GitLab, GitHub, Bitbucket, Stash, and the old SVN (it's a revolution, so switch to Git). All of the code, including infrastructure as code, should be versioned, and each version potentially corresponds to a deployment in some environment.

Long story short, have a source code repository, and it is better to have an open source and widely adopted solution.

Dependencies

The second factor is related to the dependency management tool. I'm familiar with the Java environment and, since its first release, I've been using Maven to explicitly declare and isolate dependencies.

Maven does it, concentrating everything into a file named `pom.xml`, where you can specify the library or framework you want to use and the exact version. Maven will compile and build your code by downloading the JARs you need from the internet (Maven repositories). Nevertheless, there are a lot of dependency management tools for all modern programming languages, such as Ivy, Gradle, Gemfiles, Bundler, and Godm.

Long story short, have a dependency management tool that ensures consistency in the build.

Config

The third factor is related to the configuration of the application. The application must have its configuration externalized, not shipped with the application itself. Shipping the configuration with the application requires altering the application bundle from environment to environment, breaking the integrity of the artifact.

To be completely agnostic from the environment, the configuration parameter must reside in the environment variables. In addition to environment variables, there are tools that provide better configuration distribution, such as Consul and Vault (security-related settings, such as passwords).

Long story short, have a separation of configuration from the code.

Backing services

The fourth factor is related to services that your application uses. Those backing services might be file storage, a database, or a mail server. The application should just reference the need for such a service, but have the infrastructure (the new revolutionary cloud infrastructure) do the resource binding. This kind of separation of concern helps your application to attach and detach to different backing services, thanks to the third factor—without redeploying the application. This is also the basis for the circuit breaker pattern that we will describe in `Chapter 8`, *Microservices Patterns*.

Long story short, integrate your application with resources, not implementations.

Build, release, run

The fifth factor is related to the first, second, and the third factors. It's about how a piece of code gets built, is released (packed), and runs in the target execution environment.

The preceding steps are called stages and represent the life cycle of your application. Each stage has its own specific role and isn't related to any other stage, and all together, these stages form a deployment.

So, to perform a deployment, we need the following:

- We need to build our source code pulled from a repository by identifying the code and its version. This is done by fetching dependencies and compiling the code (the first and second factors).
- To release the previous build, by identifying it by its name and version, we need to attach the appropriate configuration settings (the third factor). Every release has its own unique version (date, incrementing numbers, code name, and so on).
- To run the released build into the execution environment, we need to launch a process that grabs the previous release, by identifying it through name and version.

These stages can and should be performed by tools provided by the cloud platform. Tools such as Jenkins and GitLab **continuous integration** (**CI**) are great for such tasks. More details can be found in `Chapter 9`, *Deployments*.

Long story short, what you build is what you release is what you run.

Processes

The sixth factor is related to the states that your application might have. And a cloud-native application must be stateless to respect characteristics such as scalability, flexibility, resilience, and fault tolerance.

Every state must be kept, stored, and saved to a backing service, such as storage, or a database, which are stateful by definition.

Long story short, don't hold states.

Port binding

The seventh factor is related to port binding, which is how the application is reachable, and exposed. A cloud-native application doesn't need any runtime, such as application servers or web servers; everything is embedded, and it's self-contained and exposes its services (such as APIs) through ports via the protocol that best fits its integration functionalities (HTTP, AMQP, MQTT, XMPP, and so on).

That also means, that if you expose your application, it can be a backing service for another application. The cloud infrastructure will provide routing capabilities.

Concurrency

The eighth factor is related to concurrency, in terms of how to scale and how to run multiple instances of the same cloud-native application to respond to increasing workloads.

Depending on the runtime execution environment, a cloud-native application can be a PHP, Ruby, Python, or Java process running to serve incoming requests. Nowadays, most of the previously mentioned technologies are multi-thread capable, so they can spread the workloads internally, as long as the resources are available. If there are sufficient resources, scaling up can be a solution, but a temporary one. Sooner or later, the resource will be missing once again. The only valid solution for a cloud infrastructure is scaling out, and Linux containers (the de facto standard is Docker) really help with that. New Linux containers can be run and more workloads can be handled by your application.

Disposability

The ninth factor is related to gently stopping the application. The application can be shut down for many reasons (new version available, updates, reload, and restart), and a twelve-factor application must be capable of handling shutdowns gracefully, which means completing the running tasks without accepting new ones. Once every task is completed (aborted or terminated), the application will shut down.

These kinds of functionalities are provided through different frameworks, available for the most-used programming languages and runtimes.

Development/production parity

The tenth factor is related to the runtime execution environments; more specifically, to keep the difference between those environments as small as possible.

The difference is with regards to the running release, that is, the version of a specific application that's running. It's common to have an older release in production and a newer release in development or **user acceptance testing (UAT)**.

But a cloud-native application is built with new concepts and ideas in mind to reflect the cloud platform, so tools for continuous integration and continuous delivery should fill the gap between the environments.

Continuous deployments are also available; it's just a matter of choice. Bring your new release to environment until pre-production (continuous delivery) or bring it until production (continuous deployment); it depends on the organization and its business model.

Logs

The eleventh factor is related to application logs. Logs are the first important thing after the application itself. Without logs, your system is blind, the operational team is blind, there is no monitoring, and you won't be able to fix a single line of code, especially in a cloud infrastructure.

In a cloud environment, in our revolution, logs should change as well. A log file in the runtime execution environment is a stateful component. If the execution environment crashes, logs are gone.

Any event in your code generates a log entry, and this should be streamed out to a stateful backing service, which receives log events (from different applications) and stores them for later analysis and aggregation. There are plenty of free and open source tools that can be used to introspect the behavior of your applications over time, such as ELF, EFK, and Grafana.

Logs are also very important to trace the flow of a request/response transaction, which might bounce from service to service before it gets back to the issuer. Log tracing is an important aspect that a cloud-native application should provide and follow.

You may have heard about telemetry—what your event-stream log might carry as information and how it carries it. Monitoring is something related to application performance (also known as APM); telemetry is about what happened from a business point of view at a certain time (for example, which products are the most sold during lunch time).

Admin processes

Last but not least, the twelfth factor is related to administration in terms of running management tasks.

These tasks should be run in the runtime execution environment, hence they should be shipped with the application itself and should be used to fix/compensate migration aspects of the application. Suppose you changed your domain model; this should also be reflected at the database level, so some script to alter the database schema should be provided and executed before the app can be used/consumed.

As a twelve-factor application is self-contained, it needs some kind of mechanism to first launch the admin management process and then be available. Fortunately, with the rise of Docker, such tasks have become even easier.

That was the last factor.

But wait a second. What about security?

A cloud-native application should be aware of security aspects such as authentication and authorization. A twelve-factor application integrates with backing services; it might not be allowed, or it shouldn't be allowed, to consume or use such a service.

How could they miss such a rule? We must add one more factor and have a thirteen-factor application.

Security

The thirteenth factor is related to security—application security. The cloud environment jumps from data center to data center, and your application, which could be a backing service, needs to protect its endpoints. Your application might give access to stateful components or to business-related functionalities. You must protect them all.

Nowadays, there are lots of frameworks that help you out with such tasks, such as SSO systems, OAuth, and OpenID Connect.

Microservices

The main concepts of a microservice architecture have been described in `Chapter 2`, *Microservices and Reactive Architecture,* where microservices are deployed, exposed, and consumed. Most of the concepts described for a microservice are pretty much the same for a cloud-native application. That's why, most of the time, a cloud-native application is implemented using the microservice approach.

To recap the most important concepts, a microservice should have the following:

- **Single responsibility**: It must be responsible for only one context—a business domain context; one and well done.
- **No sharing**: It must be stateless and eventually delegate its persistency state to another backing service.
- **Black box**: Its implementation must be hidden; the only shareable information is its API and the protocol used to expose its endpoints.
- **Private data**: As per its hidden implementation, how data is stored is an implementation detail. Any data store can be used.

Based on our journey, we will design and implement a series of microservices that implement an overall application called **Cloud Football Manager**.

The application will be composed of the following components:

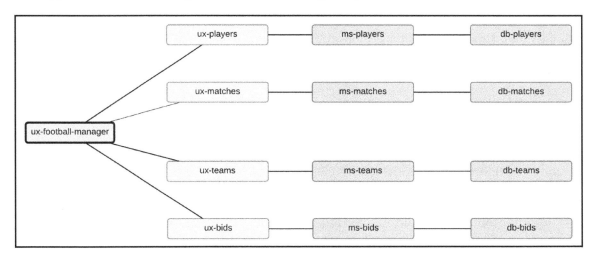

Later on, we will design and implement each component from a user interface point of view, from a microservice point of view, and from a data store point of view.

As previously mentioned, a cloud-native application can be designed and implemented with any kind of technology. As this book is oriented to Java programmers, it will focus on Spring Boot, Thorntail, and Vert.x, which are the runtime environments of the application.

From a microservice architecture perspective, each component could be implemented and run targeting a different runtime environment; the cooperation between microservices is due to communication protocols.

Runtime environments

As mentioned earlier, a cloud-native application is a self-contained unit, hence it generally contains everything it needs to run. At the time of writing, the most-used frameworks to build a cloud-native application or a microservice are the following:

- Spring Boot
- Thorntail (formerly WildFly Swarm)
- Vert.x

Spring Boot

The process of creating standalone, production-grade, and easy-to-run Spring is made convenient by Spring Boot 2. Most Spring Boot applications need very little Spring configuration.

Spring Boot offer the following features:

- Create standalone Spring applications
- Embed Tomcat, Jetty, or Undertow directly (no need to deploy WAR files)
- Dependency management through starters and various package manager integrations
- Provide opinionated *starter* dependencies to simplify your build configuration
- Automatically configure Spring and third-party libraries
- Provide production-ready features
- Absolutely no code generation and no requirement for XML configuration

With every new release of Spring Boot, versions of various dependencies of the Java ecosystem get upgraded. This is defined in the Spring Boot **Bill of Materials** (**BOM**).

Creating a microservice with Spring Boot is very simple; just add the following settings in your Maven project file (that is, pom.xml):

```
<properties>
    <project.build.sourceEncoding>UTF-8</project.build.sourceEncoding>
<project.reporting.outputEncoding>UTF-8</project.reporting.outputEncoding>
    <java.version>1.8</java.version>
</properties>
<dependencies>
    <dependency>
        <groupId>org.springframework.boot</groupId>
        <artifactId>spring-boot-starter-jersey</artifactId>
        <version>2.0.3.RELEASE</version>
    </dependency>
    <dependency>
        <groupId>org.springframework.boot</groupId>
        <artifactId>spring-boot-starter-test</artifactId>
        <version>2.0.3.RELEASE</version>
        <scope>test</scope>
    </dependency>
</dependencies>
<build>
    <plugins>
        <plugin>
        <groupId>org.springframework.boot</groupId>
        <artifactId>spring-boot-maven-plugin</artifactId>
        </plugin>
    </plugins>
</build>
```

And an example application will look like the following snippet:

```
package com.example.demo;
import org.springframework.boot.SpringApplication;
import    org.springframework.boot.autoconfigure.SpringBootApplication;
@SpringBootApplication
public class DemoApplication {
    public static void main(String[]    args) {
        SpringApplication.run(DemoApplication.class,    args);
    }
}
```

Furthermore, Spring's website offers a bootstrap page (http://start.spring.io/), where you can specify the requirements for your microservice by filling in the form with all of the dependencies you need, as shown in the following screenshot:

Thorntail

Thorntail packages the Java EE applications with the required server runtime to *java-jar* your application. This consists of the application code, a basic of the WildFly application server, and any essential dependencies. The *java-jar* can be used to run the application. It's also MicroProfile compatible.

It's well integrated with the most-used frameworks, such as Camel, Netflix OSS, Keycloak, Logstash, and Swagger. Thanks to its flexible and pluggable DNA, it lets you create your own Java EE runtime packaged as an executable JAR file (often called an Uber JAR or fat JAR), which fits the microservices approach very well. Each fat JAR is essentially a microservice that can then independently upgrade, replace, or scale. As single responsibility principle is followed by each fat JAR, only the required dependencies will be packaged for it.

Thorntail is fully compliant with the Eclipse MicroProfile specification by providing support for the following features:

- MicroProfile
- MicroProfile JWT RBAC Auth
- MicroProfile Metrics
- MicroProfile Rest Client
- MicroProfile Config
- MicroProfile Fault Tolerance
- MicroProfile Health

Creating a microservice with Thorntail is very simple; just add the following settings in your Maven project file (that is, pom.xml):

```xml
<properties>
    <version.thorntail>2.0.0.Final</version.thorntail>
  <maven.compiler.source>1.8</maven.compiler.source>
    <maven.compiler.target>1.8</maven.compiler.target>
    <failOnMissingWebXml>false</failOnMissingWebXml>
    <project.build.sourceEncoding>UTF-8</project.build.sourceEncoding>
</properties>
<dependencyManagement>
  <dependencies>
   <dependency>
   <groupId>io.thorntail</groupId>
   <artifactId>bom-all</artifactId>
   <version>${version.thorntail}</version>
   <scope>import</scope>
   <type>pom</type>
   </dependency>
  </dependencies>
</dependencyManagement>
<dependency>
    <groupid>io.thorntail</groupId>
    <artifactId>jaxrs</artifactId>
    <version>${version.thorntail}</version>
</dependency>
<plugin>
    <groupid>io.thorntail</groupId>
  <artifactId>thorntail-maven-plugin</artifactId>
  <version>${version.thorntail}</version>
  <executions>
   <execution>
   <goals>
        <goal>package</goal>
```

```
    </goals>
    </execution>
   </executions>
 </plugin>
```

The `HelloWorldEndpoint` example application is as follows:

```
package com.example.demo.rest;
import javax.ws.rs.Path;
import javax.ws.rs.core.Response;
import javax.ws.rs.GET;
import javax.ws.rs.Produces;
@Path("/hello")
public class HelloWorldEndpoint { @GET @Produces("text/plain") public
Response doGet() { return Response.ok("Hello from Thorntail!").build(); } }
```

The code snippet for `RestApplication` is as follows:

```
package com.example.demo.rest;
import javax.ws.rs.ApplicationPath;
  import javax.ws.rs.core.Application;
@ApplicationPath("/")
  publicclass RestApplication extends Application {
  }
```

Furthermore, Thorntail's website offers a bootstrap page (https://thorntail.io/ generator/), where you can specify the needs for your microservice by filling in the form with all of the dependencies you need, as shown in the following screenshot:

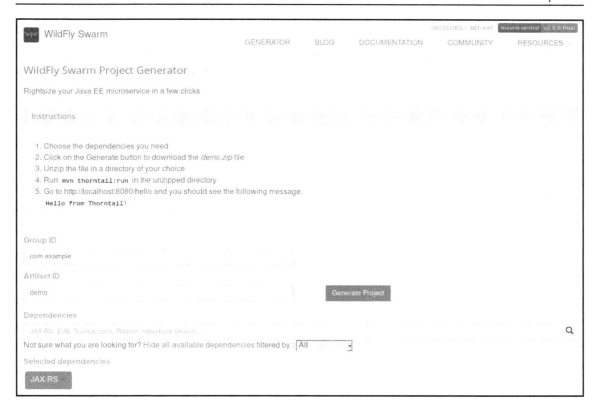

Vert.x

Vert.x is an open source framework by the Eclipse Foundation to build reactive and polyglot software. It's reactive because it uses asynchronous streams to respond to any changes or events.

It's polyglot because it supports different programming languages based also on the JVM, such as Java, Groovy, Ruby, Python, and JavaScript.

Vert.x, like its competitor Node.js, uses an event bus (technically a loop) to interact with components of the application, passing events to appropriate handlers to manage them asynchronously.

Vert.x comes with few concepts that are necessary to explain.

Verticles

A verticle is a small piece of code (at least, it should be small) executed by the Vert.x engine. The framework comes with many different abstract verticles that can be used and extended for any needs. In Java, a verticle can be implemented using the `io.vertx.core.Verticle` interface or any one of its subclasses.

Event bus

The event bus is the core of the system of a Vert.x application. Each verticle communicates with other verticles using the event bus. This means that, once a message or event is looped into the event bus, this message gets delivered to the appropriate verticle. The verticle then reacts by reading the event (it can contain objects or any primitive data type such as strings or numbers) and by taking the proper action.

Events and messages are handled asynchronously, so every time a verticle produces a message, the latter is sent to the bus in a queue and control is returned to the verticle. Later, as computational resource are available, the listening verticle gets the event and it sends back a response using `Future` and `callback` methods.

Creating a microservice with Vert.x is very simple; just add the following settings in your Maven project file (that is, `pom.xml`):

```xml
<properties>
    <java.version>1.8</java.version>
    <vertx.version>3.5.3</vertx.version>
</properties>
<build>
    <plugins>
        <plugin>
        <groupId>org.apache.maven.plugins</groupId>
        <artifactId>maven-compiler-plugin</artifactId>
        <version>3.5.1</version>
        <configuration>
            <source>${java.version}</source>
            <target>${java.version}</target>
        </configuration>
        </plugin>
        <plugin>
        <groupId>org.apache.maven.plugins</groupId>
        <artifactId>maven-shade-plugin</artifactId>
        <version>2.4.3</version>
        <executions/>
        </plugin>
        <plugin>
```

```xml
            <groupId>org.codehaus.mojo</groupId>
            <artifactId>exec-maven-plugin</artifactId>
            <version>1.5.0</version>
            <configuration>
                    <mainClass>io.vertx.core.Launcher</mainClass>
                    <arguments>
                            <argument>run</argument>
                            <argument>com.example.demo.MainVerticle</argument>
                    </arguments>
            </configuration>
            </plugin>
    </plugins>
</build>
<dependencies>
            <dependency>
            <groupId>io.vertx</groupId>
            <artifactId>vertx-unit</artifactId>
            <version>${vertx.version}</version>
            </dependency>
            <dependency>
            <groupId>io.vertx</groupId>
            <artifactId>vertx-core</artifactId>
            <version>${vertx.version}</version>
            </dependency>
            <dependency>
            <groupId>io.vertx</groupId>
            <artifactId>vertx-web</artifactId>
            <version>${vertx.version}</version>
            </dependency>
</dependencies>
```

And an example application will look like the following:

```java
package com.packt.vertx;
import io.vertx.core.AbstractVerticle;
public class MainVerticle extends   AbstractVerticle {
   @Override
   public void start() throws Exception {
           vertx.createHttpServer().requestHandler(req   -> {
                   req.response()
                   .putHeader("content-type", "text/plain")
                   .end("Running Vert.x!");
           }).listen(8080);
           System.out.println("HTTP server started on port 8080");
   }
}
```

Furthermore, Vert.x's website offers a bootstrap page (`http://start.vertx.io/`), where you can specify the needs for your microservice by filling in the form with all of the dependencies you need, as shown in the following screenshot:

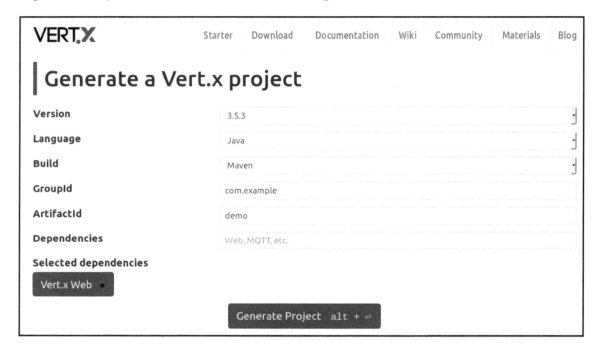

Summary

In this chapter, we've learned what a cloud-native application is and all of the features it should have to support a cloud architecture, which is distributed by nature.

We also looked at the twelve factors that should compose a cloud-native application, adding one more factor, which is about security. As technology moves very fast, the twelve-factor application concepts should also be updated by removing and adding new factors. We also described the principles for a microservice in regards to its implementation.

Lastly, we gave examples of cloud-native applications in different runtime environments using different frameworks such as Spring Boot, Thorntail, and Vert.x.

In the next chapter, we will start going into more detail about how to build a cloud-native application with microservices, building from scratch a football manager application.

Building Microservices Using Thorntail

4

In this chapter, after seeing the evolution of architectures toward the cloud, I will cover, in detail, how to create a distributed microservice architecture using the Jakarta EE and MicroProfile specifications with Thorntail. You can choose another implementation, such as Payara or Open Liberty.

The following topics will be analyzed in detail:

- **Thorntail**: The MicroProfile implementation that enables you to package your Java EE applications with just enough of the server runtime.
- **Building a fantasy football application**: I will create a set of microservice implementations based on different technologies in order to demonstrate the power of this new way to design enterprise applications.
- **User interface microservices**: I will analyze the micro frontend architecture and how to design the user experience with the microservices approach, and I will implement it with an example, based on Angular 6.

Thorntail

Thorntail, previously called WildFly Swarm, is an open source implementation of MicroProfile specifications. It's built on top of mature technologies, and it leverages existing expertise that has been derived from Jakarta EE specifications, patterns, and implementations.

The Thorntail project was born with WildFly/Jakarta EE, but it focuses on modern cloud applications, following the path made by MicroProfile.io (in certain ways). It initially implemented version 1.3 of MicroProfile. You can find its specifications at `https://github.com/eclipse/microprofile-bom/releases/download/1.3/microprofile-spec-1.3.pdf`.

At the time of writing, Thorntail is in version 2.0.0, and it includes all of the features implemented in WildFly Swarm 2018.5.0.

You can consider Thorntail as a combination of all the benefits of the mature Java EE/Jakarta EE specifications and the flexibility of the MicroProfile.io and cloud-oriented concepts, as illustrated by the following diagram:

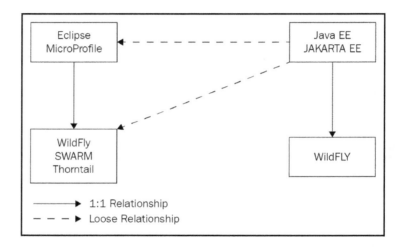

Indeed, when you build a traditional Jakarta EE application (distributed using the standard EAR or WAR), you need to install the entire application server (for example, WildFly), and then deploy your application on top of it.

It is true that with the introduction of the web profile (starting with Java EE 6), it is possible to decrease the number of APIs and components present in the initial configuration of the application server.

Further optimizations have been made by the application servers to only load the specifications (and consequently, the classes) that our application really needs. WildFly, for example, has four basic configuration profiles, which make up only a subset of the functionalities available during the start of the application server. WildFly also loads its subsystems in a lazy way, so that its footprint is very low, and the memory usage related to loaded classes is strictly related to what the application really uses.

However, in microservice architectures, this is not enough, because with a traditional Jakarta EE application server, you could have significantly more functionality than your application requires.

Thorntail gives you the ability to create a final package that contains exactly what you need for your deployment, using two different strategies, as follows:

- `Uber JAR`: A self-contained, executable Java archive that contains your application, the fractions of Thorntail required to support it, a Maven repository of dependencies, and a small library that's needed to bootstrap it all.
- `Hollow Uber JAR`: A self-contained, executable Java archive that contains no application code, but only what you need to run it. Usually, it contains a subset of APIs, Jakarta EE, and MicroProfile, that your application will use. In this way, you exclude your EAR or WAR file (with the application code) from the executable `Hollow JAR`. Then, you can deploy your application artifact in the same style as traditional Jakarta EE app servers.

One of the key elements of Thorntail is the fraction, which will be explained in the following section.

Fractions

As we explained earlier, you can consider Thorntail as a runtime environment that you can build in a pluggable way. The core unit that represents the compositional aspect in Thorntail is the **fraction**. It's a well-defined runtime capability to add to your environment. In some cases, a fraction maps directly to a subsystem from WildFly, but in other cases, it may involve a different functionality that's described in the MicroProfile.io specifications or is needed in the cloud environment.

A fraction can do the following things:

- Directly enable a WildFly subsystem as Infinispan, which is needed to implement a data caching layer
- Integrate additional frameworks or services (for example, topology using Consul, JGroups, and OpenShift)
- Provide deployments of features like API documentation (for example, Swagger) or JMX metrics access (for example, Jolokia)

- Add API dependencies as Jakarta EE (for example, JAX-RS) or MicroProfile.io (for example, config, and health check)
- Alter deployment, introducing features as single-sign on for the authentication and authorization settings of your application (for example, Keycloak).

At the time of writing, there are about 184 fractions available that are stable and experimental, and there are more in the pipeline. About 80% wrap WildFly, related components, so you are able to use some Jakarta EE specifications, and you can easily evolve your application from a monolithic to a microservice architecture.

Fractions support explicit and implicit configuration; in many cases, you won't need to configure anything. The default values will let you successfully run your application.

Fractions can be detected or explicitly declared. The simplest case is a WAR project, with just the Maven plugin. After enabling the `thorntail-maven-plugin` inside your application, Thorntail will detect which APIs you use, and will include the fractions that implement them at build time. The default behavior of `thorntail-maven-plugin` is to auto detect fractions only if you do not specify anything explicitly. You can change this setting through the `fractionDetectMode` property.

To implement the auto detection mode, you should implement the following steps:

1. Add the `thorntail-maven-plugin` to your `pom.xml` in a `<plugin>` block, with an `<execution>` specifying the package goal:

```xml
<plugins>
    <plugin>
        <groupId>io.thorntail</groupId>
        <artifactId>thorntail-maven-plugin</artifactId>
        <version>${version.thorntail}</version>
        <executions>
            <execution>
                <id>package</id>
                <goals>
                    <goal>package</goal>
                </goals>
            </execution>
        </executions>
    </plugin>
</plugins>
```

2. Specify the API that you want to use in your `pom.xml` file; for example, JAX-RS, to implement a RESTful web service, as follows:

```
<dependencies>
    <dependency>
        <groupId>javax.ws.rs</groupId>
        <artifactId>javax.ws.rs-api</artifactId>
        <version>${version.jaxrs-api}</version>
        <scope>provided</scope>
    </dependency>
</dependencies>
```

3. Build your project using the following command:

```
$ mvn package
```

4. Run the final, atomic `Uber JAR`, using the following command:

```
$ java -jar ./target/myapp-thorntail.jar
```

To use the explicit fractions, setting a specific version, you should implement the following steps:

1. Set the correct **Bill Of Material (BOM)** of the Thorntail version, as follows:

```
# Set the property relate to the Thorntail version
<properties>
    <version.thorntail>2.0.0.Final</version.thorntail>
</properties>
...
```

2. Set the BOM dependency in order to have the correct version of the fraction:

```
...
<dependencyManagement>
    <dependencies>
        <dependency>
            <groupId>io.thorntail</groupId>
            <artifactId>bom</artifactId>
            <version>${version.thorntail}</version>
            <type>pom</type>
            <scope>import</scope>
        </dependency>
    </dependencies>
</dependencyManagement>
```

3. Add the `thorntail-maven-plugin` to your `pom.xml` in a `<plugin>` block, with an `<execution>` specifying the package goal:

```
<plugins>
    <plugin>
        <groupId>io.thorntail</groupId>
        <artifactId>thorntail-maven-plugin</artifactId>
        <version>${version.thorntail}</version>
        <executions>
            <execution>
                <id>package</id>
                <goals>
                    <goal>package</goal>
                </goals>
            </execution>
        </executions>
    </plugin>
</plugins>
```

4. Add the dependency on the Thorntail fraction, for example, JAX-RS, to implement a RESTful web service, to the `pom.xml` file:

```
<dependencies>
    <dependency>
        <groupId>io.thorntail</groupId>
        <artifactId>jaxrs</artifactId>
    </dependency>
</dependencies>
```

5. Build your project, using the following command:

```
$ mvn package
```

6. Run the final, atomic `Uber JAR`, using the following command:

```
$ java -jar   ./target/myapp-thorntail.jar
```

Flexible configuration

Thorntail gives you the opportunity to easily configure your applications and your environments via different strategies, based on your background or internal policies.

You can use the following implementations:

- The `thorntail-maven-plugin` is used to set a specific fraction property (for example, the port for the default HTTP listener), as follows:

```
<swarm.http.port>8081</swarm.http.port>
```

- The traditional Java properties that you can set when you launch your application can be used as follows:

```
$ java -Dswarm.http.port=8081    myapp.jar
```

- The WildFly configuration file that you used in a previous implementation (or when you were migrating from a traditional Jakarta EE architecture to the microservice cloud native architecture) can be set with the following command:

```
$ java myapp.jar    -c standalone.xml
```

- You can also use a YML file (as implemented in most cloud environments and PaaS), by using the following command:

```
$ java myapp.jar    -s project-production.yml
```

Building a fantasy football application

Having presented Thorntail's features and its relationship with Java EE/Jakarta EE and MicroProfile.io, it's time to start to build our microservices application.

We will build a simple fantasy football application that is divided into four Maven projects, as follows:

1. A microservice application that handles the football players domain; it will expose **create**, **read**, **update**, and **delete** (**CRUD**) API, and it will store and retrieve information using a PostgreSQL database.
2. A microservice application that handles the fantasy football player domain and the presidents of the fantasy teams; it will expose a CRUD API, and it will store and retrieve information using a MySQL database.

3. A microservice application that handles the fantasy team's domain; it will expose a CRUD API, and it will store and retrieve information using a MongoDB database.

4. A microservice application that will be the web interface through which the various APIs call, in order to sign up to the fantasy league, create the fantasy team, and buy the football players.

We have decided to use a different database in order to show you that the microservice architecture works using different languages, and to confirm the concept that a microservice must own a specific data domain.

To build our application, we will use the following tools, and for each one, we will specify the information needed to install them:

1. **Apache Maven 3.5.4**: Here is the link to install (`https://maven.apache.org/install.html`)

2. **JDK 1.8.0_171**: You are free to use Oracle JDK or OpenJDK, but we recommend OpenJDK (`http://openjdk.java.net/install/`)

3. **Thorntail 2.0.0**: Here is the link to install (`https://thorntail.io/`)

4. **Docker Community edition 18.03.1** : This is so that you can easily install and use the different databases required for our application (`https://docs.docker.com/install/`)

5. **AngularJS**: This is to build the frontend layer; we will describe the instructions to install it later on.

The football player microservice

In this section, we will build the microservice related to the management of football players. In order to do so, we will need to install PostgreSQL on the system, in addition to the prerequisites described in the preceding section. As I stated previously, we will use Docker to install and handle PostgreSQL. I'm using a macOS High Sierra for my working environment, and I will describe how to install and run PostgreSQL in a Docker container.

Database installation and configuration

Having installed Docker on your machine, it's time to run the containerized version of PostgreSQL, as follows:

1. Open a new Terminal window and launch the following command:

```
$ docker run --name postgres_thorntail \
-e POSTGRES_PASSWORD=postgresPwd -e
POSTGRES_DB=football_players_registry \
-d -p 5532:5432 postgres
```

This command will trigger a pull from Docker's public registry for the PostgreSQL version labeled as the latest, downloading all of the layers that it needs to run the container on, as depicted in the following output:

```
Unable to find     image 'postgres:latest' locally
   latest: Pulling from library/postgres
   683abbb4ea60: Pull complete
   c5856e38168a: Pull complete
   c3e6f1ceebb0: Pull complete
   3303bcd00128: Pull complete
   ea95ff44bf6e: Pull complete
   ea3f31f1e620: Pull complete
   234873881fb2: Pull complete
   f020aa822d21: Pull complete
   27bad92d09a5: Pull complete
   6849f0681f5a: Pull complete
   a112faac8662: Pull complete
   bc92d0ab9365: Pull complete
   9e87959714b8: Pull complete
   ac7c29b2bea7: Pull complete
   Digest:
sha256:d99f15cb8d0f47f0a66274afe30102b5bb7a95464d1e25acb66ccf7b
d7bd8479
   Status: Downloaded newer image for postgres:latest
83812c6e76656f6abab5bf1f00f07dca7105d5227df3b3b66382659fa55b507
7
```

After that, the PostgreSQL image is launched as a container.

2. To verify this, you can launch the `$ docker ps -a` command, which gives you a list of the containers created and their relative statuses:

```
CONTAINER ID   IMAGE     COMMAND                  CREATED

1073daeefc52   postgres  "docker-entrypoint.s..." Less than a second
ago



STATUS           PORTS                              NAMES

Up 4 seconds     0.0.0.0:5532->5432/tcp
postgres_thorntail
```

The command result has been split into two lines in order to make it readable.

3. You can also check the container logs in order to retrieve information about the PostgreSQL status. Launch the following command:

```
$ docker logs   -f 1073daeefc52
```

`1073daeefc52` is the container ID. You should get the following information:

```
PostgreSQL   init process complete; ready for start up.

    2018-07-13 22:53:36.465 UTC [1] LOG:   listening on IPv4
address "0.0.0.0",    port 5432
    2018-07-13 22:53:36.466 UTC [1] LOG:   listening on IPv6
address "::",    port 5432
    2018-07-13 22:53:36.469 UTC [1] LOG:   listening on Unix
socket "/var/run/postgresql/.s.PGSQL.5432"
```

4. Now, it's time to connect to the container, in order to manage it. Launch the following command:

```
$ docker exec   -it 1073daeefc52 bash
```

`1073daeefc52` is the container ID. Now, log in to PostgreSQL with the following command:

```
$ psql -U   postgres
```

5. Now, you will be able to interact with the database server, as follows:

```
psql (10.4    (Debian 10.4-2.pgdg90+1))
   Type "help" for help.
   postgres=#
```

You should be able to see the football_players_registry database that we created when we launched the container's creation.

6. Run the \l command to verify the list of databases:

```
postgres=# \l

                                     List of databases

            Name                 | Owner   | Encoding |  Collate    |
Ctype     |   Access privileges

----------------------------+----------+----------+-------------+----
--------+----------------------

 football_players_registry   | postgres | UTF8        | en_US.utf8 |
en_US.utf8 |

 postgres                     | postgres | UTF8     | en_US.utf8 |
en_US.utf8 |

 template0                    | postgres | UTF8     | en_US.utf8 |
en_US.utf8 | =c/postgres        +

                                |          |            |
|             |    postgres=CTc/postgres

 template1                    | postgres | UTF8     | en_US.utf8 |
en_US.utf8 | =c/postgres        +

                                |          |            |
|             |    postgres=CTc/postgres

(4 rows)
```

OK. Now it's time to create a simple table that will host the football players' data.

7. From the running Docker container instance, you should connect to the `football_players` database with the following command:

```
$ \connect   football_players_registry
```

8. Create the table with the following command:

```
CREATE TABLE    FOOTBALL_PLAYER(
        ID SERIAL       PRIMARY KEY NOT NULL,
        NAME            VARCHAR(50) NOT NULL,
        SURNAME         VARCHAR(50) NOT NULL,
        AGE             INT    NOT NULL,
        TEAM            VARCHAR(50) NOT NULL,

    POSITION            VARCHAR(50) NOT NULL,
      PRICE             NUMERIC
    );
```

9. Check the table's structure with the following command:

```
$   \d+    football_player
```

You should see the following result:

```
football_players_registry=#   \d+ football_player

                              Table "public.football_player"

 Column  | Type   | Collation | Nullable | Default | Storage
 | Stats target | Description

 ----------+------------------------+-----------+----------+-----
 -----------------

 ------------------------+----------+--------------+-------------

 id       |   integer |  | not null |
 nextval('football_player_id_seq'::regclass) | plain   |
 |

  name    |   character varying(50) | | not null | | extended |
 |

  surname |   character varying(50) | | not null | | extended |
 |

  age     |   integer | | not null |   | plain | |
```

```
    team     |    character varying(50) | | not null | | extended |
|

    position |    character varying(50) | | not null | | extended |
|

    price    |    numeric | | | | main | |
Indexes:

    "football_player_pkey"    PRIMARY KEY, btree (id)
```

Creating the source code

We have installed and configured everything that's necessary to create our microservice for the management of the registry of players. Now, it's time to write the code that's needed to expose our microservice APIs.

We will use the Thorntail project generator utility, `https://thorntail.io/generator/`, in order to get a project skeleton to work on. Our microservice, as described previously, will have to display APIs that allow us to perform CRUD operations. Java EE and Jakarta EE have specifications for implementing these features, as follows:

- JAX-RS
- CDI
- JPA
- JTA

We will use `com.packtpub.thorntail` as the Maven **Group ID** of the project, and **football-player-microservice** as the **Artifact ID:**

1. Set the **Group ID**, **Artifact ID,** and **Dependencies** values in the project form generator, as shown in the following screenshot:

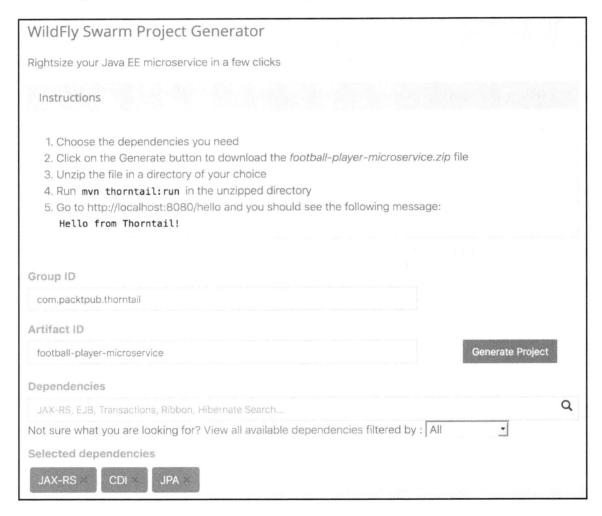

2. Click on **Generate Project** to create and download the ZIP file with the project skeleton.

3. Unzip the file in a directory of your choice, and open the Maven project with your favorite IDE (Eclipse, NetBeans, IntelliJ, and so on).

   The core element of the project is the Maven `pom.xml` file that contains all of the dependencies needed to implement our microservice.

   The project uses the BOM to correctly manage dependency management, as follows:

   ```
   <properties>
       . . .
               <version.thorntail>2.0.0.Final</version.thorntail>
               . . .
   </properties>
   <dependencyManagement>
               <dependencies>
               <dependency>
                       <groupId>io.thorntail</groupId>
                       <artifactId>bom-all</artifactId>
                       <version>${version.thorntail}</version>
                       <scope>import</scope>
                       <type>pom</type>
               </dependency>
               </dependencies>
   </dependencyManagement>
   ```

4. The default value is set to `bom-all`, which includes all of the fractions—stable, unstable, experimental, and even deprecated. We need to change it to `bom`, which only includes the stable fractions; it's recommended for daily use:

   ```
   <properties>
       . . .
               <version.thorntail>2.0.0.Final</version.thorntail>
               . . .
   </properties>
   <dependencyManagement>
               <dependencies>
               <dependency>
                       <groupId>io.thorntail</groupId>
                       <artifactId>bom</artifactId>
                       <version>${version.thorntail}</version>
                       <scope>import</scope>
                       <type>pom</type>
               </dependency>
               </dependencies>
   </dependencyManagement>
   ```

5. We will also change the value of the project name from `Thorntail Example` to `Thorntail Football player microservice`:

```
...
<modelVersion>4.0.0</modelVersion>
<groupId>com.packtpub.thorntail</groupId>
<artifactId>football-player-microservice</artifactId>
<name>Thorntail Football player microservice</name>
<version>1.0.0-SNAPSHOT</version>
<packaging>war</packaging>
...
```

6. We will change the final name of the artifact, created in the build phase, from `demo` to `football-player-microservice`, as follows:

```
<build>
    <finalName>football-player-microservice</finalName>
    ...
</build>
```

7. Now, launch the first build with the following command:

```
$ mvn clean    package
```

In this way, we will download all of the dependencies and create the WAR artifact named `football-player-microservice.war` and the super-executable JAR file, `football-player-microservice-thorntail.jar`.

To check that the project is ready to be used, we can run it by using the following command:

```
$ mvn thorntail:run
```

First of all, you will notice that all of the fractions related to JAX-RS, CDI, and JPA are installed and running, as follows:

```
2018-07-14   16:38:50,356 INFO  [org.wildfly.swarm] (main) WFSWARM0013:
Installed   fraction:                JAX-RS - STABLE
io.thorntail:jaxrs:2.0.0.Final
   2018-07-14 16:38:50,363 INFO  [org.wildfly.swarm] (main) WFSWARM0013:
Installed fraction:           Logging - STABLE
io.thorntail:logging:2.0.0.Final
   2018-07-14 16:38:50,363 INFO  [org.wildfly.swarm] (main) WFSWARM0013:
Installed fraction:           Undertow - STABLE
io.thorntail:undertow:2.0.0.Final
   2018-07-14 16:38:50,364 INFO  [org.wildfly.swarm] (main) WFSWARM0013:
Installed fraction:           Elytron - STABLE
```

```
io.thorntail:elytron:2.0.0.Final
    2018-07-14 16:38:50,364 INFO  [org.wildfly.swarm] (main) WFSWARM0013:
Installed fraction:                CDI - STABLE
io.thorntail:cdi:2.0.0.Final
    2018-07-14 16:38:50,364 INFO  [org.wildfly.swarm] (main) WFSWARM0013:
Installed fraction:        CDI Configuration - STABLE
io.thorntail:cdi-config:2.0.0.Final
    2018-07-14 16:38:50,364 INFO  [org.wildfly.swarm] (main) WFSWARM0013:
Installed fraction:        Bean Validation - STABLE
io.thorntail:bean-validation:2.0.0.Final
    2018-07-14 16:38:50,365 INFO  [org.wildfly.swarm] (main) WFSWARM0013:
Installed fraction:                Transactions - STABLE
io.thorntail:transactions:2.0.0.Final
    2018-07-14 16:38:50,365 INFO  [org.wildfly.swarm] (main) WFSWARM0013:
Installed fraction:                JPA - STABLE
io.thorntail:jpa:2.0.0.Final
    2018-07-14 16:38:50,365 INFO  [org.wildfly.swarm] (main) WFSWARM0013:
Installed fraction:                Datasources - STABLE
io.thorntail:datasources:2.0.0.Final
    2018-07-14 16:38:50,365 INFO  [org.wildfly.swarm] (main) WFSWARM0013:
Installed fraction:                JCA - STABLE
io.thorntail:jca:2.0.0.Final
```

Then, you can see that Thorntail is running, and that the application is deployed:

```
2018-07-14   16:38:55,555 INFO  [org.wildfly.extension.undertow]
(ServerService Thread   Pool -- 10) WFLYUT0021: Registered web context: '/'
for server 'default-server'
    2018-07-14 16:38:55,598 INFO  [org.jboss.as.server] (main) WFLYSRV0010:
Deployed "football-player-microservice.war" (runtime-name : "football-
player-microservice.war")
 2018-07-14 16:38:55,607 INFO [org.wildfly.swarm] (main) WFSWARM99999:
Thorntail is Ready
```

Finally, we can invoke the application at `http://localhost:8080/hello`, and see the message, `Hello from Thorntail!`. Now, let's stop Thorntail by using the *Ctrl + C* command, and start to update our project.

Entity class – JPA

We need a domain model object to map the records inserted into our database. To do this, we will use the JPA specification; so, we will create an entity class for this purpose, as follows:

1. Let's create a new Java package named `model`, in order to store the data model class. The fully qualified package name will be `com.packtpub.thorntail.footballplayermicroservice.model`.

2. Next, we will build the domain class, named `FootballPlayer`:

```java
package   com.packtpub.thorntail.footballplayermicroservice.model;

import java.math.BigInteger;
...

/**
 * Domain model class that maps the data stored into
football_player table
 * inside database.
 *
 * @author Mauro Vocale
 * @version 1.0.0 15/08/2018
 */
@Entity
@Table(name = "football_player")
@XmlRootElement
@NamedQueries({
 @NamedQuery(name = "FootballPlayer.findAll", query
            = "SELECT f FROM FootballPlayer f")
 })
public class FootballPlayer {

 @Id
 @GeneratedValue(strategy = GenerationType.IDENTITY)
 @Basic(optional = false)
 @Column(name = "id")
 private Integer id;

 @Basic(optional = false)
 @NotNull
 @Size(min = 1, max = 50)
 @Column(name = "name")
 private String name;

 @Basic(optional = false)
 @NotNull
```

```
@Size(min = 1, max = 50)
@Column(name = "surname")
private String surname;

@Basic(optional = false)
@NotNull
@Column(name = "age")
private int age;

@Basic(optional = false)
@NotNull
@Size(min = 1, max = 50)
@Column(name = "team")
private String team;

@Basic(optional = false)
@NotNull
@Size(min = 1, max = 50)
@Column(name = "position")
private String position;

@Column(name = "price")
private BigInteger price;

public FootballPlayer() {
}

public FootballPlayer(String name, String surname, int age,
        String team, String position, BigInteger price) {
    this.name = name;
    this.surname = surname;
    this.age = age;
    this.team = team;
    this.position = position;
    this.price = price;
}

...

@Override
public int hashCode() {
    int hash = 0;
    hash += (id != null ? id.hashCode() : 0);
    return hash;
}

@Override
public boolean equals(Object object) {
```

```
            if (!(object instanceof FootballPlayer)) {
                return false;
            }
            FootballPlayer other = (FootballPlayer) object;
            return !((this.id == null && other.getId() != null)
                || (this.id != null &&
    !this.id.equals(other.getId()))));
        }

        ...

    }
```

3. To complete the management of the database access operations, we need to configure the `persistence.xml` file, inside `src/main/resources/META-INF` directory, where we will store all the configurations related to our persistence layer:

```xml
<?xml    version="1.0" encoding="UTF-8" standalone="no"?>
<persistence xmlns="http://xmlns.jcp.org/xml/ns/persistence"
xmlns:xsi="http://www.w3.org/2001/XMLSchema-instance" version="2.1"
xsi:schemaLocation="http://xmlns.jcp.org/xml/ns/persistence
http://xmlns.jcp.org/xml/ns/persistence/persistence_2_1.xsd">
    <persistence-unit name="FootballPlayerPU" transaction-
type="JTA">
        <jta-data-
source>java:/jboss/datasources/FootballPlayerDS</jta-data-source>
        <properties>
            <property name="javax.persistence.schema-
generation.database.action"
                value="drop-and-create"/>
            <property name="javax.persistence.schema-
generation.drop-source"
                value="metadata"/>
            <property name="javax.persistence.schema-
generation.create-script
                source"
                value="META-INF/create.sql" />
            <property name="javax.persistence.sql-load-script-
source"
                value="META-INF/load.sql"/>
        </properties>
    </persistence-unit>
</persistence>
```

The most important elements are as follows:

- The name of the persistence unit (FootballPlayerPU)
- The transaction type, JTA (which means that we demand to the container the management of the transactions)
- The data source JNDI name to use (java:/jboss/datasources/FootballPlayerDS)
- The load script source that will preload a subset of data into the database

4. Finally, we will create the default project (the defaults.yml file) in the src/main/resources/ directory, where we will define the data source, FootballPlayerDS, which contains the configuration to connect to the database:

```
swarm:
  datasources:
    data-sources:
      FootballPlayerDS:
        driver-name: postgresql
        connection-
url:jdbc:postgresql://localhost:5532/football_players_registry
        user-name: postgres
        password: postgresPwd
        valid-connection-checker-class-name:
org.jboss.jca.adapters.jdbc.extensions.postgres.PostgreSQLValidConn
ectionChecker
        validate-on-match: true
        background-validation: false
        exception-sorter-class-name:
org.jboss.jca.adapters.jdbc.extensions.postgres.PostgreSQLException
Sorter
```

5. We will set the relative dependency in a Maven pom.xml file, as follows:

```
<properties>
    ...
    <version.postgresql>9.4.1207</version.postgresql>
</properties>
<dependency>
    <groupId>io.thorntail</groupId>
    <artifactId>datasources</artifactId>
    <scope>provided</scope>
</dependency>
<dependency>
    <groupId>org.postgresql</groupId>
```

```
              <artifactId>postgresql</artifactId>
              <version>${version.postgresql}</version>
          </dependency>
```

Declaring the vendor JDBC library dependency, Thorntail will automatically detect and install the driver.

RESTful web service – JAX-RS and CDI

Now, it's time to build our RESTful web service implementation, as follows:

1. Delete the default implementation class, `HelloWorldEndpoint.java`, created by the Thorntail generator.
2. Define a new package, named `service` (the fully qualified name will be `com.packtpub.thorntail.footballplayermicroservice.rest.service`), where we will put the RESTful web service implementation.
3. Finally, let's build the API implementations by using the CDI specifications (in order to inject the entity manager used to manage database connections) and the JAX-RS (in order to implement the RESTful operations). We will create an `AbstractFacade` class that defines the standard CRUD of our microservice:

```java
package
com.packtpub.thorntail.footballplayermicroservice.rest.service;

import java.util.List;
import javax.persistence.EntityManager;

/**
 * Abstract facade used to define the CRUD APIs of our micro
service.
 *
 * @author Mauro Vocale
 * @param <T> The type class of our entity domain.
 * @version 1.0.0 17/08/2018
 */
public abstract class AbstractFacade<T> {

    private final Class<T> entityClass;

    public AbstractFacade(Class<T> entityClass) {
        this.entityClass = entityClass;
    }

    protected abstract EntityManager getEntityManager();
```

```
public void create(T entity) {
    getEntityManager().persist(entity);
}

public void edit(T entity) {
    getEntityManager().merge(entity);
}

public void remove(T entity) {
getEntityManager().remove(getEntityManager().merge(entity));
}

public T find(Object id) {
    return getEntityManager().find(entityClass, id);
}

public List<T> findAll() {
    javax.persistence.criteria.CriteriaQuery<T> cq =
getEntityManager().getCriteriaBuilder().createQuery(entityClass);
    cq.select(cq.from(entityClass));
    return getEntityManager().createQuery(cq).getResultList();
}
}
```

4. Finally, the real implementation is as follows:

```
package
com.packtpub.thorntail.footballplayermicroservice.rest.service;

import
com.packtpub.thorntail.footballplayermicroservice.model.FootballPla
yer;
import java.util.List;
import javax.enterprise.context.ApplicationScoped;
import javax.persistence.EntityManager;
import javax.persistence.PersistenceContext;
import javax.ws.rs.Consumes;
import javax.ws.rs.DELETE;
import javax.ws.rs.GET;
import javax.ws.rs.POST;
import javax.ws.rs.PUT;
import javax.ws.rs.Path;
import javax.ws.rs.PathParam;
import javax.ws.rs.Produces;
import javax.ws.rs.core.MediaType;

/**
 * Class that exposes the APIs implementations of our CRUD micro
```

```
service.
 *
 * @author Mauro Vocale
 * @version 1.0.0 17/08/2018
 */
@ApplicationScoped
@Path("/footballplayer")
public class FootballPlayerFacadeREST extends
AbstractFacade<FootballPlayer>   {

    @PersistenceContext(unitName = "FootballPlayerPU")
    private EntityManager em;

    public FootballPlayerFacadeREST() {
        super(FootballPlayer.class);
    }

    @POST
    @Override
    @Consumes({MediaType.APPLICATION_JSON})
    @Transactional(Transactional.TxType.REQUIRES_NEW)
    public void create(FootballPlayer entity) {
        super.create(entity);
    }

    @PUT
    @Path("{id}")
    @Consumes({MediaType.APPLICATION_JSON})
    @Transactional(Transactional.TxType.REQUIRES_NEW)
    public void edit(@PathParam("id") Integer id, FootballPlayer
entity) {
        super.edit(entity);
    }

    @DELETE
    @Path("{id}")
    @Transactional(Transactional.TxType.REQUIRES_NEW)
    public void remove(@PathParam("id") Integer id) {
        super.remove(super.find(id));
    }

    @GET
    @Path("{id}")
    @Produces({MediaType.APPLICATION_JSON})
    public FootballPlayer find(@PathParam("id") Integer id) {
        return super.find(id);
    }
```

```
@GET
@Override
@Produces({MediaType.APPLICATION_JSON})
public List<FootballPlayer> findAll() {
    return super.findAll();
}

@Override
protected EntityManager getEntityManager() {
    return em;
}

}
```

5. Now, we will be able to create our Uber JAR, with the following command:

```
$ mvn clean package
```

6. Launch our microservice application by using the following command:

```
$ java -jar target/football-player-microservice-thorntail.jar
```

Let's check that the application is deployed and that Thorntail is up and running, as follows:

```
2018-07-17    16:41:31,640 INFO
[org.wildfly.extension.undertow] (ServerService Thread    Pool -
- 12) WFLYUT0021: Registered web context: '/' for server
'default-server'
    2018-07-17 16:41:31,674 INFO  [org.jboss.as.server] (main)
WFLYSRV0010:   Deployed "football-player-microservice.war"
(runtime-name : "football-player-microservice.war")
    2018-07-17 16:41:31,680 INFO  [org.wildfly.swarm] (main)
WFSWARM99999:   Thorntail is Ready
```

7. Now, invoke the API that retrieves the list of football players, as follows:

```
$ curl   http://localhost:8080/footballplayer | json_pp
```

The output should be similar to the following (for convenience, there is only a portion of it here):

```
[
    {
    "id":1,
    "name":"Gianluigi",
    "surname":"Buffon",
    "age":40,
```

```json
        "team":"Paris Saint Germain",
        "position":"goalkeeper",
        "price":2
        },
        {
        "id":2,
        "name":"Manuel",
        "surname":"Neuer",
        "age":32,
        "team":"Bayern Munchen",
        "position":"goalkeeper",
        "price":35
        },
        {
        "id":3,
        "name":"Keylor",
        "surname":"Navas",
        "age":31,
        "team":"Real Madrid",
        "position":"goalkeeper",
        "price":18
        },
        ...
    ]
```

8. Finally, we will create the JUnit test, in order to ensure that our APIs are working properly. Let's add the Maven dependencies, as follows:

```xml
<properties>
    ...
    <version.resteasy>3.0.19.Final</version.resteasy>
</properties>

<dependency>
    <groupId>io.thorntail</groupId>
    <artifactId>arquillian</artifactId>
    <scope>test</scope>
</dependency>
<dependency>
    <groupId>org.jboss.resteasy</groupId>
    <artifactId>resteasy-client</artifactId>
    <version>${version.resteasy}</version>
    <scope>test</scope>
</dependency>
```

9. Then, we will create the test class, named `FootballPlayerFacadeRESTTest`, in the package `com.packtpub.thorntail.footballplayermicroservice.rest.service`, under the `src/main/test` directory:

```
package
com.packtpub.thorntail.footballplayermicroservice.rest.service;

import
com.packtpub.thorntail.footballplayermicroservice.model.FootballPla
yer;
import
com.packtpub.thorntail.footballplayermicroservice.rest.RestApplicat
ion;
...

/**
 * Unit Test class needed to test the APIs.
 *
 * @author Mauro Vocale
 * @version 1.0.0 18/07/2018
 */
@RunWith(Arquillian.class)
public class FootballPlayerFacadeRESTTest {
    private static final String API_URL =
"http://localhost:8080/footballplayer";

    /**
     *
     * @return @throws Exception
     */
    @Deployment
    public static Archive createDeployment() throws Exception {
        JAXRSArchive deployment =
ShrinkWrap.create(JAXRSArchive.class);
        deployment.addPackage(FootballPlayer.class.getPackage());
        deployment.addPackage(AbstractFacade.class.getPackage());
        deployment.addPackage(RestApplication.class.getPackage());

        deployment.addAsWebInfResource(new ClassLoaderAsset(
            "META-INF/create.sql", FootballPlayerFacadeREST.class.
            getClassLoader()),"classes/META-INF/create.sql");

        deployment.addAsWebInfResource(new ClassLoaderAsset(
            "META-INF/load.sql",
FootballPlayerFacadeREST.class.getClassLoader()),
            "classes/META-INF/load.sql");
```

```
            deployment.addAsWebInfResource(new ClassLoaderAsset(
                "META-INF/persistence.xml",
FootballPlayerFacadeREST.class.
                getClassLoader()), "classes/META-INF/persistence.xml");

            deployment.addAsWebInfResource(new ClassLoaderAsset(
                "project-defaults.yml", FootballPlayerFacadeREST.class.
                 getClassLoader()), "classes/project-defaults.yml");

            deployment.addAllDependencies();
            System.out.println(deployment.toString(true));
            return deployment;
        }

    private final Client client =
ClientBuilder.newBuilder().build();
        private WebTarget target;

        ...
        @Before
        public void setUp() {
            target = client.target(API_URL);
        }

        /**
         * Test of create method, of class FootballPlayerFacadeREST.
         */
        @Test
        @InSequence(2)
        public void testCreate() {
            System.out.println("create");
            FootballPlayer player = new FootballPlayer("Mauro",
"Vocale", 38,
                "Juventus", "central midfielder", new
BigInteger("100"));
            Response response =
target.request().post(Entity.entity(player,
                MediaType.APPLICATION_JSON_TYPE));
            assertThat(response.getStatus(),
is(Response.Status.NO_CONTENT.
                getStatusCode()));
        }

    ...
}
```

Are some famous players missing? At the end of the chapter, we will build a graphic user interface that will help you to insert your favorite ones.

The football manager microservice

In this section, we will build the microservice related to the management of the football managers (the people that manage the fantasy teams and participate in the fantasy league). In order to do so, in addition to the prerequisites described previously, you will need MySQL installed on your system; and, like we did for PostgreSQL, we will use Docker to install and handle it. The structure of the project will be very similar to that which was already created in the previous section; for that reason, we will only focus on the aspects that are different.

Database installation and configuration

To install the MySQL Docker image, perform the following steps:

1. Open a new Terminal window and launch the following command, setting the name of the image, the port, and the credentials:

    ```
    $ docker run --name mysql_thorntail -p 3306:3306 -e
    MYSQL_ROOT_PASSWORD=root -d mysql
    ```

    After that, the MySQL image will be launched as a container.

2. To verify this, you can launch the $ docker ps -a command, which gives you a list of the containers created and their relative statuses. The status must be up.

3. You can also check the container logs, in order to retrieve information about the MySQL status. Launch the following command:

    ```
    $ docker logs   -f 6f1f54a5b932
    ```

    The 6f1f54a5b932 is the container ID. You should see the following information:

    ```
    [System] [MY-010931] [Server] /usr/sbin/mysqld: ready for
    connections. Version: '8.0.11' socket:
    '/var/run/mysqld/mysqld.sock' port: 3306 MySQL Community Server
    - GPL.
    ```

4. Now, it's time to connect to the container, in order to manage it. Launch the following command:

    ```
    $ docker exec   -it 6f1f54a5b932 bash
    ```

    The 6f1f54a5b932 is the container ID.

5. Now, log in to the MySQL with the following command:

```
$ mysql -u   root -p
```

6. Set the password that's required (in our case, root). Now, you will be able to interact with the database server:

```
Welcome to the   MySQL monitor.  Commands end with ; or \g.

Your MySQL   connection id is 18

Server   version: 8.0.11 MySQL Community Server - GPL
```

7. Let's create the database that's needed for our microservice and select it for use, as follows:

```
$ CREATE DATABASE   football_managers_registry;

$ use   football_managers_registry;
```

8. You can create the table in the container, as showing below, or delegate it to the source code implementation of your microservice. The first one is an easy but poor approach to use only in development environment:

```
CREATE TABLE    FOOTBALL_MANAGER (
        ID SERIAL       PRIMARY KEY NOT NULL,
        NAME            VARCHAR(50) NOT NULL,
        SURNAME         VARCHAR(50) NOT NULL,
        AGE             INT     NOT NULL,
        NICKNAME        VARCHAR(50) NOT NULL
    );
```

Creating the source code

We have installed and configured everything that's necessary to create our microservice for the management of the registry of fantasy manager. Now, it's time to write the code that's needed to expose our microservice APIs.

We will follow the same steps that were described for the football players' microservice:

1. We will connect to the Thorntail project generator utility, `http://wildfly-swarm.io/generator/`, in order to get our project skeleton to work on, and we will select the following dependencies:
   - JAX-RS
   - CDI
   - JPA
   - JTA

2. We will use `com.packtpub.thorntail` as the Maven **Group ID** of the project, and `fantasy-player-microservice` as the **Artifact ID**.

3. Click on **Generate Project** to create and download the ZIP file with the project skeleton.

4. Unzip the file in a directory of your choice, and open the Maven project with your favorite IDE (Eclipse, NetBeans, IntelliJ, and so on).

Remember to perform the following important steps:

1. Change the value of the BOM from `bom-all` to `bom`, in order to only include the stable fractions that are recommended for daily use.

2. Change the value of the project name from `Thorntail Example` to `Thorntail Football manager microservice`.

3. Change the final name of the artifact, created in the build phase, from `demo` to `football-manager-microservice`.

4. Now, launch the first build with the following command:

```
$ mvn clean package
```

In this way, we will download all of the dependencies and create the WAR artifact named `football-manager-microservice.war` and the `Uber` executable JAR file, `football-manager-microservice-thorntail.jar`.

Entity class – JPA

We need a domain model object to map the records that are inserted into our database. To do this, we will use the JPA specification; so, we will create an entity class for this purpose:

1. Let's create a new Java package, to store it, and name it `model`. The fully qualified package name will be `com.packtpub.thorntail.footballmanagermicroservice.model`.

2. After that, we will build the domain class, named `FootballManager` (only the `fields` section is shown here):

```
...

/**
 * Domain model class that maps the data stored into
football_manager table
 * inside database.
 *
 * @author Mauro Vocale
 * @version 1.0.0 19/08/2018
 */

@Entity
@Table(name = "FOOTBALL_MANAGER")
@XmlRootElement
@NamedQueries({
@NamedQuery(name = "FootballManager.findAll", query
        = "SELECT f FROM FootballManager f")
 })
public class FootballManager {

@Id
@GeneratedValue(strategy = GenerationType.IDENTITY)
@Basic(optional = false)
@Column(name = "ID")
private Long id;

@Basic(optional = false)
@NotNull
@Size(min = 1, max = 50)
@Column(name = "NAME")
private String name;

@Basic(optional = false)
@NotNull
@Size(min = 1, max = 50)
@Column(name = "SURNAME")
```

```
private String surname;

@Basic(optional = false)
@NotNull
@Column(name = "AGE")
private int age;

@Basic(optional = false)
@NotNull
@Size(min = 1, max = 50)
@Column(name = "NICKNAME")
private String nickname;

...

}
```

3. To complete the management of database access operations, we need to configure the `persistence.xml` file, inside the `src/main/resources/META-INF` directory, where we will store all of the configurations related to our persistence layer. Remember to set:

   - The name of the persistence unit (`FootballManagerPU`)
   - The transaction type (JTA), which means that we demand to the container the management of the transactions
   - The data source JNDI name to use (`java:/jboss/datasources/FootballManagerDS`)
   - The load script source that will preload a subset of data into the database

4. Finally, we will create the default project (the `defaults.yml` file) in the `src/main/resources/` directory, where we will define the data source, `FootballManagerDS`, that contains the configuration to connect to the database:

```
swarm:
    datasources:
    data-sources:
      FootballManagerDS:
            driver-name: mysql
            connection-url:
jdbc:mysql://localhost:3306/football_managers_registry
            user-name: root
            password: root
            valid-connection-checker-class-name:
org.jboss.jca.adapters.jdbc.extensions.mysql.MySQLValidConnectionCh
```

```
ecker
            validate-on-match: true
            background-validation: false
            exception-sorter-class-name:
    org.jboss.jca.adapters.jdbc.extensions.mysql.MySQLExceptionSorter
```

5. Let's complete the process by setting the relative dependency to `io.thorntail.datasources` and the `mysql` driver in the Maven `pom.xml` file.

6. Declaring the vendor JDBC library dependency, Thorntail will automatically detect and install the driver.

RESTful web service – JAX-RS and CDI

Now, it's time to build our RESTful web service implementation, as follows:

1. Delete the default implementation class, `HelloWorldEndpoint.java`, created by the Thorntail generator.

2. Define a new package, named `service` (the fully qualified name will be `com.packtpub.thorntail.footballmanagermicroservice.rest.service`), where we will put the RESTful web service implementation.

3. Build the API implementations by using the CDI specifications (to inject the entity manager used to manage the database connections) and JAX-RS (to implement the CRUD RESTful operations). You can follow the same steps that were implemented in the *The football player microservice* section.

4. Remember to set the `@Path` of your RESTful implementation to `/footballmanager`.

5. Before we create our `Uber JAR` and run the application, we must change the port that the Thorntail instance will use. You must remember that there is the football player microservice that runs on the default `8080` port.

6. To avoid port conflict, we will set the following property in the Maven `pom.xml` file:

```
...
    <configuration>
            <properties>
                    <swarm.port.offset>100</swarm.port.offset>
            </properties>
    </configuration>
    ...
```

7. Create our Uber JAR using the following command:

```
$ mvn clean    package
```

8. Then, launch our microservice application with the following command:

```
$ java -jar target/football-manager-microservice-thorntail.jar
```

9. Now, we can invoke the API that retrieves the list of football managers, using the following command:

```
$ curl http://localhost:8080/footballmanager | json_pp
```

10. Finally, we will create the JUnit test, in order to ensure that our APIs work properly. Let's add the Maven dependencies, as follows:

```
<properties>
    ...
    <version.resteasy>3.0.19.Final</version.resteasy>
</properties>

<dependency>
    <groupId>io.thorntail</groupId>
    <artifactId>arquillian</artifactId>
    <scope>test</scope>
</dependency>
<dependency>
    <groupId>org.jboss.resteasy</groupId>
    <artifactId>resteasy-client</artifactId>
    <version>${version.resteasy}</version>
    <scope>test</scope>
</dependency>
```

11. Then, we will create the test class, named FootballManagerFacadeRESTTest, in the package com.packtpub.thorntail.footballmanagermicroservice.rest.service, under the src/main/test directory.

Follow the same steps that were described in the *Entity class – JPA* section, and try to do it yourself. If you can't, don't worry; at the end of the section, I will give you a link to the GitHub repository to find the solution.

The football team microservice

In this section, we will build the microservice related to the management of the football teams that participate in the fantasy league. It's time to measure your skills and try to build the microservice according to the specifications that will be described in this section.

At the end of the chapter, there will be a link to the GitHub repository, where you can find the final implementation.

Database installation and configuration

The first step is to install the database. For this microservice, we will use MongoDB, and, as was done for the previous microservices, we will use Docker to install and handle it.

You should install and configure the Docker image, with the following requirements:

- Set the name of your image to `mongo_thorntail`.
- Expose, via TCP, the default MongoDB—27017.
- Run the container in the background and print the container ID.

After that, the MongoDB image should be launched as a container. Launch the command that will verify this and give you a list of the created containers and their relative statuses.

You should mainly focus on the following attributes:

- **Status**: To verify that the container is up and running
- **Ports**: To verify that the default port, 27017, is exposed

Creating the source code

We have installed and configured everything that's necessary to create our microservice for the management of the registry of teams. Now, it's time to write the Java code for our microservice APIs.

You should create a Maven project with the following dependencies:

- JAX-RS
- CDI
- MongoDB Java driver
- Arquillian
- RESTEasy client

In this case, you won't use JPA, because version 2.0.0 of Thorntail doesn't support the use of Hibernate OGM, which allows for the use of NoSQL data stores with JPA.

Refer to the documentation at `https://docs.thorntail.io/4.0.0-SNAPSHOT/#component-ogm` for more details.

Remember to also set the following properties:

- The Maven **Group ID** will be `com.packtpub.thorntail`.
- The Maven **Artifact ID** will be `football-team-microservice`.
- The BOM that will only include the stable fractions that are recommended for daily use.
- The **Project Name** will be `Thorntail Football team microservice`.
- The final name of the artifact, created in the build phase, will be `football-team-microservice`.
- The HTTP port that is used by Thorntail; there are the other two microservices, which could be up and running at the same time.

Build the project, and make sure you include the WAR artifact named `football-team-microservice.war` and the executable Uber JAR, `football-team-microservice-thorntail.jar`.

At the end of this phase, you will be ready to implement the Java classes needed to reach our target.

Design and build the classes to do this, as follows:

- A model class that simulates a JPA entity, with the following attributes:
    - `String ID`: The ID primary key used by the MongoDB collection
    - `String name`: The name of your football team
    - `String city`: The name of the city that usually hosts the matches of your team
    - **Set** `<Integer> footballManagerId`: The primary key of the football manager of your team, managed by the football manager microservice
    - **Set** `<Integer> footballPlayersId`: The list of the primary keys of the football players of your team, managed by the football player microservice

- A service class that behaves like a **Data Access Object** (**DAO**), needed to manage the MongoDB CRUD operation. Here, you should implement the following operations:
    - An initialize phase, where you do the following:
        - Connect to MongoDB
        - Create the database, if it doesn't exist
        - Create the collection, if it doesn't exist
        - Delete the previous collection's values
        - Load the collection's data
    - A destroy phase, where you close the connection to the database.
    - A `getTeams` method that retrieves all the values.
    - A `find` method that retrieves the record with the primary key.
    - An `edit` method that modifies the record.
    - A `delete` method, to remove the record.
- A RESTful web service that implements the CRUD operation with the verbs `GET`, `POST`, `PUT,` and `DELETE`.
- A `beans.xml` file, needed to activate the CDI in the container.
- A JUnit test to verify the implementations of the RESTful APIs.

OK. Now, you should be able to create your `Uber JAR`, with the following command:

```
$ mvn clean package
```

Launch our microservice application, as follows:

```
$ java -jar target/football-team-microservice-thorntail.jar
```

Try to invoke the API that retrieves the list of football teams, as follows:

```
$ curl http://localhost:8280/footballteam | json_pp
```

You will receive an output similar to the following:

```
[
  {
    "footballPlayersId": [
      1,
      4,
      6,
      7,
      10,
      12,
```

```
        14,
        16,
        18,
        19,
        20
    ],
    "city": "Turin",
    "name": "Mauryno_NewTeam",
    "footballManagerId": 1,
    "id": "5b548e7097007545c9904ce4"
  },
  {
    "footballPlayersId": [
        2,
        5,
        8,
        9,
        11,
        13,
        15,
        17,
        21,
        22,
        23
    ],
    "name": "Foogaro_Great_Lazie",
    "city": "Rome",
    "id": "5b548e7097007545c9904ce5",
    "footballManagerId": 2
  }
]
```

You will find the complete implementation of the microservice at the end of the chapter.

The user interface microservice

Modern enterprise applications are designed with the basic concept of separating the frontend from the backend.

These two layers have very different characteristics, and therefore, they require different approaches, in terms of the following:

- Software development and life cycle
- Resource management (CPU, thread, throughput)
- Scalability and service levels

For these reasons, all new applications, from those built with monolithic architectures to new ones designed with microservices, are released with components dedicated to the management of the backend and frontend.

While, for the backend components, Jakarta EE and MicroProfile have contributed to the creation of more functional specifications for the realization of cloud-oriented applications, the same cannot be said for the frontend components.

At the moment, the platform only provides full specifications for the server side while, for the frontend layer, there is only one specification based on the concepts of component model, a flexible and ready-to-use user interface element—**Java Server Faces (JSF)**.

Java EE/Jakarta EE 8 provides version 2.3 of JSF, which represents the standard user interface for building applications.

Although they have been completely revised starting from version 2.0, released in a concise form with JEE 6, JSF have progressively lost their appeal in the developer community, despite all the improvements enacted in the latest versions.

Numerous criticisms of JSF technology have been launched, the most famous of which was presented in the *Technology Radar* publication, available at https://www.thoughtworks. com/radar/languages-and-frameworks/jsf.

The main criticisms are as follows:

- The use of a shared stateful state inside the components
- The presence, in the same place, of the user interface and the business logic concepts

The JSF specification leaders have tried to respond to these criticisms (for example, in the article at https://www.primefaces.org/jsf-is-not-what-youve-been-told-anymore/), but without any great success.

To try to overcome the limitations found in JSF, it was proposed to create a new JSR, MVC 1.0/JSR 371, based on an action-based model, which should have been the answer to Spring MVC. But MVC is vetoed in the final stage and it still exists as a community-based specification.

Although I do consider Jakarta EE and extremely mature MicroProfiles for the realization of Java Enterprise and cloud-oriented applications, I do not consider it the right choice for the realization of frontend architectures.

Thorntail, from this point of view, only offers support to JSF through a specific fraction, as follows:

```
<dependency>
    <groupId>io.thorntail</groupId>
    <artifactId>jsf</artifactId>
</dependency>
```

For these reasons, the suggestion is to adopt a microservice architecture, even for frontend components, so as to be able to modify specific elements of the user experience without having to release the entire graphical interface, but with frameworks that follow the HTML 5 specifications (CSS 3 and ECMAScript).

There are numerous frameworks in this segment, as follows:

- **Angular**: https://angular.io/
- **Bootstrap**: https://getbootstrap.com/
- **ReactJS**: https://reactjs.org/

The basic idea is to divide the original monolithic frontend into multiple microservices, potentially written using different languages and frameworks, and to coordinate them using the concept of a **micro frontend**.

This term is the equivalent of a microservice backend, but related to the frontend world.

The basic idea is to build a single-page application that is a composition of features implemented by dedicated microservices.

As was described for the backend microservice, the micro frontend should be organized into vertical teams responsible for implementing specific areas of the user experience.

Every single micro frontend can be implemented with the technology that the team evaluates as being best in terms of business requirements

Finally, you can have a sort of aggregator single-page application that invokes the micro frontends, in order to build the final user experience.

This approach gives you the ability to do the following:

- **Be technologically agnostic**: Make the team free to choose the technology.
- **Isolate the team code**: The applications are independent and self-contained. In this way, every micro frontend can have a dedicated life cycle.
- **Favor native browser features over custom APIs**: In this way, you can build a more effective and easily portable user interface.
- **Build a resilient site**: Through the use of JavaScript that is asynchronous, and it's designed for native manages the failure.

Building a user experience is beyond the scope of this chapter, since we are evaluating the features of Jakarta EE in Thorntail. For that reason, I will show you a quick way to create a user interface for your specific microservice, in order to test the APIs in a way other than the JUnit test.

Building a user interface

To build a basic HTML5 application that exposes your API, you will need to implement a few steps. First of all, you need to enable your previous microservice to accept HTTP requests from different domains (a feature called **cross-origin resource sharing**).

In order to do this, I have used an open source plugin that enables CORS support for JAX-RS 2.0 in the Java EE 7 environment.

Put this fraction of XML into the `pom.xml` file of the microservices built from the previous sections, as follows:

```
<!-- CORS Support For JAX-RS 2.0 / JavaEE 7  -->

<dependency>
    <groupId>com.airhacks</groupId>
    <artifactId>jaxrs-cors</artifactId>
    <version>0.0.2</version>
    <scope>compile</scope>
```

```
</dependency>
```

This plugin creates the filter needed to implement the CORS feature inside the microservices, without writing other Java code.

You have to decide whether to build a monolith user interface that contains the user experience of all of the microservices, or split the logic into different micro frontends, and then create a single-page application that aggregates them.

Let's start to build the user interface of the football player microservice.

I used Angular 6 and Bootstrap 4 to create a new HTML 5 project, named `football-player-ui`. To accelerate the development, I used the Angular CLI, which makes the creation of the application easy.

To run the examples that you will find in the GitHub repository, or to create a user interface, you will need to install the Angular CLI and the relative dependencies.

Launch the following commands to install NVM, NPM, and NodeJS:

```
$ touch ~/.bash_profile
$ curl -o-
https://raw.githubusercontent.com/creationix/nvm/v0.32.1/install.sh | bash
```

Close your Terminal in order to make your changes effective and open a new one. Then, launch the following commands:

```
$ nvm ls-remote
$ nvm install 8.11.3
$ npm install -g @angular/cli
$ npm install --save bootstrap font-awesome
$ npm install rxjs@6 rxjs-compat@6 --save
```

Now, you are ready to create the files needed to implement the presentation view (HTML and CSS) and the business logic (JavaScript, to invoke the RESTful APIs).

Since the application is only built with HTML and JavaScript files, you can just put them into an Apache web server directory (for example, `/var/www/html`), and launch it:

```
$ /etc/init.d/httpd start
```

You should obtain a result like the following screenshot:

Football players							
Users							New Football Player
id	Name	Surname	Age	Team	Position	Price	
1	Gianluigi	Buffon	40	Paris Saint Germain	goalkeeper	2	Edit Delete
2	Manuel	Neuer	32	Bayern Munchen	goalkeeper	35	Edit Delete
3	Keylor	Navas	31	Real Madrid	goalkeeper	18	Edit Delete
4	Joao	Cancelo	24	Juventus	right back	35	Edit Delete
5	Dani	Alves	35	Paris Saint Germain	right back	4	Edit Delete
6	Sergio	Ramos	32	Real Madrid	central defender	45	Edit Delete
7	Giorgio	Chiellini	33	Juventus	central defender	10	Edit Delete
8	Mats	Hummels	29	Bayern Munchen	central defender	60	Edit Delete
9	Diego	Godín	32	Atletico de Madrid	central defender	35	Edit Delete

Summary

In this chapter, you learned how to create a microservice based on Jakarta EE specifications (JAX-RS, JPA, CDI, and JTA), using Thorntail. We also discussed the limits of the platform with regard to the client-side components, and how to overcome them. You can find the full code described in this chapter in the GitHub repository at `https://github.com/Hands-on-MSA-JakartaEE/ch4`.

In the next chapter, we will discuss the management of transactions in distributed environments, such as microservices.

5
Eclipse MicroProfile and Transactions - Narayana LRA

In the previous chapters, I discussed how to implement a microservices architecture using the Jakarta EE and MicroProfile specifications with Thorntail.

We described the techniques that are used to interact with different database types, using the JPA or **Data Access Object** (**DAO**) pattern. You learned how to commit your operations using the **Java Transaction API** (**JTA**). You saw how to expose your APIs using JAX-RS specifications to implement RESTful web services with JSON to send and receive data. Finally, we discussed how to follow the TDD approach and test our APIs with Arquillian.

Now, it's time to deal with one of the revolutionary approaches that you need to follow in an MSA architecture—the transactions. The transaction is one of the key elements of enterprise applications—maintaining data integrity and consistency, in a distributed and heterogeneous architecture like the microservice architecture, is one of the main challenges.

In this chapter, we will cover the following topics:

- Transactions
- Transactions in microservices architectures
- The saga pattern
- Saga pattern implementation
- MicroProfile **Long Running Actions** (**LRAs**)

Transactions

Transaction handling is one of the most important elements of an enterprise application.

A transaction is a unit of work that provides an *all or nothing* property to the operation that is running within its scope. Furthermore, it guarantees that shared resources (for example, database records or messages in a messaging broker) are protected from access by multiple users that try to change them concurrently. The transaction is in a block of inseparable sequences of operation—to guarantee the integrity of the data, all of the operations, included in a transaction, must be terminated with a successful change of the state of your data (in this case, the transaction is defined as committed). Otherwise, none of them must take effect (in this case, the transaction is rolled back, or aborted).

You can think of a transaction as a sort of mechanical aid to achieve data correctness.

Developers that use Java EE/Jakarta EE specifications have the ability to manage transactions in two ways, as follows:

- **Container-managed transactions**: This is the easiest way to handle transactions. Using **Enterprise Java Bean** (**EJB**) or a simple Java class with the @Transactional annotation, developers can delegate the life cycle of the transaction to a container that hides all of the complex processing necessary to handle the transaction. In this case, it's important to know and follow the rules and specifications of the platform and the container to know the exact behavior of your workflow, avoiding unexpected results.
- **Bean-managed transactions**: This is a fine-grained way to handle transactions. Developers are responsible for starting and ending the transaction, and deciding its final state (committed, aborted, or rolled back). The container will provide a transaction manager implementation, but it will not handle anything on behalf of the developer, who will have total control of the workflow, but no protection from bugs or low-quality code.

ACID properties

A transaction must have four fundamental characteristics, summarized by the acronym **ACID** (**atomicity, consistency, isolation, durability**), to correctly implement its function. Its main goal is to maintain the correctness and consistency of the data during the operations of alteration of the status of the business domain.

The characteristics are as follows:

- **Atomicity**: This property means that all operations that are included in a transaction must be executed as if they were a single block. With this behavior, the application has the ability to abort a transaction if an exception occurs, and to have all writes (performed by `insert`, `update`, and `delete` operations) discarded, preserving the original integrity state of the data. Otherwise, when the transaction commits successfully, all operations of a transaction must execute a valid commit of the operation (be it database writing, message consuming, and so on). Conversely, when the transaction fails, the system must be able to roll back the original status of the data, and all realized operations and effects must be undone.

- **Consistency**: This property is related to the logical consistency of the data. When a new transaction starts, it must ensure that the data maintains a state of logical consistency, regardless of the final outcome (`commit`, `abort`, or `roll back`). In reality, the concept of logical consistency cannot be translated into a universal, semantic algorithm, applicable by a transaction manager; it is a state that is linked to the business domain implemented by the application. We can define it as a human concept; therefore, there is no semantic knowledge to be applied by the container. The only way to implement this concept is to restore the initial state of the data (in case of a failure), or to ensure that all operations are completed, bringing the data to a new state, if successful.

- **Isolation**: This property is related to the execution of parallel transactions on the same resources. It guarantees that concurrent transactions cannot interfere with one another, like what happens for the thread-safe code. Each transaction behaves as if it was executed entirely alone. The serial execution of each transaction guarantees a consistent state, while the execution of parallel transactions cannot result in an inconsistent state of the data. The relational databases that follow the standards described in ANSI SQL-92 implement four levels of isolation with a different implementation of the locking mechanism. The four levels are as follows:
    - **Read uncommitted**: This is the lowest isolation level. Setting this property, the transaction only sets the lock when it needs to update the record item and releases it after the transaction is terminated. It's usually defined as **long write locks**. This behavior allows one transaction to read the changes of any other transactions that are not committed (a **dirty read**). However, it avoids the **dirty write** problem, which happens when a transaction overwrites a value that was previously written by another transaction and has not been committed yet.

- **Read committed:** Using this property, the application is able to avoid the dirty reads phenomenon. This isolation level allows the read of data only when it has been committed. It is the main model that's used in enterprise applications.
- **Repeatable read**: This isolation level prevents the phenomenon called **non-repeatable read** that can happen with the read committed setting. It involves reading the data values over different periods, during which a consistent data state may not be guaranteed. This means that, for example, a transaction could know of a data change at a later point in time: this could invalidate the data that was read during previous processing.
- **Serializable**: This property specifies that one transaction is unable to read the data that has been modified by another transaction, but has not yet been committed. If you want to obtain the same result without setting this value you should implement a model that guarantees that no other transaction can insert new data that has a primary key with values that could fall within a key range read from any statement. So you should choose if delegate this behavior to the database or to implement a custom solution yourself.

- **Durability**: This feature requires that all of the changes be made during a transaction; once it is committed, it must be persistent and definitive, even in the case of system crashes. Usually, the use of persistent storage, like a disk drive or the cloud, is sufficient.

In addition to the specific elements that each solution uses to implement ACID properties, you may have noticed that the common denominator is a lock, which is not one of the factors that allows us to obtain a high level of scalability in an architecture.

Who is the actor that handles the transactions? The answer is—**the transaction manager**.

Transaction managers

The **transaction manager** is responsible the coordination of transactions across one or more resources. This guarantees the completion of each transaction and decides whether to `commit` or `rollback`. Its main responsibilities are as follows:

- Starting and ending (with `commit` or `abort` state) transactions, using the `begin`, `commit`, and `rollback` methods

- Coordinating the transactions across multiple resources
- Managing the transaction context—the transaction manager creates it and attaches it to the current thread
- Recovery from failure—this concept is implemented by using `rollback` capabilities that ensure the recovery of the original data state caused by a failure

There are two types of transaction managers, local and global:

- The **local transaction manager** is responsible for coordinating the transactions over a single resource; it's not able to provide ACID features across multiple resources (for example, database updates and **Java Message Service** (**JMS**) message sending).
- The **global transaction manager** is used to coordinate transactions over multiple resources. Usually, it's provided by an external system (for example an application server) and it's able to guarantee ACID transactions between two or more different transactional resources.

Transaction managers are defined in Java EE/Jakarta EE through two specifications:

- **Java Transaction API** (**JTA**), currently in version 1.2
- **Java Transaction Service** (**JTS**)

JTA

The JTA is the specification that established the APIs of the transaction manager and the way of which it should interact with the other components involved in a distributed transaction system:

- The application
- The resource manager
- The application server

As I explained earlier, you are able to use these APIs in a container-managed way, also known as a **declarative model**, or in a bean-managed way, also known as a **programmatic model**. The recommended way of managing transactions is by the container that handles all the phases of the transaction life cycle. From my experience, managing transactions programmatically is only necessary in very exceptional use cases and needs a deep knowledge of transactions, concurrency, and recovery strategies.

In the first case (the declarative model), the developers usually ask the container to manage the transactions through the use of EJB.

Many consider EJB a complex and not very scalable technology. Personally, I do not agree with this assessment, which is based on a negative prejudice that has developed in relation to version 2 of this technology. From version 3.0 on, the use of EJB has been greatly simplified; their configuration, as well as their use, is not very different from that of the beans present in the Spring framework.

However, for those that do not want to be tied to the EJB context, two new annotations, `@Transactional` and `@TransactionScoped`, were introduced in version 1.2 of the JTA. These annotations enable simple managed beans to behave as an EJB but without any dependencies on the EJB container. They also provide feature that enables the developers to specify a standard CDI scope for the bean instances, whose life cycles are related to the currently active JTA transaction. We used them in the microservices examples we implemented in `Chapter 4`, *Building Microservices Using Thorntail*.

When the transaction manager works in JTA mode, the data is shared in the memory, and the transaction context is transferred by remote EJB calls.

Regardless of the technology used, developers are required to configure the container, setting how individual transactions should be managed by it. The permitted values are as follows:

- `MANDATORY`: The execution method of a client must happen inside of a transaction context. If there is a transaction context and the EJB method is executed inside its scope, the container uses it; otherwise, an exception is thrown.
- `REQUIRED`: The execution method of a client must happen inside of a transaction context. The specification defines that if the transaction context is already present, it must be used; otherwise, a new transaction context will be started by the container. This is the default value for all methods defined in EJB.
- `REQUIRES_NEW`: The container creates a new transaction context on every method's invocation. If a transaction context is already present, it will be suspended by the container for the duration of the execution of the new transaction.

- `NOT_SUPPORTED`: The execution of a method happens only outside of a transaction context. If a transaction's context is created before the invocation of the method, it will be suspended and then the method will be invoked. Otherwise, the method will be executed without the creation of a new transaction context.
- `SUPPORTS`: If the execution of a method happens with a transaction context, the container will behave in the same way as the `REQUIRED` attribute. Otherwise, the behavior of the container will be the same as what we described for the `NOT_SUPPORTED` attribute.

In the second case (the programmatic model), developers use the `javax.transaction.UserTransaction` interface to handle the entire transaction life cycle, mainly using the following methods:

- `begin()`: Start a new transaction, and associate it with the current thread
- `commit()`: Complete the transaction associated with the current thread
- `rollback()`: Rollback the transaction associated with the current thread
- `setRollbackOnly()`: Update the transaction status associated with the current thread so that the only possible result of the transaction is to `rollback`

JTS

JTS specifies the implementation of a transaction manager that supports the following:

- JTA specifications, at a high level
- Java mapping of the **Object Management Group** (**OMG**), and **Object Transaction Service** (**OTS**) specification at a low level

When the transaction manager works in JTS mode, the data is shared by sending **Common Object Request Broker Architecture** (**CORBA**) messages, and the transaction context is transferred by **Internet Inter-ORB Protocol** (**IIOP**) calls.

This method is less portable due to interoperability with external, third-party ORB issues. Different application server implementations may be unable to distribute transactions between themselves when using this technology.

Extended architecture

In the previous sections, we discussed how the status of the data is permanently persisted at the end of an operation.

However, enterprise applications are composed of complex operations that often involve multiple and heterogeneous data sources, such as databases, message brokers, caches, and so on.

An application functionality must be implemented to ensure the logical consistency of the data; this means that the individual operations that compose it, while insisting on different data sources, must still act as a single unit. They must complete everything successfully, or none of them can affect the status of the data.

How can we achieve this behavior?

The answer is the **Extended Architecture (XA)** specification. It's the **X/Open Common Applications Environment** (CAE) standard specification that was developed to define a transaction that uses more than one backend data store. Its goal is to define the specifications to make the transaction manager coordinate all of the transactions associated with a single data source (application servers, databases, caches, and message queues) as a single, global XA transaction.

In an XA architecture, there are two main actors involved, as follows:

- The global transaction manager, who is responsible for coordinating the different transactions as a single unit
- The XA resource, which represents the data source target of the single transaction

In Java EE/Jakarta EE, the XA standard, related to the handling of the distributed transactions across multiple resources, is implemented by the `javax.transaction.xa.XAResource` interface. It defines how the resource manager and the transaction manager should communicate in a **Distributed Transaction Processing** (DTP) environment.

The distributed transaction, also known as XA Transaction, is an ACID transaction that is executed across of independent participants, who are connected to each other through a communication network.

In a global distributed transaction, each node has its own transaction manager that manages a local transaction—after completion, the transaction manager communicates with the transaction managers of the other participants to share the state of the transaction to decide the final outcome.

Usually, in an extended architecture, one transaction manager is elected as a global transaction coordinator—it administers the other participants in the distributed transaction and it can be one of the participating nodes, or an independent service.

By what rules does the global transaction manager use to decide the outcome of an XA transaction?

The decision strategy is known as the consensus protocol.

Consensus protocol

The **consensus protocol** is the way, for different components of a distributed system, to achieve an agreement about a shared data value. A transaction environment is used by the transaction manager to establish whether a transaction can be committed or aborted, using the following three conditions:

- **Agreement**: All nodes decide on the same value
- **Validity**: If all of the nodes have the same value, then a consensus must be obtained on this value
- **Termination**: All nodes decide about a transaction's outcome

In enterprise architectures, there are three major consensus protocols, as follows:

- **Two-phase commit (2PC)** protocol
- **Three-phase commit (3PC)** protocol
- Paxos

2PC protocol

2PC is the most commonly used consensus algorithm. In this scenario, the global transaction manager contacts every participant, suggests a possible value, collects a response from every participant, and, if everyone agrees, decides on a `commit`; otherwise, it communicates to `abort` about the consensus and performs a `rollback` on the transaction.

The procedure consists of two phases, as follows:

- **The prepare phase**: All participants send their proposals to the coordinator, stating whether they are able to proceed and commit their single operation, or whether the transaction should be aborted. This phase is implemented by the `prepare()` method of the `javax.transaction.xa.XAResource` interface.
- **Commit or abort phase**: All participants communicate the result of the vote, and tell the coordinator to either go ahead and decide to `commit`, or to `abort` the transaction. The coordinator specifies the behavior of the resources. The resources notify the coordinator when they finished to do this and when the transaction has finished. This is implemented by the `commit` and `rollback` methods of the `javax.transaction.xa.XAResource` interface.

The 2PC consensus protocol has the ability to manage node failures through the transaction log. Usually, a periodic recovery thread processes all of the unfinished transactions.

One of the main disadvantages of the 2PC protocol is that it is a lock-based protocol. If the coordinator fails after the first phase has completed, all of the participants will be blocked waiting for the coordinator's decision, and will not be able to progress until it recovers.

3PC protocol

The 3PC protocol is an extension of the 2PC protocol, and its goal is to overcome its limits, which are related to its blocking nature.

One of the main features of this consensus protocol is that it is non-blocking; this doesn't mean that the participants are not blocked during processing, but it means that the protocol can proceed in spite of failures.

It consists of three phases; the prepare phase and the commit (or abort) phase are the same as those of the 2PC protocol.

However, it introduces a new phase, which we can define as a **prepared state**, where all of the participants of the transaction will define their statuses. The status can be either waiting or pre-commit. This means that the final phase can only have one, final state—aborted, if the previous phase was waiting, or commit, if the previous phase was pre-commit.

3PC mitigates the blocking nature of 2PC. The problem is that it obtains it with a more complicated protocol, and with a need to send another message before deciding to commit or abort the transaction. Furthermore, it does not solve the issue with network partitions.

3PC is not widely used in production environments.

The Paxos consensus

The Paxos consensus protocol was introduced by Leslie Lamport in 1998, with a goal of overcoming the limits of the 2PC and 3PC protocols. When most of participants in a system are present and the delays in messages are minimal, in such cases the system is not blocked.

It is composed of three main actors, as follows:

- **Proposer**: This component has the responsibility to initiate the protocol. It proposes, as name says, the possible values of which the client wants the entire system to agree on. It send a proposal number to the acceptors and it waits for a response from a majority of them. In case most of the acceptors `agree`, the value of any previously accepted proposal will be returned; if the majority reply with `reject`, or fail to reply, they abandon the proposal and start again.

- **Acceptor**: This component responds to the proposal performed by the proposer. All of the nodes that participate in the transaction are required to know the quorum of acceptors that form a majority. Once the acceptor receives a proposal, it compares its value to the highest value proposal that the client has already accepted. If the new proposal is higher, it replies `agree`; otherwise, it replies `reject`.

- **Learner**: This component is responsible to learn which value was chosen by the acceptors in the consensus phase.

The protocol is based on two phases, as follows:

- **Promise phase**: In this phase, the proposer proposes a value on which to establish a consensus. Then, it communicates this value to all of the acceptors (or to the quorum) using a unique identification number generated from a sequence. The acceptor receives the proposed value and checks if it is higher than the last ID that the client has already agreed to. If this evaluation returns true, the acceptors will respond to the proposer with a promise message; otherwise, no action will be taken.

- **Commit phase**: In this phase, the proposer collects all the answers it received by the acceptors. If the majority answered with a promise, the proposer sends them an `accept-request`. The majority of acceptors reply with an `accept` message to the proposer and learners that finally accept it. In this way, all the members involved in a distributed environment reach the consensus and decide to commit the transaction. Otherwise, a `rollback` operation will be performed.

Paxos was the first protocol that was resilient in asynchronous networks; it prefers to sacrifice liveness when the network is behaving asynchronously rather than correctness. It terminates the operations only when synchronicity returns.

In spite of this, it has some issues; the concurrency competition of two proposers trying to obtain the highest proposal number can cause the system to be blocked until the conflict is resolved.

The consensus is a very sophisticated and complex problem; at the time of writing this book, in the Java EE/Jakarta EE environment, the most commonly applied protocol is 2PC.

Transactions in microservices architecture

The benefits related to microservice architectures are there for all to see, from the reduction of the time to market, to the simpler management of the source life cycle, to the punctual management of resources, according to the actual workload.

However, at the end of every discussion on microservices, before proceeding to the design of the application architecture, a question always comes up—how are the transactions managed within microservices?

Distributed system interactions can be complex for many reasons, some of which are as follows:

- A microservices architecture involves many parties, realized using different technologies that adhere to different specifications
- A business function can span many different organizations that can have different service-level agreements, and, for this reason, can be implemented with various strategies
- A business function potentially lasting for hours or days, a logic that hardly reconciles with scalability—indeed it's very difficult to scale an application that has a logic based on the lock, performed by a transaction, which makes the system irresponsive for a long time

To preserve its high scalability feature, a microservice may not be able to lock resources indefinitely.

A business function can be composed of numerous microservices, each of which is responsible for managing a specific data domain. In complex cases, in which a business feature to be implemented needs to implement more steps, it may be required to undo only a subset of work which was previously done.

However, the concepts expressed in the previous sections (relating to the ACID properties of transactions) have always worked correctly in previous architectural models, including that of SOA; so, why give those up? And, if we are forced to do so, how can the data's integrity be managed?

It is not easy to use the JTA (and, especially, the XA) in microservices architecture. The reasons lie in the nature of ACID transactions, which implicitly assume the following:

- Have a closely coupled environments where all entities involved in a transaction span a LAN
- Have activities with a short execution time that must be able to work properly when the resources are locked for periods of time

Microservices are based on diametrically opposed concepts, such as loosely coupled environments and long-duration activities. Furthermore, microservices are distributed systems, and communication over the network brings a few complications, such as network failures and communication performance issues due to network overhead. Failure and performance are two aspects in which transactions can have a high incidence rate.

In 1997, James Gosling, the father of Java, extended a draft created by Peter Deutsch, which stated incorrect assumptions that were commonly made about distributed systems.

These assumptions are known as *The eight fallacies of distributed computing*, and they are as follows:

- The network is reliable
- The latency is zero
- The bandwidth is infinite
- The network is secure
- The topology doesn't change
- There is one administrator
- The transport cost is zero
- The network is homogeneous

All of these factors have important implications in the management of transactions, as was already discussed in the *Consensus protocols* section.

The microservices architecture tackles this series of problems with one word: relaxation.

It proposes a less rigid approach regarding the ACID properties, as follows:

- **Atomicity**: The microservices architecture approach prefers to undo a portion of work rather than cancel all of the work. For example, imagine you're booking a holiday—I'm sure that you prefer to buy an airline ticket, maybe when it has a very good price, even without travel insurance, rather than failing to book the trip and, consequently, stay at home only because the insurance service is temporarily unavailable. This model is similar to that of nested transactions where the work performed within their scope is provisional. A nested transaction represents a problem from a JTA point of view; support for nested transactions is not required, as declared in the specifications, and XAResource does not support nested transactions. So, it's very difficult to implement this concept in the Java EE/Jakarta EE environment. In the end, the mantra must be that failure does not affect enclosing the transaction.

- **Consistency**: ACID transactions, and the two phase commit protocol, are based on strong global consistency. All participants stay in the lock step and they must retrieve the same transaction outcome. But this approach doesn't scale, and weak consistency replication protocols were developed for large scales. A weak or relaxed consistency is the approach proposed by microservice architectures. This model is known as **eventual consistency**, also known as optimistic replication—its main concept is that the system guarantees that, if no new updates are performed to the requested object, all of the data reads will return the last updated value. With this approach, the system does not provide any guarantees about the consistency of data for a limited period, also defined as **inconsistency window**. Microservices must manage the eventual consistency model to avoid to make decisions based on inconsistent information. Distributed systems, such as microservices, are unable to guarantee both strong consistency and high availability at the same time. For this reason, distributed business applications are often chosen to tolerate temporary data inconsistencies in favor of promoting availability. This approach is also classified as **Basically Available, Soft state, Eventual consistency** (**BASE**) in contrast to traditional ACID semantic.

- **Isolation**: In this case, the microservice approach is to delegate the isolation of the resources to a service provider. It could decide to commit early and perform a compensation actions later. The important thing is that the undo operation, which is needed for the system to come back to its original state, must be always available.

The saga pattern

The saga pattern is the solution, proposed by microservice architectures to manage transactions in distributed systems.

A **saga** is a sequence of operations that represent a unit of work that can be undone by the compensation action. When an operation is successful, it publishes a message or event to trigger the next local transaction in the saga; otherwise, the saga executes a series of compensating transactions that undo the changes that were made by the preceding. Each operation can be seen as a local transaction; so, it performs a `commit` or `rollback` to its own data source, but communicates with all other operations or local transactions that build the saga.

The saga guarantees that either all of the operations complete successfully, or the corresponding compensation actions are run for all of the executed operations, to cancel partial processing.

This approach is different than the one followed by the 2PC protocol, where a global distributed transaction (XA) is created, involving all of the resources/services that build the business function. The saga pattern implements the concept of *divide et impera*—each single service runs in a local transaction and provides a compensate action. The set of all of the individual operations that make up the business functionality communicates by using events (events/choreography pattern) or a **Saga Execution Coordinator** (command/orchestration).

It is immediately possible to notice that the approach, implemented by the saga pattern violates the principle of the isolation of ACID transactions; the ability to commit a partial operation breaks the isolation, since it makes the segment changes available before the saga ends. Saga overcomes this approach by using the eventual consistency model that, as I described previously, guarantees that the state will eventually become consistent, after the saga completes.

So, the saga pattern utilizes an alternative to ACID; we can define it as **BASE**. This acronym summarizes the following properties:

- **Basically available**: The system guarantees availability, as defined in the **CAP theorem**, published by Seth Gilbert and Nancy Lynch in 2002, stating that network shared data systems can only guarantee support for two of the following three properties:
    - **Consistency**: Every node in a distributed cluster returns the same, most recent, successful write, so that every client has the same view of the data

- **Availability**: Every available node returns a response for all read and write requests in a reasonable amount of time
- **Partition tolerant**: The system continues to function and maintains its consistency guarantees, in spite of network partitions

- **Soft state**: The state may change as time progresses, even without any immediate modification requests, due to the eventual consistency.
- **Eventual consistency**: As I described earlier, the state of the system is allowed to be in inconsistent states for short periods of time. If the system does not receive any new update requests, then it guarantees that the state will eventually get to a consistent state.

One of the key elements in the saga pattern is the compensation. Its role is to undo the work performed by the original operation, but with another operation, and not with the common approach of the transaction's `rollback`.

The reason is related to not only technical aspects, as was described previously, but also to a different functional approach. The compensation action does not necessarily have to restore the status of the data to the initial situation; its function is to set the status of the data to a value that is consistent for the business domain that is processing, in the case of the failure of a saga operation that prevented the successful completion of the original operation requested.

The important thing is that the compensation must be idempotent, because that is the only way to intercept the failures and to implement strong recovery management.

The main reason is that even the compensation may fail; it gives no guarantees to always work, unlike with the traditional transaction `rollback` that is guaranteed by the database or application server. The causes of the failure are heterogeneous, so it's difficult to implement an algorithm that's able to intercept all.

You can implement two different strategies, as follows:

- **Backward recovery**: This is the most common approach, and it requires that all operations define a compensation handler. In the case of failure, the saga execution component aborts the currently executed operation, and then, for every previous successful operation, in the reverse order of the original execution, it calls its respective compensation action.

- **Forward recovery**: This strategy requires that the system is able to produce a checkpoint that represents a snapshot of the system state at that particular point in time, to which the system can always be restored. This concept is similar to the one used in business process management applications. This effectively eliminates the need to define any compensation actions, since the system, in the case of a failure, will always have a safe point from which it can try to complete the business operation. Using this approach, the saga execution component is reduced to a basic, persistent transaction executor, losing most of the saga's benefits.

It is also possible to combine the two approaches to get the benefits of each one.

The transaction system makes checkpoints in predefined intervals, which can be periodical or based on different criteria. In the case of a failure, the system performs backward recovery to the last defined checkpoint, and then continues saga execution in a forward recovery mode.

Saga implementations

As we described in the *Saga pattern* section, the saga pattern is becoming the de facto standard for transaction management in microservices.

There are several frameworks that implement the saga pattern. In following sections, we will quickly analyze the main ones, focusing on the implementation proposal that is developing in the MicroProfile community.

The Axon framework

Axon is a lightweight framework, implemented as a Java Spring Boot microservices application, built in independent Maven projects, and distributed as an executable JAR; it is based on the **Command Query Responsibility Segregation** (**CQRS**) principles. The main concept here is that you can use a different data model for `update` operations (`update` or `insert`) and `read` operations.

Axon uses two different channels to exchange information between services:

- A command bus
- An event bus

The command bus is the actor that has the target receive the command object, containing all of the data relative to the operation to execute; it forwards it to the command handler. The command handler executes the operation (and the business methods) specified by the command object.

The result of this operation is the generation of the domain events that form the domain model.

The event bus dispatches events, synchronously or asynchronously, to event listeners, which execute the operations (for example, to update a data source or send a message to an external system).

The command handlers are completely unaware of the components that are interested in the changes they make; in this way, you are able to build a loosely coupled architecture.

Axon uses two different implementations for the command bus—JGroups Connector and Spring Cloud Connector, based on the Netflix Eureka Discovery client and Eureka Server combination.

For the event bus, the framework uses RabbitMQ, an external open source messaging system that supports multiple messaging protocols; in the Axon implementation, the event bus is built on top of the **Advanced Message Queuing Protocol** (**AMQP**).

Axon is a very powerful framework, but if you want to use it to handle the transactions in your system, you must be aware of the following challenges:

- **Maintenance of the saga life cycle**: Axon provides only the implementation to start and stop the saga execution. The handling of some important aspects of the saga pattern is up to the developer—for example, the invocation of participants, the relative collection of responses to define the final state of the transaction or the handling of the compensations actions, in order to recover the original data state after a failure, are delegate to the developer since the framework implements the communication between the participants of the saga only through events. This implementation model of the saga specification could become a potential bottleneck of the saga pattern's maintenance.
- **CQRS restrictions**: In Axon, the sagas are only a specialized type of event listener: this implementation model could be too restrictive in an environment that doesn't use the CQRS pattern.

Eventuate

Eventuate is a platform for developing asynchronous microservices and, like the Axon framework, it used the event sourcing model and the CQRS pattern. The main difference between the two approaches is that in the Eventuate platform, the command and event buses are local and not distributed. Another difference is that Eventuate allows only the use of the REST protocol for the remote communication.

The platform consists of two products, as follows:

- **Eventuate ES**: This product uses an approach similar to the one of the Axon framework, which is based on an event sourcing programming and a persistence model.
- **Eventuate Tram**: This is especially suitable for microservices that perform CRUD operations through the use of JPA/JDBC. It is easily integrated with the Spring framework, and it overcomes some limits of Eventuate ES, for saga handling in particular.

Eventuate ES

An Eventuate ES application consists of the following types of modules:

- **Command-side module**: It creates, updates, and aggregates objects that implement business logic and are persisted using event sourcing, in response to external update requests (usually HTTP POST, HTTP PUT, and HTTP DELETE requests) using services objects, and events published by command-side aggregates.
- **Query-side module**: It maintains the materialized CQRS views of command-side aggregates. This module has two sub-modules, as follows:
  - **View update module**: This subscribes to events to update the view
  - **View query module**: This handles query requests by querying the view
- **Outbound gateway module**: This processes events by invoking external services.

Eventuate ES has some limitations in relation to saga management, mainly involving the complexity of the platform and the restrictions placed by the CQRS pattern.

Eventuate Tram

The Eventuate Tram platform implements different solutions for saga management, all of which have been built using the Eventuate platform. The main idea is sending messages as a part of a database transaction; in this way, you can atomically `update` the state and send a message or a domain event, maintaining data consistency.

The architecture of the Eventuate Tram application, taken from the example that's available at `https://bit.ly/2UtmFp4`

In the figure observed, you can see two different services: **Todo Service** and **Todo View Service.** The first one implements functionalities related to the change of the state of the domain (`insert`, `update`, and `delete`) and, after one of these, publishes an event that will be stored in the **MESSAGE table** in a traditional, ACID-transaction way.

The **Eventuate Tram CDC service** tracks inserts into the **MESSAGE table**, usually using the database log, as a sort of change data capture, and publishes messages to a distributed topic using **Apache Kafka**.

Finally, the **Todo View Service** subscribes to the events and updates **ElasticSearch,** in order to retrieve the last version of the data.

As you can see, the overall architecture merges the benefits of saga orchestration and the CQRS pattern.

MicroProfile LRA

The MicroProfile specification aims to propose a standard solution about the management of the transactions in distributed systems as microservices, based on the saga pattern.

The specification is **Long Running Actions (LRA)** for MicroProfile: it's built by the Narayana team under the Eclipse MicroProfile initiative. Currently, it is in a "in progress" state, and it is one of the main topics under discussion in the community.

It proposes a new API for the coordination of long-running activities: the approach would be totally different from the one implemented, for example, in the Extended Architecture. The target is to guarantee a globally consistent outcome without the need to set locks on data that limits the scalability of the system.

The Narayana LRA implementation is based on the standard specifications provided by Java EE/Jakarta EE and MicroProfile (in particular, **Context and Dependency Injection (CDI)** and JAX-RS).

Unlike the frameworks we described previously, Narayana (and, in general, the LRA specification) uses an orchestration saga model.

The main actors in Narayana frameworks are as follows:

- **LRA coordinator**: This manages the saga processing, and can be a standalone service or embedded within an application service. Its main responsibilities are the LRA's initialization, participant enlisting, and either saga completion or compensation.
- **Saga participant**: This is a service that is involved in the LRA. Each one is required to provide at least one REST endpoint that serves as the compensation handler.

The execution of the LRA operation is done via an invocation to an LRA coordination service. This service responds with a unique identification value related to the initiating service.

When a business service is built by multiple microservices, there is the need to group and coordinate all the actors involved in the functionality. In an LRA implementation, the system enlists the participants with the LRA coordinator, using the ID returned by the coordinator. At the end of the process, either in case of success or in case of failure, one of the participating services that knows the LRA identification (the ID) contacts the coordinator to close (success) or compensate (failure) the LRA. The coordinator performs the corresponding requested action for each enlisted participant.

The participants that are involved in a saga transaction can have two states, as follows:

- **Success**: The activity has completed successfully, so the participants can consider the transaction closed
- **Fail**: The activity has completed unsuccessfully, and all participants involved in the LRA must perform compensation in the reverse order

Let's start to implement an example scenario.

The football market microservice

In this section, we will implement an LRA scenario.

The use case is related to purchasing the players that are necessary for the creation of our fantasy team.

We will build five actors, as follows:

- The LRA coordinator
- A microservice that handles the football player registry (`football-player-microservice-lra`)
- A microservice that handles the purchase offers for the football players (`football-player-offer-microservice-lra`)
- A microservice that simulates an API gateway that is responsible for implementing the business logic related to the football player market season (`football-player-market-microservice-lra`)
- A simple client that performs the offers to buy the football players (`Football_Player_Market_client`)

LRA coordinator

To manage the LRA, we need a coordinator that manages the saga processing. We have chosen a Narayana implementation, as a standalone service, to implement this concept.

You can download it at `http://narayana.io/downloads/index.html`; for our implementation, we will use version 5.9.0.

After downloading it, you will need to unzip it to a directory of your choice, which, from now on, will be defined as `$NARAYANA_HOME`.

Finally, you should run the Narayana LRA coordinator by using the following command:

```
$ java -jar $NARAYANA_HOME/rts/lra/lra-coordinator-swarm.jar  -
Dswarm.http.port=8580
```

We have now launched the coordinator as a standalone service that listens on port `8580` to avoid port conflicts with the services that we implemented in `Chapter 3`, *Cloud Native Applications*, and with the new services that we will build in the following sections.

In the service's log, at the end, you should notice the following messages that confirm that the Narayana coordinator is up and running:

```
2018-08-23   16:43:52,134 INFO   [io.narayana.lra] (ServerService Thread
Pool -- 6)   LRAClient assuming the LRA coordinator and recovery
coordinator are on the    same endpoing
   2018-08-23 16:43:52,170 INFO   [org.wildfly.extension.undertow]
(ServerService   Thread Pool -- 6) WFLYUT0021: Registered web context: /
   2018-08-23 16:43:52,199 INFO   [org.jboss.as.server] (main) WFLYSRV0010:
Deployed "lra-coordinator.war" (runtime-name : "lra-coordinator.war")
   2018-08-23 16:43:52,200 INFO   [org.wildfly.swarm] (main) WFSWARM99999:
WildFly Swarm is Ready
```

Football-player-microservice-lra

This service is an evolution of the service that we implemented in `Chapter 3`, *Cloud-Native Applications*.

Its goal is to handle the football player registry; in this version, we will use the MicroProfile specifications to build the LRA saga specifications. To make it easy to understand the use of the specifications, we will only change the `edit` method's management of the transaction.

To use LRA specifications, we will change the Maven `pom.xml`; the following code snippet shows the changes we've made:

```xml
<?xml version="1.0"   encoding="UTF-8"?>
    <project xmlns="http://maven.apache.org/POM/4.0.0"
xmlns:xsi="http://www.w3.org/2001/XMLSchema-instance"
          xsi:schemaLocation="http://maven.apache.org/POM/4.0.0
http://maven.apache.org/maven-v4_0_0.xsd">
    ...

    <properties>
       <version.thorntail>2.1.0.Final</version.thorntail>
       ...
       <lra.http.host>localhost</lra.http.host>
       <lra.http.port>8580</lra.http.port>
    </properties>

    <build>
       <finalName>football-player-microservice-lra</finalName>
       <plugins>
          <plugin>
             <groupId>io.thorntail</groupId>
             <artifactId>thorntail-maven-plugin</artifactId>
             <version>${version.thorntail}</version>
```

```
                    <executions>
                        <execution>
                            <goals>
                                <goal>package</goal>
                            </goals>
                        </execution>
                    </executions>
                    <configuration>
                        <properties>
                            <lra.http.host>${lra.http.host}</lra.http.host>
                            <lra.http.port>${lra.http.port}</lra.http.port>
                        </properties>
                    </configuration>
                </plugin>
            </plugins>
        </build>

        <dependencies>
            ...
            <dependency>
                <groupId>io.thorntail</groupId>
                <artifactId>microprofile</artifactId>
            </dependency>
            ...
            <!-- LRA JAXRS filters -->
            <dependency>
                <groupId>org.jboss.narayana.rts</groupId>
                <artifactId>lra-filters</artifactId>
                <version>5.9.0.Final</version>
            </dependency>
            ...
        </dependencies>
    </project>
```

The main changes are as follows:

- The Thorntail version needed to use the MicroProfile specification—2.1.0
- The host and port needed to connect with the LRA coordinator (in our case, localhost and 8580)
- The new dependencies related to MicroProfile and lra-filters

Then, we need to update the domain model, FootballPlayer.java, introducing two new fields—the status of the football player (free, reserved, or purchased) and the lraId that represents the unique identifier of the long-running action that's needed to update the status of the record associated with the right action.

Also, in this case, we will propose the code of the changes made, as follows:

```
public class FootballPlayer {
    ...

    @Column(name = "status")
    private String status;

    @Basic(optional = true)
    @Size(min = 1, max = 100)
    @Column(name = "lraId")
    private String lraId;

    ...

    public FootballPlayer(String name, String surname, int age, String
team, String position,
            BigInteger price, String status, String lraId) {
        this.name = name;
        this.surname = surname;
        this.age = age;
        this.team = team;
        this.position = position;
        this.price = price;
        this.status = status;
        this.lraId = lraId;
    }

    public String getStatus() {
        return status;
    }

    public void setStatus(String status) {
        this.status = status;
    }

    public String getLraId() {
        return lraId;
    }

    public void setLraId(String lraId) {
        this.lraId = lraId;
    }

    ...

}
```

Finally, we will change the REST endpoint (only the `edit`/`PUT` method) to handle the saga implementation with the LRA model. The code is as follows:

```
@ApplicationScoped
@Path("/footballplayer")
public class FootballPlayerFacadeREST extends
AbstractFacade<FootballPlayer>   {
    ...

    @PUT
    @Path("{id}")
    @Consumes({MediaType.APPLICATION_JSON})
    @Transactional(Transactional.TxType.REQUIRES_NEW)
    @LRA(LRA.Type.SUPPORTS)
    public void edit(@PathParam("id") Integer id, FootballPlayer   entity)
{
        super.edit(entity);
    }

    ...

    @GET
    @Path("lraId/{id}")
    @Produces({MediaType.APPLICATION_JSON})
    public FootballPlayer findByLraId(@PathParam("id") String   lraId) {
        TypedQuery<FootballPlayer> query =
getEntityManager().createQuery(
                "SELECT f FROM FootballPlayer f WHERE f.lraId = :lraId",
                FootballPlayer.class);
        return query.setParameter("lraId", lraId).getSingleResult();
    }

    ...
}
```

I have introduced the `@LRA` annotation with the `SUPPORTS` value; this means that, if called outside of an LRA context, the bean method's execution must then continue outside of an LRA context. Otherwise, it must continue inside of that LRA context. The LRA context will be created by the coarse-grained API gateway that we will build later on.

I have also implemented the `findByLraId` method, which is needed to retrieve the record associated with the LRA context to perform the operation.

Now, we are ready to run the microservice with the following command:

```
$ java -jar target/football-player-microservice-lra-thorntail.jar -
Dlra.http.port=8580
```

Remember to set the `lra.http.port` parameter to connect your service with the LRA coordinator.

You can find the full code implementation in the GitHub repository, at `https://github.com/Hands-on-MSA-JakartaEE/ch5.git`.

Football-player-offer-microservice-lra

This microservice implements the business domain of the offer to buy football players.

The Maven `pom.xml` file is similar to the one that was described previously.

We will use MySQL, not PostgreSQL to enforce the concept of a dedicated database schema for each microservice.

The following is the code for the attributes of the entity `FootballPlayerOffer.java`, which is used to display the information, managed by this microservice:

```
@Entity
@Table(name = "FOOTBALL_PLAYER_OFFER")
@XmlRootElement
@NamedQueries({
 @NamedQuery(name = "FootballPlayerOffer.findAll", query
        = "SELECT f FROM FootballPlayerOffer f")
 })
public class FootballPlayerOffer {

    @Id
    @GeneratedValue(strategy = GenerationType.IDENTITY)
    @Basic(optional = false)
    @Column(name = "ID")
    private Long id;

    @Basic(optional = false)
    @NotNull
    @Column(name = "ID_FOOTBALL_PLAYER")
    private Long idFootballPlayer;

    @Basic(optional = false)
    @NotNull
    @Column(name = "ID_FOOTBALL_MANAGER")
```

```
                private Long idFootballManager;

                @Column(name = "price")
                private BigInteger price;

                @Basic(optional = true)
                @Size(min = 1, max = 50)
                @Column(name = "status")
                private String status;

                @Basic(optional = true)
                @Size(min = 1, max = 100)
                @Column(name = "lraId")
                private String lraId;

                public FootballPlayerOffer() {
                }

                public FootballPlayerOffer(Long id, Long idFootballPlayer,
                        Long idFootballManager, BigInteger price, String status,
        String lraId) {
                        this.id = id;
                        this.idFootballPlayer = idFootballPlayer;
                        this.idFootballManager = idFootballManager;
                        this.price = price;
                        this.status = status;
                        this.lraId = lraId;
                }

        . . .
}
```

Like we did for the `football-player-microservice-lra` microservice, we will only associate the `@LRA` annotation on the `edit/PUT` method to handle the saga implementation with the LRA model. The following code is required:

```
@ApplicationScoped
@Path("/footballplayeroffer")
public class FootballPlayerOfferFacadeREST extends
AbstractFacade<FootballPlayerOffer>     {
    . . .

    @PUT
    @Path("{id}")
    @Consumes({MediaType.APPLICATION_JSON})
    @Transactional(Transactional.TxType.REQUIRES_NEW)
    @LRA(value = LRA.Type.SUPPORTS)
    public void edit(@PathParam("id") Long id, FootballPlayerOffer
```

```
entity) {
        super.edit(entity);
    }

    ...

    @GET
    @Path("lraId/{id}")
    @Produces({MediaType.APPLICATION_JSON})
    public FootballPlayerOffer findByLraId(@PathParam("id") String    lraId)
{
        TypedQuery<FootballPlayerOffer> query =
getEntityManager().createQuery(
                    "SELECT f FROM FootballPlayerOffer f WHERE f.lraId =
:lraId",
                    FootballPlayerOffer.class);
        return query.setParameter("lraId",    lraId).getSingleResult();
    }

    ...

}
```

Now, you are ready to run the microservice with the following command; the reasons behind the use of the SUPPORTS value in the @LRA annotation and the introduction of the findByLraId method are the same as those seen when using football-player-microservice-lra:

```
$ java -jar   target/football-player-offer-microservice-lra-thorntail.jar -
Dlra.http.host=localhost   -Dlra.http.port=8580
```

Also, in this case, you must remember to set the lra.http.port and lra.http.host parameters so that you can connect your service with the LRA coordinator.

You can find the full code implementation in the GitHub repository, at https://github.com/Hands-on-MSA-JakartaEE/ch5.git.

Football-player-market-microservice-lra

This is the key module of our scenario.

Here, we will organize the invocations to the microservices football-player-microservice-lra and football-player-offer-microservice-lra microservices as is required to implement our business logic.

We will analyze the two key points of this microservice, in detail:

- The Maven `pom.xml`, with the right dependencies
- The RESTful endpoint to understand the logic of the LRA specifications

Let's start with `pom.xml`, as follows:

```xml
<?xml    version="1.0" encoding="UTF-8"?>
    <project xmlns="http://maven.apache.org/POM/4.0.0"
xmlns:xsi="http://www.w3.org/2001/XMLSchema-instance"
            xsi:schemaLocation="http://maven.apache.org/POM/4.0.0
http://maven.apache.org/maven-v4_0_0.xsd">
        <modelVersion>4.0.0</modelVersion>
        <groupId>com.packtpub.thorntail</groupId>
        <artifactId>football-player-market-microservice-lra</artifactId>
        <name>Thorntail Football player market microservice LRA</name>
        <version>1.0.0-SNAPSHOT</version>
        <packaging>war</packaging>

        <properties>
                <version.thorntail>2.1.0.Final</version.thorntail>
                <maven.compiler.source>1.8</maven.compiler.source>
                <maven.compiler.target>1.8</maven.compiler.target>
                <failOnMissingWebXml>false</failOnMissingWebXml>
<project.build.sourceEncoding>UTF-8</project.build.sourceEncoding>
                <version.resteasy>3.0.19.Final</version.resteasy>
                <lra.http.host>localhost</lra.http.host>
                <lra.http.port>8580</lra.http.port>
        </properties>

        <dependencyManagement>
                <dependencies>
                <dependency>
                        <groupId>io.thorntail</groupId>
                        <artifactId>bom</artifactId>
                        <version>${version.thorntail}</version>
                        <scope>import</scope>
                        <type>pom</type>
                </dependency>
                </dependencies>
        </dependencyManagement>

        <build>
                <finalName>football-player-market-microservice-lra</finalName>
                <plugins>
                <plugin>
                        <groupId>io.thorntail</groupId>
```

```xml
                    <artifactId>thorntail-maven-plugin</artifactId>
                    <version>${version.thorntail}</version>

                    <executions>
                            <execution>
                            <goals>
                                    <goal>package</goal>
                            </goals>
                            </execution>
                    </executions>
                    <configuration>
                            <properties>
                            <lra.http.host>${lra.http.host}</lra.http.host>
                            <lra.http.port>${lra.http.port}</lra.http.port>
                            <swarm.port.offset>400</swarm.port.offset>
                            </properties>
                    </configuration>
            </plugin>
            </plugins>
</build>

<dependencies>
    <dependency>
        <groupId>io.thorntail</groupId>
        <artifactId>microprofile</artifactId>
    </dependency>
    <dependency>
        <groupId>io.thorntail</groupId>
        <artifactId>transactions</artifactId>
        <scope>provided</scope>
    </dependency>
    <!-- LRA JAXRS filters -->
    <dependency>
        <groupId>org.jboss.narayana.rts</groupId>
        <artifactId>lra-filters</artifactId>
        <version>5.9.0.Final</version>
    </dependency>
    <dependency>
        <groupId>io.thorntail</groupId>
        <artifactId>jaxrs</artifactId>
        <scope>provided</scope>
    </dependency>
    <dependency>
        <groupId>io.thorntail</groupId>
        <artifactId>cdi</artifactId>
        <scope>provided</scope>
    </dependency>
    <dependency>
```

```
            <groupId>org.jboss.resteasy</groupId>
            <artifactId>resteasy-client</artifactId>
            <version>${version.resteasy}</version>
            <scope>provided</scope>
        </dependency>
        <!-- CORS Support For JAX-RS 2.0 / JavaEE 7  -->
        <dependency>
            <groupId>com.airhacks</groupId>
            <artifactId>jaxrs-cors</artifactId>
            <version>0.0.2</version>
            <scope>compile</scope>
        </dependency>
    </dependencies>
</project>
```

The key points are as follows:

- The minimum Thorntail version that's required is 2.1.0
- `lra.http.port` and `lra.http.host` are needed to connect to the LRA coordinator
- The dependencies are needed to perform RESTful invocations and to handle the LRA

Now, we will analyze the RESTful endpoint.

We will categorize a four-part class to analyze the key elements of the implementation, given as follows:

- Initialize
- A business method that represents our LRA
- The complete phase
- The compensate phase

Initialize

In this phase, the class initializes all of the elements needed to perform the invocations to other microservices, and obtains, with the LRA implementation, the `LRAClient` that's needed to interact with the LRA coordinator:

```
@ApplicationScoped
@Path("/footballplayer-market")
public class FootballPlayerMarketREST {

    private static final Logger LOG =
        Logger.getLogger(FootballPlayerMarketREST.class.getName());
```

```
    private Client footballPlayerClient;

    private Client footballPlayerOfferClient;

    private WebTarget footballPlayerTarget;

    private WebTarget footballPlayerOfferTarget;

    @Inject
    private LRAClient lraClient;

    @PostConstruct
    private void init() {
        footballPlayerClient = ClientBuilder.newClient();
        footballPlayerOfferClient = ClientBuilder.newClient();
        footballPlayerTarget = footballPlayerClient.target(
                "http://localhost:8080/footballplayer");
        footballPlayerOfferTarget = footballPlayerOfferClient.target(
                "http://localhost:8680/footballplayeroffer");
    }

    @PreDestroy
    private void destroy() {
        footballPlayerClient.close();
        footballPlayerOfferClient.close();
    }
    ...
}
```

The most important thing to notice is that the LRAClient will be automatically injected into the container, and, using the lra.http.port and lra.http.host properties given upon startup, will automatically connect to the LRA coordinator. Clearly, the URLs relating to the microservices to be invoked should be parameterized so that they are correctly configured according to the execution environment.

The LRA business method

The LRA business method is where we will define the business logic.

We will organize the invocation into other microservices, implementing the following steps:

1. Create the offer for the desired football player, and set its status to "SEND".
2. Retrieve the football player data.

3. Set the status of the football player to "Reserved"; in this phase, the player is in negotiation, and therefore, cannot be sought after by other football managers.

4. Persist the "Reserved" intermediate status, and mark the record with the LRA ID to be associated with this LRA context.

5. Simulate the outcome of the negotiation with a check of the value of the offer made; if it is less than 80% of the value of the football player, the offer will be refused, and the LRA coordinator will execute the compensate phase. Otherwise, it will be accepted, and the LRA coordinator will execute the complete phase:

```java
/**
 * Business method that performs the send offer business logic.
 * The method implement the business logic related to create the football
 * player offer domain record and sets the status to a non final status,
"SEND".
 * It also set the status of the football player to Reserved.
 * The LRA coordinator, based on the Response.Status, will decide how to
 * complete or compensate the business logic setting the definitive status.
 *
 * @param footballPlayerOffer The POJO that maps the football player offer
data.
 */
@POST
@Consumes({MediaType.APPLICATION_JSON})
@Produces({MediaType.APPLICATION_JSON})
@LRA(value = LRA.Type.REQUIRED,
     cancelOn = {Response.Status.INTERNAL_SERVER_ERROR}, // cancel on a
500    code
     cancelOnFamily = {Response.Status.Family.CLIENT_ERROR} // cancel on
any    4xx code)
 public void sendOffer(FootballPlayerOffer footballPlayerOffer) {
     LOG.log(Level.INFO, "Start method sendOffer");
     LOG.log(Level.FINE, "Retrieving football player with id {0}",
             footballPlayerOffer.getIdFootballPlayer());

     String lraIdUrl = lraClient.getCurrent().toString();
     String lraId = lraIdUrl.substring(lraIdUrl.lastIndexOf('/') + 1);

     LOG.log(Level.FINE, "Value of LRA_ID {0}", lraId);

     // Create the offer
     LOG.log(Level.FINE, "Creating offer ...");
     footballPlayerOffer.setStatus("SEND");
     footballPlayerOffer.setLraId(lraId);
     Response response =
footballPlayerOfferTarget.request().post(Entity.entity(
             footballPlayerOffer, MediaType.APPLICATION_JSON_TYPE));
```

```
    LOG.log(Level.FINE, "Offer created with response code {0}",
response.getStatus());

    if (response.getStatus() ==
Response.Status.NO_CONTENT.getStatusCode()) {
        FootballPlayer player =
footballPlayerTarget.path(footballPlayerOffer.
                        getIdFootballPlayer().toString()).
                        request().get(new
GenericTypeFootballPlayerImpl());

        LOG.log(Level.FINE, "Got football player {0}", player);

        player.setStatus("Reserved");
        player.setLraId(lraId);

        LOG.log(Level.FINE, "Changing football player status ...");

        footballPlayerTarget.path(footballPlayerOffer.
            getIdFootballPlayer().toString()).request().put(Entity.
                entity(player, MediaType.APPLICATION_JSON_TYPE));

        // Check about the price of the offer: if it is less than 80% of
the
        // value of the football player I will refuse the offer
        BigInteger price = footballPlayerOffer.getPrice();

        LOG.log(Level.FINE, "Value of offer price {0}", price);
        LOG.log(Level.FINE, "Value of football player price {0}",
player.getPrice());

        if ((price.multiply(new
BigInteger("100")).divide(player.getPrice())).intValue() < 80) {
            throw new WebApplicationException("The offer is
unacceptable!",
                Response.Status.INTERNAL_SERVER_ERROR);
        }
    } else {
        throw new
WebApplicationException(Response.Status.INTERNAL_SERVER_ERROR);
    }
    LOG.log(Level.INFO, "End method sendOffer");
}
```

We defined the value of `LRA.Type.REQUIRED`; this means that, if it is called outside of an LRA context, a JAX-RS filter will begin a new LRA for the duration of the method call; and, when the call completes, another JAX-RS filter will complete the LRA. The key point of the method is the use of the `@LRA` annotation that handles the life cycles of LRAs.

We also defined the cases in which the business method can be considered failed to instruct the LRA coordinator to execute the compensate phase through `cancelOn =` `{Response.Status.INTERNAL_SERVER_ERROR}`, which cancels the operation on a `500` code, and `cancelOnFamily = {Response.Status.Family.CLIENT_ERROR}`, which cancels on any `4xx` code.

The complete phase

In the complete phase, the LRA coordinator invokes the method annotated with `@Complete` and performs the business operations needed to make the business operation consistent, in terms of data status.

In our scenario, the method will set the status of the offer to `"ACCEPTED"` and the status of the football player to `"Purchased"`.

The following code is required to do so:

```
/**
    * LRA complete method: it sets the final status of the football player
offer
    * and football player based on a successful response of the send offer
    * method.
    *
    * @param lraId The Long Running Action identifier needed to retrieve
    * the record on which perform the operation.
    */
@PUT
@Path("/complete")
@Produces(MediaType.APPLICATION_JSON)
@Consumes(MediaType.APPLICATION_JSON)
@Complete
public void confirmOffer(@HeaderParam(LRAClient.LRA_HTTP_HEADER) String
lraId) {
       LOG.log(Level.INFO, "Start method confirmOffer: I'm in LRA complete
phase");
       LOG.log(Level.FINE, "Value of header lraId {0}", lraId);

       String lraIdParameter = lraId.substring(lraId.lastIndexOf('/') + 1);

       LOG.log(Level.FINE, "Value of lraIdParameter {0}",
```

```
lraIdParameter);

        // Set the offer to accepted
        LOG.log(Level.FINE, "Setting the offer as ACCEPTED ...");
        FootballPlayerOffer fpo = footballPlayerOfferTarget.path("lraId/"
+
            lraIdParameter).request().get(new
GenericTypeFootballPlayerOfferImpl());

        fpo.setStatus("ACCEPTED");

footballPlayerOfferTarget.path(fpo.getId().toString()).request().put(
                Entity.entity(fpo, MediaType.APPLICATION_JSON_TYPE));

        LOG.log(Level.FINE, "Set the offer as ACCEPTED ...");

        // Set the football player status to purchased
        FootballPlayer player = footballPlayerTarget.path("lraId/" +
lraIdParameter).request().get(new GenericTypeFootballPlayerImpl());

        LOG.log(Level.FINE, "Got football player {0}", player);

        player.setStatus("Purchased");
        player.setLraId(null);

        LOG.log(Level.FINE, "Changing football player status ...");

        footballPlayerTarget.path(player.getId().toString()).request().put(
                Entity.entity(player, MediaType.APPLICATION_JSON_TYPE));

        LOG.log(Level.INFO, "End method confirmOffer: LRA complete phase
                        terminated");
}
```

The main element of the method is the @Complete annotation; in this way, the method is considered a participant of the LRA, and the LRA coordinator will automatically invoke it in the case of the success of the operation that starts the LRA context.

The compensate phase

In the compensate phase, the LRA coordinator invokes the method annotated with @Compensate and performs the business operations needed to make the business operation consistent, in terms of the data status after a condition that determines the operation as failed.

In our scenario, the method will set the status of the offer to "REFUSED" and the status of the football player to "Free". We have decided to set "Free" and not null, in order to show that the record is updated by a method invoked by the LRA coordinator.

The following code is required to do so:

```
/**
 * LRA compensate method: it sets the final status of the football
player   offer
 * and football player based on a failed response of the send offer
method.
 *
 * @param lraId The Long Running Action identifier needed to retrieve
 * the record on which perform the operation.
 * @return the Response of the operation.
 */
@PUT
@Path("/compensate")
@Produces(MediaType.APPLICATION_JSON)
@Compensate
public Response compensateWork(@HeaderParam(LRAClient.LRA_HTTP_HEADER)
String   lraId) {

    LOG.log(Level.INFO, "Start method compensateWork: I'm in LRA
compensate                          phase");

    String lraIdParameter = lraId.substring(lraId.lastIndexOf('/') + 1);

    LOG.log(Level.FINE, "Value of lraIdParameter {0}",
lraIdParameter);

    LOG.log(Level.FINE, "Setting the offer as REFUSED ...");
    // Set the offer to REFUSED
    FootballPlayerOffer fpo = footballPlayerOfferTarget.path("lraId/"
                    + lraIdParameter).request().get(
                                    new
GenericTypeFootballPlayerOfferImpl());

    fpo.setStatus("REFUSED");

footballPlayerOfferTarget.path(fpo.getId().toString()).request().put(
                Entity.entity(fpo, MediaType.APPLICATION_JSON_TYPE));

    LOG.log(Level.FINE, "Set the offer as REFUSED ...");

    FootballPlayer player = footballPlayerTarget.path("lraId/"
                    + lraIdParameter).
                    request().get(new GenericTypeFootballPlayerImpl());
```

```
        LOG.log(Level.FINE, "Got football player {0}", player);

        player.setStatus("Free");
        player.setLraId(null);

        LOG.log(Level.FINE, "Changing football player status ...");

        footballPlayerTarget.path(player.getId().toString()).request().put(
                Entity.entity(player, MediaType.APPLICATION_JSON_TYPE));

        LOG.log(Level.INFO, "End method compensateWork: LRA compensate
phase                               terminated");

        return Response.ok().build();
    }
```

The main element of the method is the @Compensate annotation; in this way, the method is considered a participant of the LRA, and the LRA coordinator will automatically invoke it in the case of a failure of the operation that starts the LRA context.

To run the microservice, you should launch the following command:

```
$ java -jar target/football-player-market-microservice-lra-thorntail.jar -
Dlra.http.port=8580
```

Football_Player_Market_client

This module is a simple Java client, which was created to test our scenario.

You can specify two parameters—the ID of the football player that you want to buy, and the value of your offer. If you don't specify these parameters, the default values will be 1 (Gianlugi Buffon) and 22 million, respectively.

Now, it's time to test it. Run the following command:

```
$ java -jar target/Football_Player_Market_client-1.0.0.jar 18 1
```

I am offering 18 million to try buy Gianluigi Buffon; my offer will be considered valid, since 18 million is more than 80% of the value of the player. For this reason, the Narayana LRA coordinator will perform the complete phase.

The following is an extract of `football-player-market-microservice-lra`, showing the workflow performed by the LRA coordinator against the microservice:

```
2018-08-24   17:32:47,851 INFO
[com.packtpub.thorntail.footballplayermicroservice.rest.service.FootballPla
yerMarketREST]   (default task-1) Start method sendOffer
     2018-08-24 17:32:47,851 FINE
[com.packtpub.thorntail.footballplayermicroservice.rest.service.FootballPla
yerMarketREST]   (default task-1) Retrieving football player with id 3
     2018-08-24 17:32:47,853 FINE
[com.packtpub.thorntail.footballplayermicroservice.rest.service.FootballPla
yerMarketREST]   (default task-1) Value of LRA_ID
0_ffff7f000001_-595eb3c1_5b80245b_17
     2018-08-24 17:32:47,853 FINE
[com.packtpub.thorntail.footballplayermicroservice.rest.service.FootballPla
yerMarketREST]   (default task-1) Creating offer ...
     2018-08-24 17:32:48,452 FINE
[com.packtpub.thorntail.footballplayermicroservice.rest.service.FootballPla
yerMarketREST]   (default task-1) Offer created with response code 204
     2018-08-24 17:32:48,874 FINE
[com.packtpub.thorntail.footballplayermicroservice.rest.service.FootballPla
yerMarketREST]   (default task-1) Got football player FootballPlayer{id=3,
name=Keylor,   surname=Navas, age=31, team=Real Madrid,
position=goalkeeper, price=18,   status=null, lraId=null}
     2018-08-24 17:32:48,874 FINE
[com.packtpub.thorntail.footballplayermicroservice.rest.service.FootballPla
yerMarketREST]   (default task-1) Changing football player status ...
     2018-08-24 17:32:49,018 INFO   [stdout] (default task-1) Value of offer
price:   18
     2018-08-24 17:32:49,018 INFO   [stdout] (default task-1) Value of
football   player price: 18
     2018-08-24 17:32:49,018 FINE
[com.packtpub.thorntail.footballplayermicroservice.rest.service.FootballPla
yerMarketREST]   (default task-1) Value of offer price 18
     2018-08-24 17:32:49,018 FINE
[com.packtpub.thorntail.footballplayermicroservice.rest.service.FootballPla
yerMarketREST]   (default task-1) Value of football player price 18
     2018-08-24 17:32:49,018 INFO
[com.packtpub.thorntail.footballplayermicroservice.rest.service.FootballPla
yerMarketREST] (default task-1) End method sendOffer
     2018-08-24 17:32:49,131 INFO
[com.packtpub.thorntail.footballplayermicroservice.rest.service.FootballPla
yerMarketREST] (default task-2) Start method confirmOffer: I'm in LRA
complete phase
     2018-08-24 17:32:49,132 FINE
[com.packtpub.thorntail.footballplayermicroservice.rest.service.FootballPla
yerMarketREST]   (default task-2) Value of header lraId
http://localhost:8580/lra-coordinator/0_ffff7f000001_-595eb3c1_5b80245b_17
```

```
     2018-08-24 17:32:49,132 FINE
[com.packtpub.thorntail.footballplayermicroservice.rest.service.FootballPla
yerMarketREST]    (default task-2) Value of lraIdParameter
0_ffff7f000001_-595eb3c1_5b80245b_17
     2018-08-24 17:32:49,132 FINE
[com.packtpub.thorntail.footballplayermicroservice.rest.service.FootballPla
yerMarketREST]    (default task-2) Setting the offer as ACCEPTED ...
     2018-08-24 17:32:49,306 FINE
[com.packtpub.thorntail.footballplayermicroservice.rest.service.FootballPla
yerMarketREST]    (default task-2) Set the offer as ACCEPTED ...
     2018-08-24 17:32:49,335 FINE
[com.packtpub.thorntail.footballplayermicroservice.rest.service.FootballPla
yerMarketREST]    (default task-2) Got football player FootballPlayer{id=3,
name=Keylor,   surname=Navas, age=31, team=Real Madrid,
position=goalkeeper, price=18,    status=Reserved,
lraId=0_ffff7f000001_-595eb3c1_5b80245b_17}
     2018-08-24 17:32:49,335 FINE
[com.packtpub.thorntail.footballplayermicroservice.rest.service.FootballPla
yerMarketREST]    (default task-2) Changing football player status ...
     2018-08-24 17:32:49,353 INFO
[com.packtpub.thorntail.footballplayermicroservice.rest.service.FootballPla
yerMarketREST] (default task-2) End method confirmOffer: LRA complete phase
terminated
```

I have highlighted the log messages that show the start and end of the business method and the complete phase organized by the LRA coordinator.

If you execute a check on the database side, you will notice that the status of Gianluigi Buffon is "purchased":

```
$ SELECT * FROM   football_player where id = 1
```

The output of the preceding command is as follows:

```
id  name       surname  age        team              position      price
1   Gianluigi  Buffon   40    Paris Saint Germain    goalkeeper     2

status       lraid
Purchased      " "
```

If you check the football player offer, as follows, you will be able to verify that the status is ACCEPTED:

```
$ SELECT * FROM FOOTBALL_PLAYER_OFFER WHERE ID_FOOTBALL_PLAYER = 1
```

The output of the preceding command is as follows:

```
ID ID_FOOTBALL_PLAYER ID_FOOTBALL_MANAGER PRICE STATUS
1 1 1 18 ACCEPTED
```

Now, we will simulate a failure scenario.

I will offer 5 million to try and buy Manuel Neuer; my offer will not be considered valid, since 5 million is less than 80% of the value of the player. For this reason, the Narayana LRA coordinator will perform the compensate phase.

Let's run the following command:

```
$ java -jar target/Football_Player_Market_client-1.0.0.jar 5 2
```

The following is an extract of football-player-market-microservice-lra, showing the workflow performed by the LRA coordinator against the microservice:

```
2018-08-25 00:18:20,007 INFO
[com.packtpub.thorntail.footballplayermicroservice.rest.service.FootballPla
yerMarketREST] (default task-4) Start method sendOffer
 2018-08-25 00:18:20,008 FINE
[com.packtpub.thorntail.footballplayermicroservice.rest.service.FootballPla
yerMarketREST] (default task-4) Retrieving football player with id 2
 2018-08-25 00:18:20,008 FINE
[com.packtpub.thorntail.footballplayermicroservice.rest.service.FootballPla
yerMarketREST] (default task-4) Value of LRA_ID
0_ffff7f000001_205e9dee_5b808159_53
 2018-08-25 00:18:20,008 FINE
[com.packtpub.thorntail.footballplayermicroservice.rest.service.FootballPla
yerMarketREST] (default task-4) Creating offer ...
 2018-08-25 00:18:20,104 FINE
[com.packtpub.thorntail.footballplayermicroservice.rest.service.FootballPla
yerMarketREST] (default task-4) Offer created with response code 204
 2018-08-25 00:18:20,105 INFO [org.apache.http.impl.execchain.RetryExec]
(default task-4) I/O exception (org.apache.http.NoHttpResponseException)
caught when processing request to {}->http://localhost:8080: The target
server failed to respond
 2018-08-25 00:18:20,106 INFO [org.apache.http.impl.execchain.RetryExec]
(default task-4) Retrying request to {}->http://localhost:8080
 2018-08-25 00:18:20,113 FINE
[com.packtpub.thorntail.footballplayermicroservice.rest.service.FootballPla
yerMarketREST] (default task-4) Got football player FootballPlayer{id=2,
name=Manuel, surname=Neuer, age=32, team=Bayern Munchen,
position=goalkeeper, price=35, status=null, lraId=null}
 2018-08-25 00:18:20,113 FINE
[com.packtpub.thorntail.footballplayermicroservice.rest.service.FootballPla
yerMarketREST] (default task-4) Changing football player status ...
```

```
2018-08-25 00:18:20,129 INFO [stdout] (default task-4) Value of offer
price: 5
2018-08-25 00:18:20,129 INFO [stdout] (default task-4) Value of football
player price: 35
2018-08-25 00:18:20,129 FINE
[com.packtpub.thorntail.footballplayermicroservice.rest.service.FootballPla
yerMarketREST] (default task-4) Value of offer price 5
2018-08-25 00:18:20,129 FINE
[com.packtpub.thorntail.footballplayermicroservice.rest.service.FootballPla
yerMarketREST] (default task-4) Value of football player price 35
2018-08-25 00:18:20,130 ERROR [org.jboss.resteasy.resteasy_jaxrs.i18n]
(default task-4) RESTEASY002010: Failed to execute:
javax.ws.rs.WebApplicationException: The offer is unacceptable!
 at
com.packtpub.thorntail.footballplayermicroservice.rest.service.FootballPlay
erMarketREST.sendOffer(FootballPlayerMarketREST.java:142)
 at
com.packtpub.thorntail.footballplayermicroservice.rest.service.FootballPlay
erMarketREST$Proxy$_$$_WeldClientProxy.sendOffer(Unknown Source)
 ...
2018-08-25 00:18:20,152 INFO
[com.packtpub.thorntail.footballplayermicroservice.rest.service.FootballPla
yerMarketREST] (default task-5) Start method compensateWork: I'm in LRA
compensate phase
2018-08-25 00:18:20,152 FINE
[com.packtpub.thorntail.footballplayermicroservice.rest.service.FootballPla
yerMarketREST] (default task-5) Value of lraIdParameter
0_ffff7f000001_205e9dee_5b808159_53
2018-08-25 00:18:20,153 FINE
[com.packtpub.thorntail.footballplayermicroservice.rest.service.FootballPla
yerMarketREST] (default task-5) Setting the offer as REFUSED ...
2018-08-25 00:18:20,196 FINE
[com.packtpub.thorntail.footballplayermicroservice.rest.service.FootballPla
yerMarketREST] (default task-5) Set the offer as REFUSED ...
2018-08-25 00:18:20,203 FINE
[com.packtpub.thorntail.footballplayermicroservice.rest.service.FootballPla
yerMarketREST] (default task-5) Got football player FootballPlayer{id=2,
name=Manuel, surname=Neuer, age=32, team=Bayern Munchen,
position=goalkeeper, price=35, status=Reserved,
lraId=0_ffff7f000001_205e9dee_5b808159_53}
2018-08-25 00:18:20,203 FINE
[com.packtpub.thorntail.footballplayermicroservice.rest.service.FootballPla
yerMarketREST] (default task-5) Changing football player status ...
2018-08-25 00:18:20,227 INFO
[com.packtpub.thorntail.footballplayermicroservice.rest.service.FootballPla
yerMarketREST] (default task-5) End method compensateWork: LRA compensate
phase terminated
```

I have highlighted the log messages that show the start and end of the business method and the compensate phase organized by the LRA coordinator.

If you execute a check on the database side, you will notice that the status of Manuel Neuer is Free:

```
$ java -jar target/Football_Player_Market_client-1.0.0.jar 5 2
```

The output of the preceding command is as follows:

```
id name surname age     team          position  price status lraid
2  Manuel Neuer  32 Bayern Munchen goalkeeper 35   Free       ""
```

If you check the football player offer, you can verify that the status will be REFUSED:

```
$ SELECT * FROM FOOTBALL_PLAYER_OFFER WHERE ID_FOOTBALL_PLAYER = 2
```

The output of the preceding command is as follows:

```
2 2 1 5 REFUSEDID ID_FOOTBALL_PLAYER ID_FOOTBALL_MANAGER PRICE STATUS
```

Limitations

As you can see, the LRA specification has a lot of potential; it can help to manage the consistency of data within microservice architectures.

At the time of writing this book, the specification is still in a draft form, and there are numerous areas for improvement.

Having gone over the use case of our application, in my opinion, the following important limitations must be resolved:

- **Single point of failure**: In the case of Narayana implementation, there is no way to set the LRA coordinator in high availability. The object store that it used to store the LRA information cannot be shared between instances, so unavailability of the LRA coordinator could be a severe issue. I think that this problem will be overcome quickly, since the Narayana team is working to provide scalability and failover for the coordinator.
- **Passing parameters to the** @Compensate **and** @Complete **methods is very complicated**: For this reason, in our scenario, I used a workaround and stored the LRA ID in the domain model to perform operations against the right data. This problem makes the implementation a little more complicated.

Summary

In this chapter, we discussed implementing and handling transactions in a microservices architecture; in particular, we covered the ACID principle, XA transactions, application compensations, and the saga pattern. We implemented an example of handling transactions using Narayana as an implementation of LRA specifications.

In the next chapter, we will discuss container technology, and how it can help developers build microservice infrastructures.

6
Linux Containers

Linux containers are a mash-up of functionalities available with the Linux kernel (that's why you often hear the phrase, *Containers are Linux*). Linux containers provide a lot of flexibility in regards to application deployment. As matter of fact, not just the application gets deployed, but the entire software stack. And the software stack is made of the application itself, its dependencies, the operative system, and the tools and processes running in the operative system. Freezing the complete software stack gives tremendous portability capability. That's why this never-ending hype around Docker and Linux containers in general has been going on for years.

In this chapter, we will cover the following concepts:

- Linux containers
- Containers
- Docker
- Kubernetes

Linux Containers

The Linux kernel is made up of several components and functionalities; the ones related to containers are as follows:

- **Control groups (cgroups)**
- Namespaces
- **Security-Enhanced Linux** (**SELinux**)

Cgroups

The cgroup functionality allows for limiting and prioritizing resources, such as CPUs, RAM, the network, the filesystem, and so on. The main goal is to not exceed the resources—to avoid wasting resources that might be needed for other processes.

Namespaces

The namespace functionality allows for partitioning of kernel resources, such that one set of processes sees one set of resources, while another set of processes sees a different set of resources. The feature works by having the same namespace for these resources in the various sets of processes, but having those names refer to distinct resources. Examples of resource names that can exist in multiple spaces (so that the named resources will be partitioned) are process IDs, hostnames, user IDs, filenames, and some names associated with network access and inter-process communication.

When a Linux system boots; that is, only one namespace is created. Processes and resources will join the same namespace, until a different namespace is created, resources assigned to it, and processes join it.

SELinux

SELinux is a module of the Linux kernel that provides a mechanism to enforce the security of the system, with specific policies.

Basically, SELinux can limit programs from accessing files and network resources. The idea is to limit the privileges of programs and daemons to a minimum, so that it can limit the risk of system halt.

The preceding functionalities have been around for many years. Namespaces were first released in 2002, and cgroups in 2005, by Google (cgroups were first named process containers, and then cgroups). For example, SunSolaris 5.10, released at the beginning of 2005, provided support for Solaris containers.

Nowadays, Linux containers are the new buzzword, and some people think they are a new means of virtualization.

Virtualization has a totally different approach. Virtualization emulates; it doesn't run processes directly on the CPU. Virtualization emulates a resource; it does not own the resource. The emulation creates an overhead in the execution phase, which might still be performant, but it'll surely need more resources. Each VM has its own dedicated OS, as shown in the following diagram:

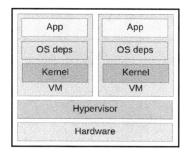

Stack virtualization

Containerization uses resources directly, and does not need an emulator at all; the fewer resources, the more efficiency. Different applications can run on the same host: isolated at the kernel level and isolated by namespaces and cgroups. The kernel (that is, the OS) is shared by all containers, as shown in the following diagram:

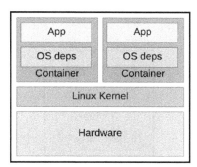

Stack containerization

Containers

When we talk about containers, we are indirectly referring to two main concepts—a container image and a running container image.

A **container image** is the definition of the container, wherein all software stacks are installed as additional layers, as depicted by the following diagram:

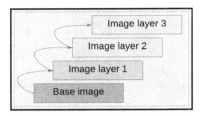

Layers of containers

A container image is typically made up of multiple layers.

The first layer is given by the base image, which provides the OS core functionalities, with all of the tools needed to get started. Teams often work by building their own layers on these base images. Users can also build on more advanced application images, which not only have an OS, but which also include language runtimes, debugging tools, and libraries, as shown in the following diagram:

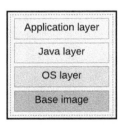

Example of container image layers

Base images are built from the same utilities and libraries that are included in an OS. A good base image provides a secure and stable platform on which to build applications. Red Hat provides base images for Red Hat Enterprise Linux. These images can be used like a normal OS. Users can customize them for their applications as necessary, installing packages and enabling services to start up just like a normal Red Hat Enterprise Linux Server.

Red Hat also provides more advanced application images that already include extra software. Examples include language runtimes, databases, middleware, storage, and **independent software vendor** (**ISV**) software. The software included in these images are tested, preconfigured, and certified to work out of the box. These prebuilt images make it easy to deploy multi-tier applications from existing components, without the effort of building your own application images.

The layering structure significantly simplifies patching procedures, since a layer needs to be patched only once, and then any image built using that layer will contain the applied patch.

Container platforms like OpenShift have the ability to track existing containers that use a certain layer, and, if patched, trigger a series of image builds and deployments for existing and running containers, in order to apply the patched layer across all containers and prevent security breaches.

Although it is possible to run every application on a single VM, the operational overhead and resource cost of the multitude of extra VMs required generally invalidates the perceived benefits.

VMs have the advantage of providing hypervisor-level isolation for the application. However, that comes at the cost of running a complete OS for each application, which consumes more memory and CPU utilization. Furthermore, VM compute and memory capacity is predefined, and does not provide any elasticity or consuming more when an application requires more memory or computing power.

Containers provide isolation by taking advantage of kernel technologies, like cgroups, kernel namespaces, and SELinux, which have been battle-tested and used for years at Google and the US Department of Defense, in order to provide application isolation.

Since containers use a shared kernel and container host, they reduce the amount of resources required for the container itself, and are more lightweight when compared to VMs. Therefore, containers provide an unmatched agility that is not feasible with VMs; for example, it only takes a few seconds to start a new container. Furthermore, containers support a more flexible model when it comes to CPU utilization and memory resources, and allow for resource burst modes, so that applications can consume more resources when required, within the defined boundaries.

Linux containers are, in a way, a virtualization technology. VMs are for virtualizing the hardware, while containers are for virtualizing application processes, no matter where they run (bare metal, virtualized, or in the cloud).

Containers provide application portability, due to the standard image format (Open Container Initiative) and the fact that they are only dependent on Linux. This gives teams better control over the infrastructure in which they deploy applications. A container host provides a common ground for running containers on any infrastructure, from your own laptop to bare-metal, virtualization, and private and public clouds.

Nevertheless, portability does not guarantee compatibility. Portability is often believed to mean that you can take a container image and run it on any container host built from any Linux distribution, but that is not technically accurate. Linux container images are collections of files, including libraries and binaries that are specific to the hardware architecture and OS. When the container image is run, the binaries inside of the image run just like they would on a normal Linux OS. There must be compatibility between the container image and the container host. For example, you cannot run 64-bit binaries on a 32-bit host.

These inconsistencies can range from sporadic failure (which is hard to debug) to complete failure, wherein the container will not run at all. Worse, incompatibilities can lead to performance degradation or security issues. The portability of Linux containers is not absolute; using different Linux distributions, or widely differing versions of the same Linux distribution, can lead to serious problems.

In order to guarantee portability and compatibility, it is a best practice to run a consistent version and distribution of Linux in all containers and on all container hosts, across environments and infrastructures. This guarantees compatibility, both horizontally and vertically.

OCI standard containers, when combined with a standard container host like Red Hat Enterprise Linux, provide a portable and compatible application delivery combination that guarantees that your applications run in the exact same way across all environments and infrastructures.

Immutability is also one of the key benefits of OCI—standard container images, without being tied to a specific machine image format, like you have with VM images (such as AMI on AWS). That's why you have even seen Netflix adopting containers to enable the same CD workflows, but in a more portable and efficient manner.

However, the term *Linux containers* is mainly associated with Docker.

Docker

Docker is a piece of software that lets you create Linux containers with a specific image format, that is, the Docker image format.

Docker brought Linux containers to a large scale, providing a toolkit for developers and administrators.

In Chapter 4, *Building Microservices Using Thorntail,* and Chapter 5, *Eclipse MicroProfile and Transactions – Narayana LRA,* we saw our cloud-native application as microservices. We split the overall application into two frontends and three backends, also using a backing service, such as MySQL, Mongo, and PostreSQL databases run inside a Docker container as a persistence layer. Before running the application itself, we had to run the databases, and then the applications.

This kind of scenario leads to complex governance of the overall system. A first step toward easing the system is to containerize as much as possible. Let's first dockerize our backend microservices.

football-player-microservice

The following is the Dockerfile for the football-player-microservice:

```
FROM docker.io/openjdk
ADD football-player-microservice/target/football-player-microservice-
thorntail.jar /opt/service.jar
ENTRYPOINT ["java","-jar","/opt/service.jar"]
CMD [""]
```

Now, within the same path of the Docker file, build the Docker image, as follows:

```
docker build -f football-player-microservice.dockerfile -t
foogaro/football-player-microservice
```

Check that the image is actually on your local Docker registry, issuing the following command:

```
docker images
```

If the image that was just built is listed (it should appear at the top of the list), run the container, as follows:

```
docker run -it --rm=true --name="football-player-microservice" -p 8180:8180
foogaro/football-player-microservice -Dswarm.http.port=8180 -
Dweb.primary.port=8180
```

The application should not start properly, due to an error while connecting to the Postgres database, shown as follows:

```
Caused by: org.postgresql.util.PSQLException: Connection to localhost:5432
refused. Check that the hostname and port are correct and that the
postmaster is accepting TCP/IP connections.
```

We need to hook the database running on a different container, and thus potentially on a different network.

To achieve this, we need to link those two containers, `football-player-microservice` and `postgres_thorntail`, so that they can communicate with each other. The best scenario would involve them sharing the same network layer; this can be achieved in two ways with plain Docker, as follows:

- Sharing the network provided by the host (that is, the server running Docker; your laptop, in the case)
- Creating a dedicated network (a dedicated Docker network) for the two containers

The first option is probably the easiest, but in big environments, it will not scale. On the other hand, the second option adds a little complexity, but it provides a more scalable solution; and, if we are dealing with containers, we want to scale.

So, let's create a dedicated Docker network, as follows:

```
docker network create football
c59ac3a846920891ce092868945caf316e5adbb4007715f9f0c38f8d2954583e
docker network inspect football
[
{
"Name": "football",
"Id": "c59ac3a846920891ce092868945caf316e5adbb4007715f9f0c38f8d2954583e",
"Created": "2018-10-23T10:08:03.496371735+02:00",
"Scope": "local",
"Driver": "bridge",
"EnableIPv6": false,
"IPAM": {
"Driver": "default",
```

```
"Options": {},
"Config": [
{
"Subnet": "172.18.0.0/16",
"Gateway": "172.18.0.1"
}
]
},
"Internal": false,
"Attachable": false,
"Containers": {},
"Options": {},
"Labels": {}
}
]
```

If you have the Postgres container up and running, stop it, and then run it again using the `football` network, as follows:

```
docker run --name postgres_thorntail --net="football" --rm="true" -e
POSTGRES_PASSWORD=postgresPwd -e POSTGRES_DB=football_players_registry -d -
p 5532:5432 postgres
```

If we inspect the network again, we should see the Postgres instance belonging to it:

```
docker network inspect football
[
{
"Name": "football",
"Id": "c59ac3a846920891ce092868945caf316e5adbb4007715f9f0c38f8d2954583e",
"Created": "2018-10-23T10:08:03.496371735+02:00",
"Scope": "local",
"Driver": "bridge",
"EnableIPv6": false,
"IPAM": {
"Driver": "default",
"Options": {},
"Config": [
{
"Subnet": "172.18.0.0/16",
"Gateway": "172.18.0.1"
}
]
},
"Internal": false,
"Attachable": false,
"Containers": {
"7a69aa8c0d700110d0ea4a49a2ee3f590f07856de4d060469758cf09fbdebf43": {
```

```
"Name": "postgres_thorntail",
"EndpointID":
"0a0d0a55d5d3141babff26a2917ae8c838af4518cc842ac6da2afd1f56d8e4b7",
"MacAddress": "02:42:ac:12:00:02",
"IPv4Address": "172.18.0.2/16",
"IPv6Address": ""
}
},
"Options": {},
"Labels": {}
}
]
```

Now, we need to link our microservice with the database that it uses as a backing service, as follows:

```
docker run -it --rm=true --net="football" --link="postgres_thorntail" --
name="football-player-microservice" -p 8180:8180 foogaro/football-player-
microservice -Dweb.primary.port=8180 -Dswarm.http.port=8180
```

If we inspect the network again, we should also see the `football-player-microservice` belonging to it, as follows:

```
Docker network inspect football
[
{
"Name": "football",
"Id": "c59ac3a846920891ce092868945caf316e5adbb4007715f9f0c38f8d2954583e",
"Created": "2018-10-23T10:08:03.496371735+02:00",
"Scope": "local",
"Driver": "bridge",
"EnableIPv6": false,
"IPAM": {
"Driver": "default",
"Options": {},
"Config": [
{
"Subnet": "172.18.0.0/16",
"Gateway": "172.18.0.1"
}
]
},
"Internal": false,
"Attachable": false,
"Containers": {
"7a69aa8c0d700110d0ea4a49a2ee3f590f07856de4d060469758cf09fbdebf43": {
"Name": "postgres_thorntail",
"EndpointID":
```

```
"0a0d0a55d5d3141babff26a2917ae8c838af4518cc842ac6da2afd1f56d8e4b7",
"MacAddress": "02:42:ac:12:00:02",
"IPv4Address": "172.18.0.2/16",
"IPv6Address": ""
},
"962c79c46821204345ab86a3cb40a5691140ccf100112904e678c044a68e5138": {
"Name": "football-player-microservice",
"EndpointID":
"0d1232f4c3cfc3f82ddefa2bd4c0ceaf994aa6b87292341f761009c56ccbe80f",
"MacAddress": "02:42:ac:12:00:03",
"IPv4Address": "172.18.0.3/16",
"IPv6Address": ""
}
},
"Options": {},
"Labels": {}
}
]
```

Now, we are sure that the containers can communicate with each other, but the football-player-microservice application needs to bind to the database at a specific IP and port.

This can be achieved by passing those parameters to the container as environment variables, as follows:

```
docker run -it --rm=true --net="football" --link="postgres_thorntail" --name="football-player-microservice" -e FOOTBALL_POSTGRES_IP=172.18.0.2 -e FOOTBALL_POSTGRES_PORT=5432 -p 8180:8180 foogaro/football-player-microservice -Dweb.primary.port=8180 -Dswarm.http.port=8180
```

These environment variables must be picked up by the application; so, the code needs to change a little.

Open the source code of the football-player-microservice application, and edit the YAML file project-defaults.yml; replace the connection-url with the following definition:

```
docker run -it --rm=true --net="football" --link="postgres_thorntail" --name="football-player-microservice" -e FOOTBALL_POSTGRES_IP=172.18.0.2 -e FOOTBALL_POSTGRES_PORT=5432 -p 8180:8180 foogaro/football-player-microservice -Dweb.primary.port=8180 -Dswarm.http.port=8180
```

Now, compile the application again, as described in Chapter 5, *Eclipse MicroProfile and Transactions – Narayana LRA,* and rebuild the Docker image; then, run the container, as follows:

```
docker run -it --rm=true --net="football" --link="postgres_thorntail" --
name="football-player-microservice" -e FOOTBALL_POSTGRES_IP=172.18.0.2 -e
FOOTBALL_POSTGRES_PORT=5432 -p 8180:8180 foogaro/football-player-
microservice -Dweb.primary.port=8180 -Dswarm.http.port=8180
```

Now, let's containerize the `football-player-ui` frontend application.

football-player-ui

First, build the frontend application, as described in Chapter 5, *Eclipse MicroProfile and Transactions – Narayana LRA*; then, create the Dockerfile for the `football-player-ui`, as follows:

```
FROM docker.io/httpd
ADD football-player-ui/dist/football-player-ui/* /usr/local/apache2/htdocs/
```

Now, within the same path of the Docker file, build the Docker image, as follows:

```
docker build -f football-player-ui.dockerfile -t foogaro/football-player-ui
```

Check that the image is actually on your local Docker registry, issuing the following command:

```
docker images
```

If the image that was just built is listed (it should appear at the top of the list), run the container, as follows:

```
docker run -it --rm=true --name="football-player-ui" --net="football" -p
80:80 foogaro/football-player-ui
```

Upon opening your browser and pointing to the URL at `http://172.18.0.4/`, the following page should appear:

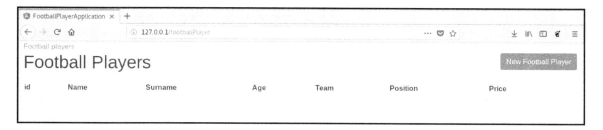

As you can see in the preceding screenshot depicting the `football-player-ui` application, the page is blank, with no data in the table.

That's because we also need to hook the frontend with the backend `football-player-microservice`. To achieve such integration, we need to modify the file `src/app/footballPlayer/football-player.service.ts` and update the private member, named `apiUrl`, with the following statement:

```
private apiUrl = 'http://172.18.0.3:8180/footballplayer';
```

The IP and port refer to the backing service. After rebuilding the frontend, rebuilding the Docker image `foogaro/football-player-ui`, and rerunning the container, the overall system should now work with no issues, as shown in the following screenshot:

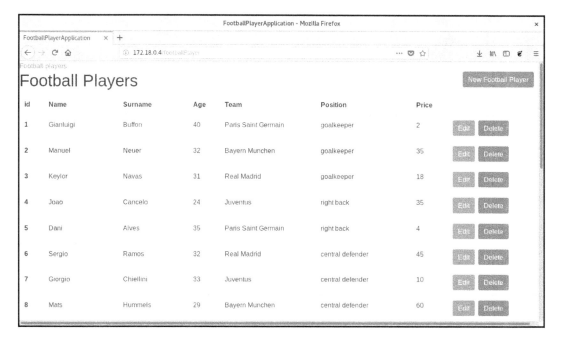

As you must have figured out while reading this chapter, dealing with containers requires some extra work, and adds some complexity to your systems, but you will surely benefit from the automation, scalability, consistency, and integrity of the overall system.

Docker itself is very useful for developing and testing purposes, but in large environments, such as production, you need to orchestrate all of the containers yourself, and it can be very tedious and error-prone, which is something that you really do not want in a production environment.

Nowadays, there is software that provides container orchestration, such as Kubernetes.

Kubernetes

Kubernetes is a portable, extensible, open source platform for managing containerized workloads and services, facilitating both declarative configuration and automation. Kubernetes was developed by Google, and the first committer after Google was Red Hat.

Kubernetes manages application integrity, replicates load balancing, and allocates hardware resources. One of the fundamental tasks of Kubernetes is the work of maintaining an application, making it work, and responding to all user requests. Apps that become unhealthy or do not complete the health check that you decide for them can be flushed automatically. Another advantage offered by Kubernetes is maximizing the use of hardware resources, including the memory, storage, and network bandwidth. Applications can have varying limits regarding the use of resources. Many apps that use minimal resources can be grouped together in the same hardware, while apps that need the resources to grow can instead be placed in systems where they have enough space to evolve. Also, the actions of deploying updates through members of clusters and executing `rollback` if the updates have issues can be automated.

Kubernetes Helm graphs facilitate the deployment of preconfigured applications. Package managers, such as the APT of Debian Linux and PIP of Python, can help the user to install and configure an application. This is particularly useful when an application has more external dependencies. Helm is a sort of package manager for Kubernetes. Many software applications must be performed to be multiple containers and grouped in Kubernetes. Helm provides a mechanism, a so called chart, such that a given piece of software being executed as a container group within Kubernetes. You can create your own Helm charts, and you may need to if you are building a custom app to be distributed internally. However, if you're deploying an application using a popular distribution model with a common one, there's a good probability that someone has already created a Helm chart that's ready to use; it may be published on `https://kubeapps.com/`.

Kubernetes simplifies storage management and other resources for applications. The containers are designed to be immutable; anything that you ship with a container should never change. However, applications need a reliable way to manage external storage volumes. This is an even more complicated scenario, wherein containers run, die (probably crash), and restart throughout the life of an application. Kubernetes has abstractions to allow for an email application container to manage the storage space in the same decoupled method of other resources. You can access many archiving types of storage, from Amazon EBS volumes to the simple NFS shares, through the Kubernetes storage drivers, called **volumes**. Most of the time, volumes are associated with a specific pod, but a volume subtype, called the **persistent volume**, can be used for data that needs to live independently of any pod. Containers often need to work with so-called secrets (credentials such as PAI tokens). While there are third-party solutions for such credentials, like Docker secrets and HashiCorp Vault, Kubernetes has its own mechanism to manage secrets natively.

Kubernetes can be implemented in hybrid and multicloud environments. One of the ambitious goals of the cloud is the possibility to run any application in any cloud environment, or in any combination of public and private cloud. This is not just to avoid supplier lock-in, but is also meant to take advantage of the specific features of individual clouds. Kubernetes provides a set of primitives, well-known federation to keep synchronized clusters between multiple site and multiple cloud regions. For example, it may be a certain distribution of the app, kept consistent between multiple bunches. Clusters and diversification can share service discovery so that a cluster backend resource can be accessed by anyone. The federation can also be used to create high availability or fault-tolerant Kubernetes distributions, regardless of the fact that you are moving in multiple cloud environments.

Nonetheless, as described previously, Kubernetes introduces a lot of new concepts and abstractions, which gives the user a high learning curve. For that reason, we don't want you to spend too much time learning the command-line tools for it; rather, you should switch directly to the enterprise-level software that integrates and uses the Kubernetes API, in order to provide an efficient and easy to use platform, such as OpenShift.

Summary

In this chapter, we covered Linux containers, and why they are so powerful and useful in support of a cloud architecture.

We also described what Docker is, and how we can Dockerize our application and run it everywhere. You learned how to create a Docker file, how to build a Docker image, and how to run a Docker container.

Finally, we described how Docker adds some complexity to the platform; we mentioned that a tool like Kubernetes is needed.

In the next chapter, we will look at how to migrate a cloud-native application with microservices to a PaaS, such as OpenShift, which leverages and eases the use of Kubernetes.

Platform as a Service 7

As the name suggests, a **Platform as a Service** (**PaaS**) is a software solution capable of providing platforms on demand. Those platforms can be any platform enable to expose services, such as database platform, Java platform, Java EE platform, .NET platform, Node.js platform, and much more.

Organizations having a PaaS can easily and quickly provide for their needs and business platform to run their application, processes, and manage everything from one single point.

In this chapter, we will cover the following topics:

- An introduction to OpenShift
- **OKD** (**The Origin Community Distribution of Kubernetes**)
- OKD installation
- Templates
- Networking
- Monitoring

An introduction to OpenShift

OpenShift is a container platform that leverages the Kubernetes orchestrator, enabling container software life cycle and management. OpenShift is the right solution for developers and operational teams.

OpenShift for developers

Test your code as it would go to production environment. Do not skip any test; be focused and give as much commitment as you can.

Each developer works in their own way, and in a team that is composed of several developers, coding, using different third-party tools, preparing the environment, and deploying the application can all be done in different ways. This can lead to heterogeneous environments across the entire development infrastructure with a lot of distinct scenarios and issues to address and solve. OpenShift helps developers to rely on standard tools, standard environments, and standard deployment processes.

One of the most appreciated features of OpenShift is the so-called **source-to-image** (**S2I**), which automatically builds an application from source and creates a container image that can be shipped easily and quickly without issues.

Of course, OpenShift provides the features to ship your own container images—you can create a Docker file, build the image, and push it to the OpenShift registry.

OpenShift application life cycle management provides consistency from the development to the production environment, with built-in pipelines improving continuous integration and continuous delivery and deployment.

Teams can choose from standard tools such as Jenkins, GitLab, GitLab-CI, Nexus, and more to integrate them with OpenShift.

New projects can be created based on the technology of choice, by using standard templates or by creating new ones, either based on JSON or YAML files. By standardizing tools and life cycle management, a simple Git push in S2I can trigger the building of an application and then deploy it directly in the environment of choice.

OpenShift for operations

OpenShift is secure, stable, and scalable. It offers consistency and stability everywhere you operate.

OpenShift relies on Kubernetes, which is the de facto standard in terms of container orchestration. Installing and maintaining a Kubernetes cluster can be very challenging, especially when dealing with underlying resources such as networking, routing, storage, security, and monitoring. OpenShift provides all these out of the box, providing consistency across environments easily and at speed. With such features and integrations, operational teams can work on adding new nodes, scaling applications, and creating new clusters.

OpenShift provides two main control tools:

- Web console
- CLI

We will describe all the functionalities that these tools give to administer your OpenShift cluster later in the chapter.

OpenShift comes in three different flavors:

- **OpenShift Enterprise**, which requires a Red Hat subscription
- **OpenShift Origin**, which is the open source community project (renamed OKD since August 2018)
- **OpenShift Online**, which is powered by Red Hat and available only online with various plans

For ease of use, and of course for free cost control, in this book, we will use the open source community flavor OKD; from now on, any OpenShift wording will refer to OKD, if not otherwise specified. All source code for the OKD project is available under the Apache License (version 2.0) on GitHub.

OKD

OKD leverages on the Kubernetes technology, and extends it by providing security and networking features. You may find Origin wording in OKD in online documentation and on GitHub. An OKD release corresponds to the Kubernetes distribution—for example, OKD 1.10 includes Kubernetes 1.10.

OKD is built around a core of Docker container packaging and Kubernetes container cluster management. All the preceding statements describing OpenShift apply to OKD; as a matter of fact, OpenShift is built on top of OKD.

Now it's time to get our hands on something more practical to continue our journey with cloud-native application environments.

Installing OKD

First of all, you will need to download and install the bundle for your operating system, whether it's any of the following:

- Linux
- macOS X
- Windows

Here is the link https://www.okd.io/download.html.

At the time of writing, the latest version of OKD is v3.11.0 build 0cbc58b. You may download a newer version, with a few updates and changes.

Also, keep in mind that in this book, we will provide instructions and examples that will run on a Linux system, so there might be some differences if you are running a different OS platform:

1. Once we have downloaded the bundle and unpacked it wherever we want, we will refer to its installation folder as OKD_HOME.

   Let's check the bundle by looking at what it contains:

   ```
   # cd $OKD_HOME
   # ll
   total 235116
   -rwxrwxr-x. 1 luigi luigi 120350344 Oct 10 18:48 kubectl
   -rw-rwxr--. 1 luigi luigi 10759 Oct 10 18:48 LICENSE
   -rwxrwxr-x. 1 luigi luigi 120350344 Oct 10 18:48 oc
   -rw-rwxr--. 1 luigi luigi 15834 Oct 10 18:48 README.md
   ```

   Apart from the README.md and LICENSE files, we have the main files, which are the Kubernetes control tool named kubectl.exe and the OKD command-line tool named oc.

   The oc tool is our first management tool to start, stop, configure, and manage the OpenShift cluster. OpenShift uses the Kubernetes API to orchestrate containers in its way, so that's why we also have the Kubernetes control tool.

2. Test the installation as follows:

```
# cd $OKD_HOME
# ./oc version
oc v3.11.0+0cbc58b
kubernetes v1.11.0+d4cacc0
features: Basic-Auth GSSAPI Kerberos SPNEGO
```

3. One important thing: you absolutely need Docker installed on your PC. In my environment, I'm running the following Docker version:

```
# docker version
Client:
Version: 1.13.1
API version: 1.26
Package version: docker-1.13.1-60.git9cb56fd.fc27.x86_64
Go version: go1.9.7
Git commit: 9c9378f-unsupported
Built: Sun Jul 8 08:52:30 2018
OS/Arch: linux/amd64
Server:
Version: 1.13.1
API version: 1.26 (minimum version 1.12)
Package version: docker-1.13.1-60.git9cb56fd.fc27.x86_64
Go version: go1.9.7
Git commit: 9c9378f-unsupported
Built: Sun Jul 8 08:52:30 2018
OS/Arch: linux/amd64
Experimental: false
```

If you don't have Docker, you can download it from https://www.docker.com/get-started.

Let's go back to our container platform OKD and let's run it for the first time. It might take some time as it will need to download all the Docker images to run our platform as containerized.

4. Open a Terminal window and do the following:

```
# ./oc cluster up
Getting a Docker client ...
Checking if image openshift/origin-control-plane:v3.11 is available
...
Checking type of volume mount ...
Determining server IP ...
Checking if OpenShift is already running ...
Checking for supported Docker version (=>1.22) ...
```

```
Checking if insecured registry is configured properly in Docker ...
Checking if required ports are available ...
Checking if OpenShift client is configured properly ...
Checking if image openshift/origin-control-plane:v3.11 is available
...
Starting OpenShift using openshift/origin-control-plane:v3.11 ...
I1107 10:02:17.533327 29872 config.go:40] Running "create-master-
config"
I1107 10:02:19.950416 29872 config.go:46] Running "create-node-
config"
I1107 10:02:20.837991 29872 flags.go:30] Running "create-kubelet-
flags"
I1107 10:02:21.342993 29872 run_kubelet.go:49] Running "start-
kubelet"
I1107 10:02:21.596927 29872 run_self_hosted.go:181] Waiting for the
kube-apiserver to be ready ...
ae999762568bI1107 10:06:21.628135 29872 interface.go:26] Installing
"kube-proxy" ...
I1107 10:06:21.628195 29872 interface.go:26] Installing "kube-dns"
...
I1107 10:06:21.628235 29872 interface.go:26] Installing "openshift-
service-cert-signer-operator" ...
I1107 10:06:21.628275 29872 interface.go:26] Installing "openshift-
apiserver" ...
I1107 10:06:21.628576 29872 apply_template.go:81] Installing "kube-
dns"
I1107 10:06:21.628571 29872 apply_template.go:81] Installing
"openshift-service-cert-signer operator"
I1107 10:06:21.628571 29872 apply_template.go:81] Installing
"openshift-apiserver"
I1107 10:06:21.628861 29872 apply_template.go:81] Installing "kube-
proxy"
I1107 10:06:24.734288 29872 interface.go:41] Finished installing
"kube-proxy" "kube-dns" "openshift-service-cert-signer-operator"
"openshift-apiserver"
I1107 10:08:05.759760 29872 run_self_hosted.go:242] openshift-
apiserver available
I1107 10:08:05.759791 29872 interface.go:26] Installing "openshift-
controller-manager" ...
I1107 10:08:05.759814 29872 apply_template.go:81] Installing
"openshift-controller-manager"
I1107 10:08:08.170568 29872 interface.go:41] Finished installing
"openshift-controller-manager"
Adding default OAuthClient redirect URIs ...
Adding centos-imagestreams ...
Adding router ...
Adding persistent-volumes ...
Adding registry ...
```

```
Adding sample-templates ...
Adding web-console ...
I1107 10:08:08.206912 29872 interface.go:26] Installing "centos-
imagestreams" ...
I1107 10:08:08.206937 29872 interface.go:26] Installing "openshift-
router" ...
I1107 10:08:08.206949 29872 interface.go:26] Installing
"persistent-volumes" ...
I1107 10:08:08.206960 29872 interface.go:26] Installing "openshift-
image-registry" ...
I1107 10:08:08.206971 29872 interface.go:26] Installing "sample-
templates" ...
I1107 10:08:08.206979 29872 interface.go:26] Installing "openshift-
web-console-operator" ...
I1107 10:08:08.207255 29872 apply_list.go:67] Installing "centos-
imagestreams"
I1107 10:08:08.207622 29872 interface.go:26] Installing "sample-
templates/mongodb" ...
I1107 10:08:08.207642 29872 interface.go:26] Installing "sample-
templates/mariadb" ...
I1107 10:08:08.207651 29872 interface.go:26] Installing "sample-
templates/mysql" ...
I1107 10:08:08.207661 29872 interface.go:26] Installing "sample-
templates/cakephp quickstart" ...
I1107 10:08:08.207673 29872 interface.go:26] Installing "sample-
templates/dancer quickstart" ...
I1107 10:08:08.207684 29872 interface.go:26] Installing "sample-
templates/django quickstart" ...
I1107 10:08:08.207695 29872 interface.go:26] Installing "sample-
templates/nodejs quickstart" ...
I1107 10:08:08.207705 29872 interface.go:26] Installing "sample-
templates/postgresql" ...
I1107 10:08:08.207715 29872 interface.go:26] Installing "sample-
templates/rails quickstart" ...
I1107 10:08:08.207725 29872 interface.go:26] Installing "sample-
templates/jenkins pipeline ephemeral" ...
I1107 10:08:08.207735 29872 interface.go:26] Installing "sample-
templates/sample pipeline" ...
I1107 10:08:08.207790 29872 apply_list.go:67] Installing "sample-
templates/sample pipeline"
I1107 10:08:08.208061 29872 apply_list.go:67] Installing "sample-
templates/mongodb"
I1107 10:08:08.208226 29872 apply_list.go:67] Installing "sample-
templates/mariadb"
I1107 10:08:08.208246 29872 apply_template.go:81] Installing
"openshift-web-console-operator"
I1107 10:08:08.208475 29872 apply_list.go:67] Installing "sample-
templates/cakephp quickstart"
```

```
I1107 10:08:08.208677 29872 apply_list.go:67] Installing "sample-
templates/nodejs quickstart"
I1107 10:08:08.208703 29872 apply_list.go:67] Installing "sample-
templates/postgresql"
I1107 10:08:08.210179 29872 apply_list.go:67] Installing "sample-
templates/dancer quickstart"
I1107 10:08:08.210319 29872 apply_list.go:67] Installing "sample-
templates/rails quickstart"
I1107 10:08:08.210321 29872 apply_list.go:67] Installing "sample-
templates/django quickstart"
I1107 10:08:08.208377 29872 apply_list.go:67] Installing "sample-
templates/mysql"
I1107 10:08:08.208401 29872 apply_list.go:67] Installing "sample-
templates/jenkins pipeline ephemeral"
I1107 10:08:17.213093 29872 interface.go:41] Finished installing
"sample-templates/mongodb" "sample-templates/mariadb" "sample-
templates/mysql" "sample-templates/cakephp quickstart" "sample-
templates/dancer quickstart" "sample-templates/django quickstart"
"sample-templates/nodejs quickstart" "sample-templates/postgresql"
"sample-templates/rails quickstart" "sample-templates/jenkins
pipeline ephemeral" "sample-templates/sample pipeline"
I1107 10:08:39.004121 29872 interface.go:41] Finished installing
"centos-imagestreams" "openshift-router" "persistent-volumes"
"openshift-image-registry" "sample-templates" "openshift-web-
console-operator"
Login to server ...
Creating initial project "myproject" ...
Server Information ...
OpenShift server started.
```

The server is accessible via the Web console at `https://127.0.0.1:8443`.

You are logged in as the following:

```
User: developer
Password: <any value>
```

5. To log in as `administrator`, use the following:

```
oc login -u system:admin
```

Let's analyze the most important aspects. There are a lot of logs, but it has done many tasks for you.

First of all, the command—we rely on the `oc cluster` command to run the cluster. Why a cluster? Because `oc` runs several containers, that is, several servers, with networks, routing, storage, container registry, and so on. It is much, much easier than providing everything yourself and then configuring a Kubernetes cluster.

The `oc` command also comes with several other flags to help you out, as follows:

```
# ./oc --help
```

The OpenShift client

The OpenShift client helps manage the platform from an operational point of view. You can deploy new applications, scale existing ones, to any Kubernetes or OpenShift cluster.

The client tool also includes a special sub-command, `adm`, to do administrative tasks.

Here is how it's used:

```
oc [flags]
```

The basic commands are as follows:

- `types`: An introduction to concepts and types
- `login`: Log in to a server
- `new-project`: Request a new project
- `new-app`: Create a new application
- `status`: Show an overview of the current project
- `project`: Switch to another project
- `projects`: Display existing projects
- `explain`: Documentation of resources
- `cluster`: Start and stop OpenShift cluster

The build and deploy commands are as follows:

- `rollout`: Manage a Kubernetes deployment or OpenShift deployment config
- `rollback`: Revert part of an application back to a previous deployment
- `new-build`: Create a new build configuration
- `start-build`: Start a new build

- `cancel-build`: Cancel running, pending, or new builds
- `import-image`: Import images from a Docker registry
- `tag`: Tag existing images into image streams

The application management commands are as follows:

- `get`: Display one or many resources
- `describe`: Show details of a specific resource or group of resources
- `edit`: Edit a resource on the server
- `set`: Commands that help set specific features on objects
- `label`: Update the labels on a resource
- `annotate`: Update the annotations on a resource
- `expose`: Expose a replicated application as a service or route
- `delete`: Delete one or more resources
- `scale`: Change the number of pods in a deployment
- `autoscale`: Auto scale a deployment config, deployment, replication controller, or replica set
- `secrets`: Manage secrets
- `serviceaccounts`: Manage service accounts in your project

The troubleshooting and debugging commands are as follows:

- `logs`: Print the logs for a resource
- `rsh`: Start a shell session in a pod
- `rsync`: Copy files between local filesystem and a pod
- `port-forward`: Forward one or more local ports to a pod
- `debug`: Launch a new instance of a pod for debugging
- `exec`: Execute a command in a container
- `proxy`: Run a proxy to the Kubernetes API server
- `attach`: Attach to a running container
- `run`: Run a particular image on the cluster
- `cp`: Copy files and directories to and from containers.
- `wait`: Wait for one condition on one or many resources (this is still experimental)

The advanced commands are as follows:

- `adm`: Tools for managing a cluster
- `create`: Create a resource from a file or from standard input
- `replace`: Replace a resource by filename or standard input
- `apply`: Apply a config to a resource by filename or standard input
- `patch`: Update field(s) of a resource using strategic merge patch
- `process`: Process a template into list of resources
- `export`: Export resources so they can be used elsewhere
- `extract`: Extract secrets or config maps to disk
- `idle`: Idle scalable resources
- `observe`: Observe changes to resources and react to them (this is still experimental)
- `policy`: Manage authorization policy
- `auth`: Inspect authorization
- `convert`: Convert config files between different API versions
- `import`: Commands that import applications
- `image`: Useful commands for managing images
- `registry`: Commands for working with the registry
- `api-versions`: Print the supported API versions on the server, in the form of `group/version`
- `api-resources`: Print the supported API resources on the server

The settings commands are as follows:

- `logout`: End the current server session
- `config`: Change configuration files for the client
- `whoami`: Return information about the current session
- `completion`: Output shell completion code for the specified shell (bash or zsh)

Some other commands are as follows:

- `ex`: Experimental commands under active development
- `help`: Get help with any command
- `plugin`: Run a command-line plugin
- `version`: Display client and server versions

Use `oc <command> --help` for more information about a given command.

In our case, we run the command `oc cluster` with the flag up. To check any composite commands such as `oc cluster`, use the `--help` directive, as follows:

```
# ./oc cluster --help
```

You can refer to the following link for more information: `https://rasor.github.io/developing-with-openshift.html`

Managing a local OpenShift cluster

The OpenShift cluster will run as an all-in-one container on a Docker host. The Docker host may be a local **virtual machine** (**VM**), remote machine, or the local Unix host.

Use the `up` command to start a new cluster on a Docker host.

Ensure that Docker commands are working and that you can create new containers before you try to use an existing Docker connection.

Default routes are set up using `nip.io` and the host IP of your cluster. Use the `--routing-suffix` flag to use a different routing suffix.

The syntax is as follows:

```
oc cluster ACTION [flags]
```

The available commands are as follows:

- `add`: Add components to an `oc cluster up` cluster
- `down`: Stop OpenShift on Docker
- `status`: Show OpenShift on Docker status
- `up`: Start OpenShift on Docker with reasonable defaults

Use `oc <command> --help` for more information about a given command. Use `oc options` for a list of global command-line options (this applies to all commands).

We will not dive into all composite commands; we will just explain the ones we will use along our journey. If you need more information, take a look at the documentation at `https://docs.okd.io/latest/welcome/index.html`.

To check what is really running, we can first check which containers are running, as follows:

```
# docker ps
```

This will give the output depicted in the following screenshot:

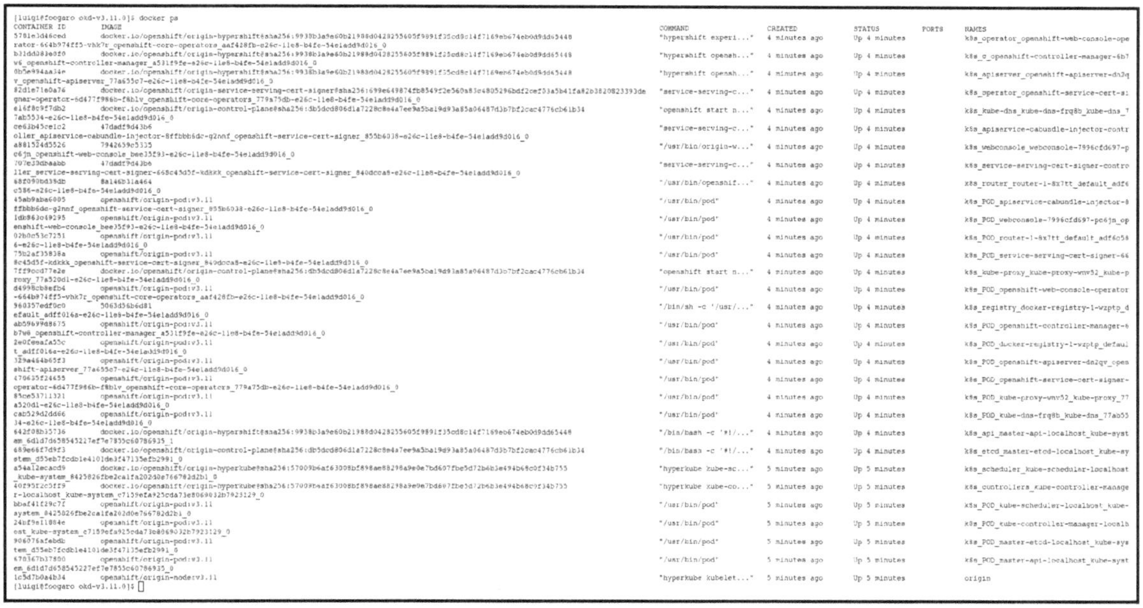

Output showing the containers that are running

Toward the end of the log, we can see something about the `web-console`, which is the other management tool provided automatically by the OKD platform.

Furthermore, the log provides the coordinates of our OKD cluster accessible at `https://127.0.0.1:8443`.

The same URL is valid for both the graphic interface and the command-line tool, and by default the `oc` automatically logs you in with a developer account, as shown at the end of the log:

```
You are logged in as:
User: developer
Password: <any value>
```

By default, the user `admin` with any password is also created. The super user, who is the real administrator of the system, is the user called `super:admin`, which is available only with the CLI, as it uses a certificate to log in.

We will go back to the `oc` command later in the chapter, and switch to the Web console.

To access the system via the UI, point your browser at the URL described earlier, and you should see the login form, shown as follows:

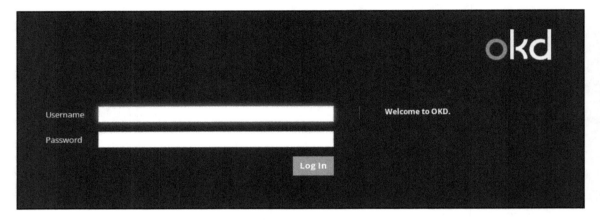

Log in as `developer` and you should see the following page:

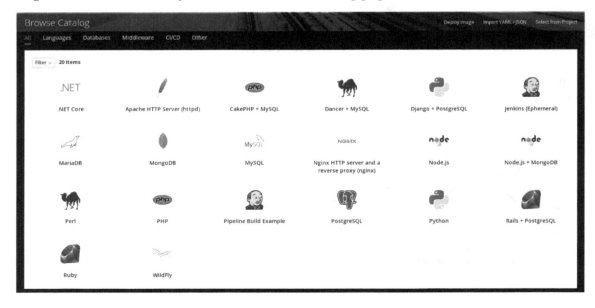

As you can see from the preceding screenshot, OKD provides, by default, various ready-to-use templates for different platforms (such as WildFly, Node.js, and Ruby) and databases (such as MongoDB and MariaDB) with which to deploy your application as a container.

Of course, you can provide your own template to the technology you need to run your applications.

Templates

For the moment, we will use the templates provided by default from the platform, and in `Chapter 8`, *Microservices Patterns*, we will see how to create templates for our cloud-native application football manager—composed of three databases, three backend microservices, and two frontend Angular applications.

Let's try the WildFly template:

1. If you are not already logged in as `developer`, log in and from the catalog choose the WildFly icon.
2. You should read through the following wizard; just go through and rely on the defaults:

3. Click on the **Try Sample Repository** link, as follows:

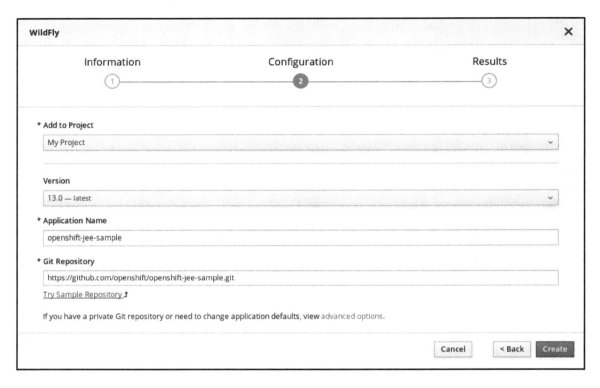

4. The template for the WildFly application will prepare the runtime environment in a few seconds, as follows:

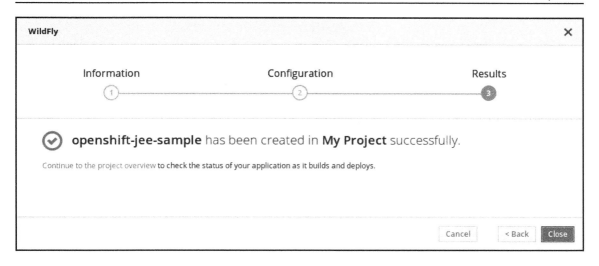

5. If you click on the **Continue to the project overview** link, you will see your project with an overview of all deployments (in this case, only this one), as shown in the following screenshot:

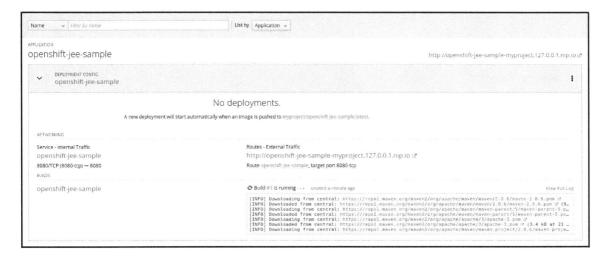

List of deployments in the project

As you can see in the preceding screenshot, the build is in place, downloading the source code and compiling the application. Once the build is complete, the OKD platform should deploy a **pod** with a container running our application in it. A properly running **pod** is shown with a blue ring, as follows:

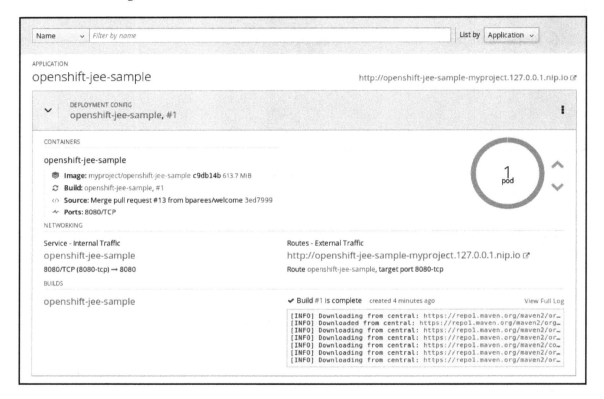

The overview shows a lot of different information.

6. At the top right, there is the URL to access the application; if you click on `http://openshift-jee-sample-myproject.127.0.0.1.nip.io`, the following page should be displayed:

Welcome to your JavaEE application on OpenShift

How to use this example application

For instructions on how to use this application with OpenShift, start by reading the Developer Guide.

Deploying code changes

The source code for this application is available to be forked from the OpenShift GitHub repository. You can configure a webhook in your repository to make OpenShift automatically start a build whenever you push your code:

1. From the Web Console homepage, navigate to your project
2. Click on Browse > Builds
3. Click the link with your BuildConfig name
4. Click the Configuration tab
5. Click the "Copy to clipboard" icon to the right of the "GitHub webhook URL" field
6. Navigate to your repository on GitHub and click on repository settings > webhooks > Add webhook
7. Paste your webhook URL provided by OpenShift
8. Leave the defaults for the remaining fields — that's it!

After you save your webhook, if you refresh your settings page you can see the status of the ping that Github sent to OpenShift to verify it can reach the server.

Note: adding a webhook requires your OpenShift server to be reachable from GitHub.

Working in your local Git repository

If you forked the application from the OpenShift GitHub example, you'll need to manually clone the repository to your local system. Copy the application's source code Git URL and then run:

```
$ git clone <git_url> <directory_to_create>

# Within your project directory
# Commit your changes and push to OpenShift

$ git commit -a -m 'Some commit message'
$ git push
```

After pushing changes, you'll need to manually trigger a build if you did not setup a webhook as described above.

Managing your application

Documentation on how to manage your application from the Web Console or Command Line is available at the Developer Guide.

Web Console

You can use the Web Console to view the state of your application components and launch new builds.

Command Line

With the OpenShift command line interface (CLI), you can create applications and manage projects from a terminal.

Development Resources

- OpenShift Documentation
- Openshift Origin GitHub
- Source To Image GitHub
- Getting Started with Node.js on OpenShift
- Stack Overflow questions for OpenShift
- Git documentation

Built on

 OPENSHIFT
by Red Hat

The application after performing the set up

Getting back to the overview of our WildFly deployment example, you should also see the following *Networking* section, which is one of the most important aspects of any application.

Networking

OKD provides a routing layer to expose the application to the outside world. You can find the routing information of our example in the networking section on the right, labeled as **Routes - External Traffic**. You may have also noticed another element on the left, called **Service - Internal Traffic**, which is used by OKD for pod-to-pod communication. In that manner, different pods can talk to each other using the internal OKD network.

Services

If you click on a service name, a new page should appear, showing detailed information about how the application is internally visible and reachable, as follows:

The service page itself also references the route used by the system to expose the internal service. In this case, the internal traffic is bound to the **openshift-jee-sample.myproject.svc Hostname** on port 8080, and it is mapped to the **Route** named **openshift-jee-sample** on the same port with a different **Hostname** (the one showing the application).

If you follow the link on the **Route** name, you should see detailed information about the **Route**, as described in the next section.

Routes

As already mentioned, the **Route** provides external traffic routing, that is, exposing the application to the world. The **Route** of the WildFly application should be as follows:

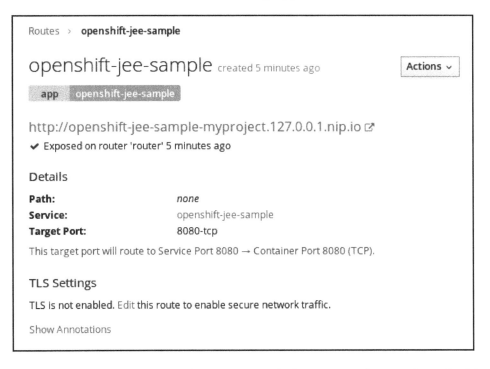

The **Route** also references the internal mapping with the service, the one described in the *Services* section.

Monitoring

The OKD platform also provides basic monitoring for the workflow of the application, as depicted in the following screenshot:

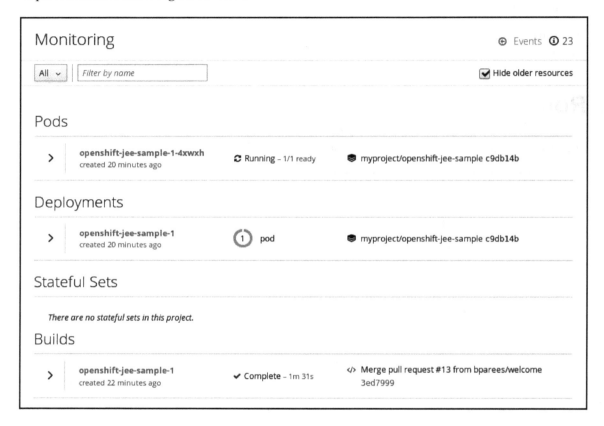

Later in the book, we will set up the Prometheus monitoring tool to get more detailed information about the status of the OKD cluster, and about the applications.

Summary

In this chapter, we have learned about OKD, the community project on which OpenShift is based.

We also described and learned how an application can be internally called by its service name, and how an application is reachable from outside the platform by relying on the **Route** component.

In the next chapter, we will describe the common patterns used when designing and building microservices using containers; more specifically, using OpenShift as PaaS. We will also implement and test the efficiency of those patterns with real-time examples.

8
Microservices Patterns

A pattern is something that can be repeated regularly and in a predictable manner.

This concept applies in all contexts—in building, in designing, in IT, and in every context where something needs to be done.

The concept of patterns started late in the 70s in regards to architecture and building designs, but patterns have always been around. Look at nature, for example—it is full of patterns, both repeatable and predictable. They occur in spirals, waves, and broccoli, and in mathematics with symmetric geometry, fractals, and so on.

However, in our context—the IT context—we first found patterns in the middle of the 90s in one of the books I read.

The pattern language continued to evolve to keep up with the speed of the evolution and revolution of IT, and at the beginning of the new millennium, new tools and systems were coming out. The internet was exploding and distributed systems went public with new infrastructures, new architectures, and new patterns.

Before we start, it's worth mentioning that the microservices architecture is an alternative to monolithic architecture, in the sense that every architecture has its own pros and cons—it's all about the trade-off.

The old principles and patterns, such as service discovery and routing from the SOA, are still valid and in use on both monolithic and microservice architectures. However, with microservices and containers, methods to design, implement, and deploy software have changed drastically. Applications are now optimized for flexibility, scalability, failure, elasticity, and to adapt to new requests and businesses rapidly. Driven by new principles, these new architectures require a different set of patterns and practices to be applied.

In this chapter, we will not visit and describe the complete lists of patterns to be used with the microservices approach, but we will concentrate on the most used ones to get you started and interested in the topic of patterns. There are tons of books about patterns, and if you care about cloud environments, you should read the *Java EE 8 Design Patterns and Best Practices* by Packt (`https://www.packtpub.com/application-development/java-ee-8-design-patterns-and-best-practices`).

The patterns that will be covered in this chapter are as follows:

- Decomposition
- API gateway
- Bulkheads
- Circuit breaker
- Sidecar

Decomposition

Decomposition isn't really the best of words—it recalls something going bad. However, in this context, it means to split apart a service, such as our football manager application; that is, splitting it into different microservices and decoupling components that follow the **Single Responsibility Principle (SRP)**. The SRP relies on the fact that one component does one and one thing only, and that it does very well. The following diagram gives us an idea about decomposition:

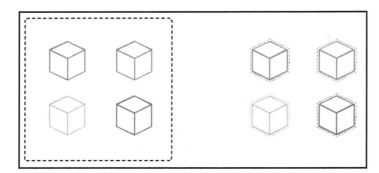

In our example, the overall application could have been designed and deployed as a monolith, where we group all of the pieces together. Of course, it would have worked well, but with a lot of drawbacks (flexibility, scalability, failure, elasticity, and so on).

How do you decompose an application?

There is no real answer to such a question—as usual, it depends on what's best for the governance of the microservices architecture, the teams involved, the current infrastructure, and cost control. There are many aspects to consider and there is no *one-fits-all* solution.

By functionality

An application can be decomposed by functionalities, that is, taking each functionality out of the application and transforming it into a microservice. To be able to follow such a fussy approach, a complete and deep knowledge of the core components is required. Don't forget that a monolith application might not have one single point of integration; rather, integration points can be spread all over the source code.

By integration

An application can be decomposed by its integration points, or how it communicates with the other components and subcomponents. Here, more components could be merged together. Another aspect to consider in such an approach is to eventually take apart only the components that are very slow from the ones that are faster in processing requests. Furthermore, merge components that interact slowly.

By resource consumption

An application can be decomposed by its resource consumption level. The greedy components can be isolated to increase control and reduce resource harvesting. Feed only the greedy ones.

All of the aforementioned approaches lead to a flexible and scalable system, if deployed in a microservice architecture. However, considering a service or a microservice for what it does is not always the right choice. Nowadays, there are new trends in deployment coming out for microservices (we should probably call them nanoservices if they are really small), and this is known as **serverless deployment**.

Serverless

The idea behind such a solution is to consider how often/how long a service is called. For example, suppose you have a shop and you have special discounts during the Easter and Christmas holidays. It does not make sense to have the special discount service active all the time, as it would result in a loss of money. It would be nice to have an infrastructure that deploys your service on demand when other services request it. That's the main point of being server less, and it deals well with microservice and cloud environments. Big cloud vendors provide these new technologies, some of which are as follows:

- AWS Lambda
- Google Cloud Functions
- Azure Functions

API gateway

The API gateway is a service that's responsible for routing requests from clients to applications, and is very similar to a design pattern called *facade*, from object-oriented design, which is best described in the book *Java EE 8 Design Patterns and Best Practices*.

The API gateway encapsulates logic to call the proper backend services. As it is the single entry point, it can also have other capabilities such as securing services, transforming payloads, monitoring, throttling, caching, and rating the number of requests per service, and so on. The API gateway is also responsible for exposing services with different protocols.

Another scenario in which it can be used is to call multiple services, aggregate the result, and return the proper output (API composition implementation) as shown in the following diagram:

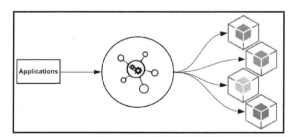

Bulkhead

This pattern is named bulkhead because it behaves as the partition of a ship to prevent the ship from sinking. It basically isolates the various compartments of a ship to avoid or minimize the risk of sinking.

The same applies to software, where one failure does not compromise the entire system. In IT, specifically when implementing a data access layer, the bulkhead pattern should be used for connection pools. Either a database, or HTTP connections that have one single connection pool, could compromise the entire system. Suppose your code does not release connections properly—the connection pool would be full of active connections very quickly, and in that case, services dealing with databases or other services via HTTP connections will not be able to function properly, even if they have to deal with different resources.

The following image depicts various applications relying on the same connection pool. All of a sudden, a bug in one application saturates the connection pool. The consequence is that the connections in the pool are all locked by one application, and the other applications cannot use it:

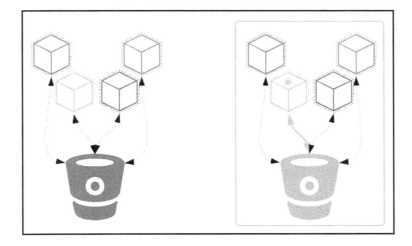

Instead, by creating a connection pool for each service, it avoids entire system failing with failure instead, compromising just one functionality, as illustrated in the following diagram:

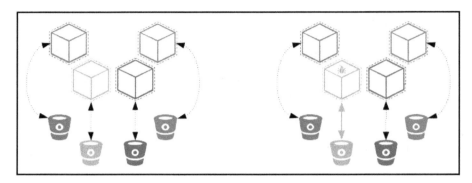

In our football manager application, we dedicated pools for each service, and we also used a different database for each service to actually show that you can rely on different tools for the right job—homogeneity is not mandatory anymore with microservices and with a PaaS providing heterogeneous runtime.

The bulkhead pattern is surely a good approach, but sometimes your system still needs to provide some kind of minimum capability for that functionality. In that case, the circuit breaker is the pattern you need.

Circuit breaker

As the name suggests, this pattern is named like this because it comes from the electronic circuit context.

It sounds familiar, doesn't it?

The purpose of the circuit breaker pattern is the same as bulkheads, but with a different approach. Here, too, a service calling another service that is not responding or is very slow might decrease the performance of the overall system.

There is also another reason to implement the circuit breaker, which is to avoid having to keep on calling a service that you already know is broken or not reachable.

Suppose service A is calling service B, and service B is down—service A should prevent such integration and respond with a timeout error or cached data. Electronically speaking, this is the open state in the circuit, that is, no more connection between the two points.

The circuit breaker implementation should poll service B periodically to check its healthiness. Once service B is up again, the circuit breaker should reset the flow, having service A calling service B once more. Electronically speaking, this is the **close** state in the circuit.

The way the circuit breaker checks the integration point depends on the use case. It might suspend service B after a certain number of invocations go wrong. If so, it's best to wait and retry.

The most well-known implementation of the circuit breaker is given by Netflix Hystrix. However, this library has no more active development and is in maintenance mode. Of course, there are alternatives to Netflix Hystrix, such as Resilience4j, Sentinel, and Istio.

The latter is the one that's used by OpenShift., the PaaS supported by Red Hat, we will be describing it in the next section.

Istio

Here is the definition of Istio from its site, `https://istio.io/`:

> *"Istio addresses the challenges developers and operators face as monolithic applications transition toward a distributed microservice architecture."*

With the increase in complexity of microservice architecture, it is mandatory to rely on resilience patterns, such as circuit breaking, load balancing, throttling, and so on.

Istio implements all of these behavioral patterns using pluggable policies via the Envoy proxy, which can be configured for the specific use case/policy at hand. Here is an example:

```
metadata:
name: circuit-breaker-policy
namespace: default
spec:
destination:
name: circuit-breaker
labels:
version: v1
```

```
circuitBreaker:
simple-circuit-breaker:
maxConnections: 100
httpMaxRequests: 1000
httpMaxRequestsPerConnection: 10
httpConsecutiveErrors: 7
sleepWindow: 15m
httpDetectionInterval: 5m
```

This means that a service mesh acts at application level (in network terms, L7), thus implementing retries, timeouts, circuit breaker, bulkheads, and routing control.

Sidecar

The first thing that comes to mind when we say the word sidecar is a pilot on a motorbike who has their co-pilot in a small capsule attached to the motorbike itself.

The same kind of suggestion can be applied to software. Suppose you have an application with a component attached to it. However, in software context, the sidecar is a component that can be plugged and unplugged from the main application, because it must be isolated and cannot impact the application in case it starts misbehaving. This will be something that's collateral to the application. The most used scenarios for a sidecar are monitoring, logging, metrics, and so on.

A sidecar container should be configurable so that it can be plugged into any application—it doesn't have to be just a single application, either. The best match for sidecars are containers. The application container can be bolted to the sidecar container and run as container groups, which are called pods in the Kubernetes and OpenShift worlds.

For decades, one of the main implementations of the sidecar pattern involved an agent, like an agent monitoring application memory, health checks, and CPU usage.

Nowadays, the most popular sidecar implementation is Istio, which deploys a proxy as a sidecar for your service. All of the requests for the service go to the proxy—the Envoy proxy, which uses its configuration to set a policy for how and when the requests should reach your service.

The diagram for Envoy proxy is shown as follows:

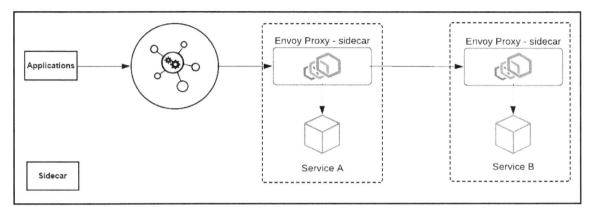

With Istio, taking control of the service, and thus of your service mesh, is very easy. Any capabilities such as traffic monitoring, access control, discovery, security, resiliency, tracing, circuit breakers, routing, load balancing, fault injection, retries, timeouts, mirroring, and rate limiting can be added without touching the original application, regardless of the runtime environment and the programming language it is implemented with.

In the end, the sidecar pattern is very helpful, but has a little overhead in terms of implementation. If you are running a small piece of software, adding a sidecar might be too much, and a bit too complex.

Summary

In this chapter, we went through the basic patterns that are needed to implement a microservice architecture. Of course, there are more patterns to study, learn, test, and use, but to get started, those that have been described so far are enough.

In the next chapter, we will start building the template for our football manager application and we will see how to deploy the whole system in OKD.

9
Deployment

Once a team has implemented a software solution, it's time to see that particular piece of software in action. To see the software in action, you basically need to install and run that software in an environment that's available to end users. Such a process is called **deployment**.

Deployment involves a lot of things. In the past, it was just a matter of copying a binary file somewhere and running it, probably using an FTP server and an SSH session.

As we described earlier in this book, software has changed drastically in terms of languages, capabilities, functionalities, and integration points. All software is connected using various protocols and systems. Thus, deploying a piece of software has become a complex process.

Today, especially in the microservices era, software is distributed in the cloud and every component needs to interact with others; this means a quick and dirty copy and paste of the binary is not a valid option anymore.

Software needs to be flexible, adaptable to business change, consistent, reliable, and performant, and it needs to respond quickly to new business needs. Therefore, software must be bug-free, and before you can deploy it to a production environment, you need to make sure it works properly both from a functional and infrastructure point of view, it integrates perfectly with the other systems involved, and it can be managed by a DevOps team. Testing is the key to success, and a proper platform to manage the entire process is mandatory.

As you can see, deploying a piece of code is a complex process, but fortunately there are lots of tools and patterns you can follow to automate the entire process and make sure your software is bug-free.

Fortunately, we have OpenShift, which is the right platform to manage such processes, leveraging the microservices in container deployment.

In this chapter, we will cover the following topics:

- Continuous integration and continuous delivery
- Blue-green deployment
- Canary deployment
- A/B testing deployment
- Rolling deployment

Continuous integration and continuous delivery

Continuous integration (CI) and **continuous delivery (CD)** (eventually deployment) are the processes that are used to build, package, and deploy your application.

Here is a diagram depicting the flow of CI/CD:

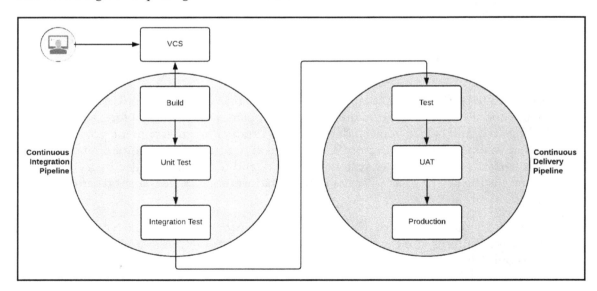

Essentially, the developer team commits the source code to a version control system—hopefully a GitHub repository; the CI tool polls down the latest version of the code and builds the application.

Building also involves unit testing and integration testing. There are different frameworks out there to use for both unit and integration testing. Of course, it depends on your runtime environment. For example, in Java, you can rely on JUnit and Arquillian for unit testing and integration testing, respectively.

The build phase also includes code inspection for quality, spotting anti patterns, optimizations, coverage, style, and so on.

Once you have the green light from the test, you can actually release your application to your first environment, which most of the time is development/test.

Typically, the environments are development, test, **user acceptance test** (**UAT**), preproduction, and production. But this is really dependent on the organization in terms of cost control and policy.

However, as long as you have test, UAT, and production, you have enough environments to manage the life cycle of your deployment.

What's the difference between CI, CD, and CD?

As you could have imagined, CI is the phase in which your application gets built, tested, and packaged (whatever the package format is—web application, binary, container, and so on). The de facto standard tool for this phase is Jenkins.

The first CD stands for continuous delivery, and is the phase where your final artifact gets delivered to an environment. Continuous means that your artifact gets delivered, that is, promoted, from environment to environment until the preproduction environment, or at least at the last environment before production, which then needs a manual promotion—typically a manager approval for deploying to production.

Again, Jenkins helps out in this phase, as it can directly promote the application from environment to environment by relying on pipelines.

The last CD stands for continuous deployment, and it is exactly the same as continuous delivery, except for the fact that the artifact, once built, gets promoted from the first stage environment to production directly in an automated way.

Which one to choose depends on which one is right for your organization.

However, there are four golden rules for the deployment process:

- **Build the final artifact only once**: What needs to be deployed from environment to environment must be exactly the same thing. To achieve such goals easily, OpenShift relies on Jenkins.
- **Keep deployment the same**: Always deploy in the same manner for each environment. Less configuration, better automation, less risk.
- **Test, test, and test**: Testing is essential for CI and CD. Testing must be part of the deployment process.
- **Similar environments**: Environments should differ only in terms of available resources. All software stack layers should be the same to minimize any differences that could eventually impact the stability and misconfiguration of your system. Clean and safe. Here as well, container technology is a godsend.

In the following sections, we will look at different ways to deploy an application for different purposes.

Blue-green deployment

Blue-green deployment is a technique that's used to reduce downtime to deploy a new version of the application. Martin Fowler described this technique at the beginning of 2010 on his site at `https://martinfowler.com/bliki/BlueGreenDeployment.html`. The following is a quote taken from this site:

> *"One of the challenges with automating deployment is the cut-over itself, taking software from the final stage of testing to live production. You usually need to do this quickly in order to minimize downtime. The blue-green deployment approach does this by ensuring you have two production environments, as identical as possible. At any time one of them, let's say blue for the example, is live. As you prepare a new release of your software you do your final stage of testing in the green environment. Once the software is working in the green environment, you switch the router so that all incoming requests go to the green environment - the blue one is now idle."*

Here is a logical architecture of the blue-green deployment:

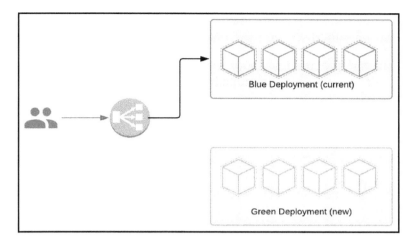

The key point in blue-green deployment is to have a route or load balancer that's able to switch from the blue environment to the green environment on demand:

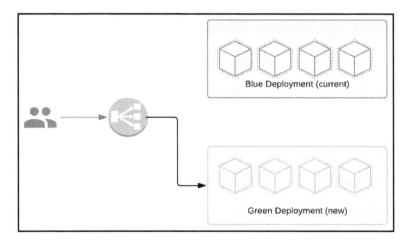

This will surely have some benefits, such as zero downtime and a ready-to-use rollback environment. On the other hand, this new environment will also be fresh and new in terms of session application, thus all user sessions will be lost. To mitigate such loss, setting the application in read-only mode could help, or waiting for all of the sessions to drain.

However, blue-green deployment is about testing the production environment, not testing the application itself, which should be done in test and/or UAT.

Let's try a blue-green deployment with an example:

1. First of all, if you don't have your OpenShift platform up and running, start it as follows:

   ```
   oc cluster up
   ```

2. Once everything has started, open your browser and point it to https://127.0.0.1:8443/console/.

3. Log in as developer, and click on the **Nginx** icon in **Browse Catalog**, as follows:

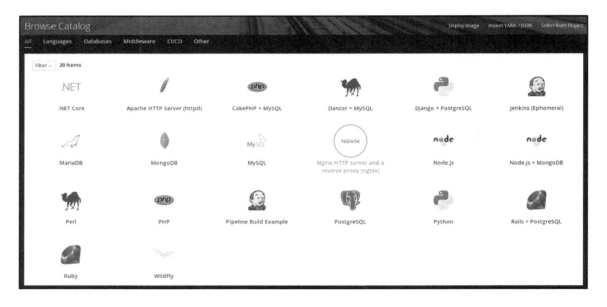

4. In the pop-up wizard, click **Next** and fill in the next form, as shown in the following screenshot:

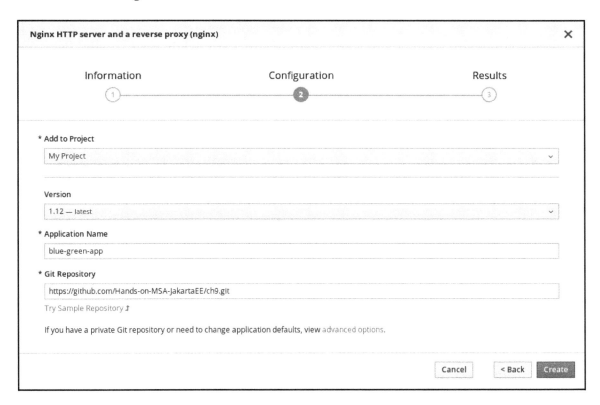

5. In the last step, the platform confirms the creation of the application, which is already being deployed in your project.

6. Click on the link labeled **Continue to the project overview** to see its overview and progress:

The overview of the application created

7. Once the application has been successfully deployed in the platform as a container in a **pod**, click on the route stating `http://blue-green-app-myproject.127.0.0.1.nip.io`, which should load our example application.

The page should display some text in blue, as follows:

8. To simulate our new version of the application, and thus simulate a switch between the two versions—the blue (the one we just deployed) and the green (the one we are about to deploy)—go back to the catalog and select the **Nginx** icon, and click **Next** in the pop-up wizard.

9. This time, click on the **Advanced options** link and fill in the form, as follows:

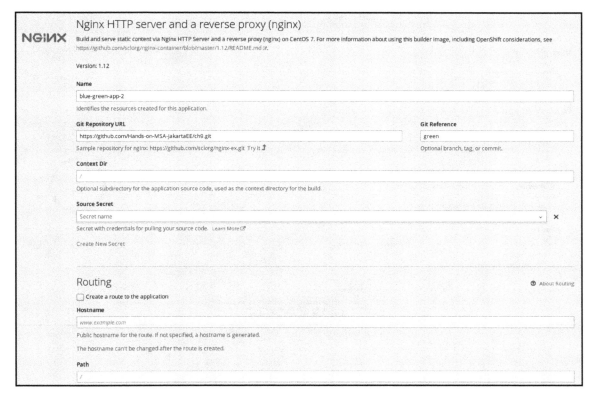

The Advanced options page

The difference from the previous deployment is, of course, the name, which is **blue-green-app-2**. Furthermore, the deployment is now pointing to the branch named **green** of our Git repository, and so we do not create a route automatically for our application.

In this way, the application will not be exposed externally. However, without sharing the route, users will not know the new URL, but as this is an automated task, the URL is predictable based on application names, and curious users might be able to spoil your new features. For this reason, we will disable automatic route creation:

10. Once the application has been deployed, we can test how it behaves in the new environment, and once we are satisfied, we can proceed with the switchover.

   To achieve that, we click on the left-hand side vertical menu **Applications | Routes** and then click on the route named **blue-green-app**.

   We should now see the detail of the route, as follows:

11. On the page, in the top-right corner, there is a drill-down menu called **Actions**; click on it and select **Edit**.

On the **Edit** page, we change all the settings for the route, even the service layer that is pointing to, which is the one that we need to change to switch from the blue environment to the green environment, as depicted in the following screenshot:

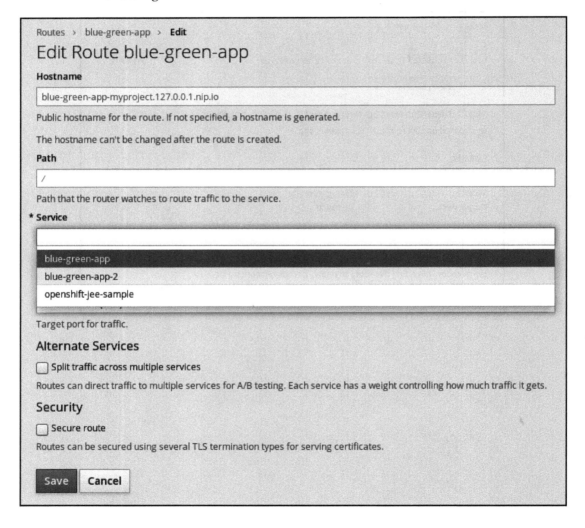

12. Then, click **Save**, and refresh the page of our application. We should now see the web page displaying some text in green, as follows:

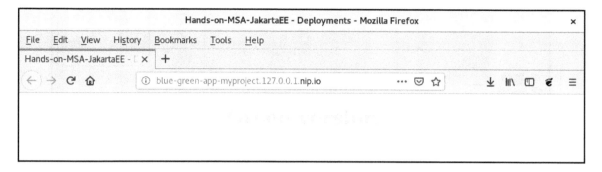

The URL for your current application didn't change, and the new fancy version is finally online.

Congratulations! You successfully performed a blue-green deployment.

Remember that if the data model between the two version changes even slightly, the blue-green deployment should be done in a different way, that is, by putting the blue version of the application in read-only mode and waiting for it to drain all the pending write requests, then switching to the new green version.

Canary deployment

Canary deployment is a technique that's used to gradually increase the load for the new version of the application.

Danilo Sato described this technique at the beginning of 2014, which was reported on Martin Fowler's site at `https://martinfowler.com/bliki/CanaryRelease.html`. The following is a quote that's been that's been taken from this site:

> *"A benefit of using canary releases is the ability to do capacity testing of the new version in a production environment with a safe rollback strategy if issues are found. By slowly ramping up the load, you can monitor and capture metrics about how the new version impacts the production environment. This is an alternative approach to creating an entirely separate capacity testing environment, because the environment will be as production-like as it can be."*

Here is a logical architecture of the canary deployment:

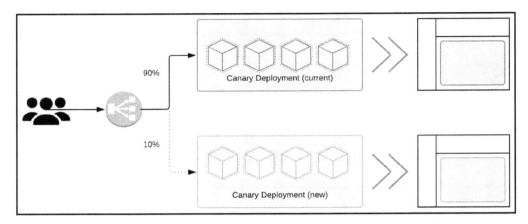

The key point here is to slowly increase the load for the application and monitor its behavior. This process may take a few hours or a few days; it depends on how fast you want to go, and the time your users need to adapt to these new changes.

From OpenShift's perspective, what has been done in the blue-green deployment example is still valid. So, in case you didn't follow the *Blue-green deployment* section, please do so, and then continue with these new instructions:

1. In **My Project**, in the left-hand sidebar, click on **Applications** | **Route** and select the route named **blue-green-app**.
2. In the top-right corner of the page, click on the drill-down menu named **Actions** and select **Edit**.

Scroll down to the bottom of the page and enable the check box that states **Split traffic across multiple services** in the **Alternate Services** section, as follows:

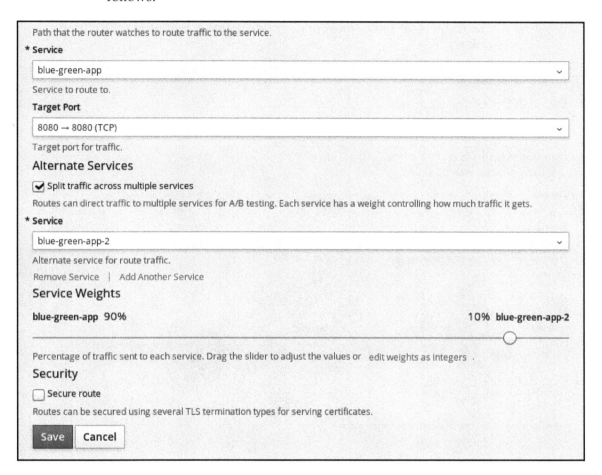

3. Set **Service** to **blue-green-app**, set the **Service Weights** so that **10%** of the load goes to **blue-green-app-2** and that the **90%** of the load goes to **blue-green-app**, and click the **Save** button at the bottom of the page.

The route page should now evidence how traffic is split graphically, as follows:

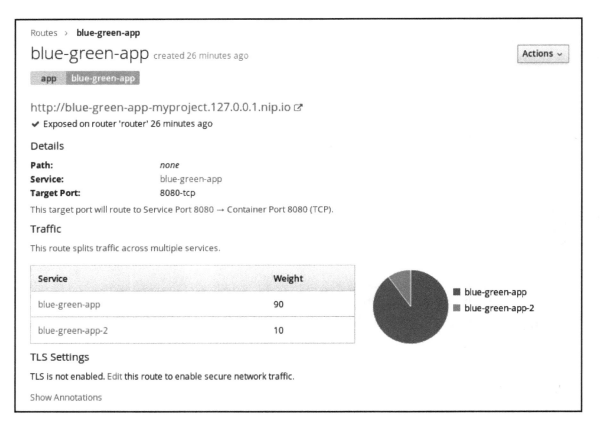

4. Try to reload our page 10 times. If you see the page with green text once, you successfully performed a canary deployment.

Once the audit and monitor tools fulfill your organization needs, you can gradually increase the load until a full rollout is reached, which means that only the green version is online.

A/B testing deployment

A/B testing deployment is a technique that's used to test features in your application.

This means that A/B testing is suitable for frontend applications that are introducing new interfaces, or changing the look and feel of the applications. Feedback from users is very important, thus doing it directly in production is the best test environment you can have. The users' reaction can show whether changes you have done are intuitive or not, and you can eventually adapt your software according to the feedback.

From OpenShift's perspective, this is literally the same as canary deployment, except that you set the weights between the two services to **50%** each:

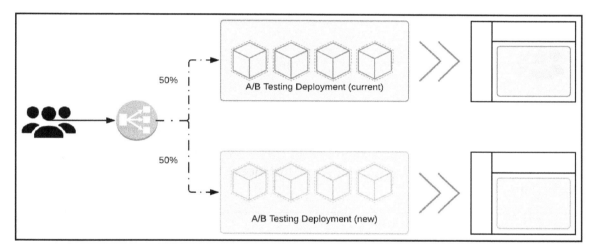

So, if you didn't follow `Chapter 8`, *Microservices Patterns*, please do so, and set **50%** for the service weights.

As you can see, in OpenShift, it is very easy to achieve such deployment techniques, as they all have the route component as the kingmaker.

Rolling deployment

Rolling deployment is a technique that's used to gradually replace the current application with the newer version of it.

This kind of deployment technique allows you to have no downtime during the update, but also requires you to have the old and the new versions of the application running at the same time. This is only possible with data model compatibility.

Here are three diagrams depicting the beginning, the process, and the final stage of the deployment. At first, one instance of the new version of the application is deployed:

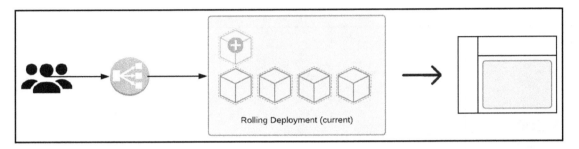

Once the new version of the application is ready to be used, which means that readiness and health checks are passed successfully, one instance of the old version is scheduled to be destroyed:

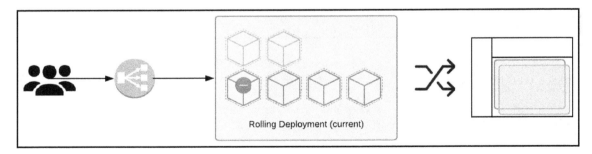

In the final stage, once the last expected instance of the new version of the application is ready to use, the last instance of the old version is destroyed, and only the new version is available:

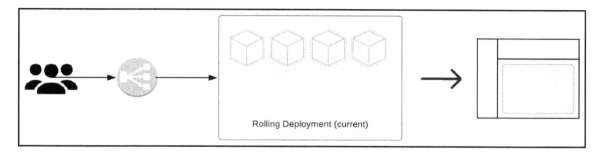

Summary

In this chapter, we went through the basic deployment strategy you can adopt in OpenShift to deploy your microservices.

We also described the basic concepts related to DevOps and the methodology that's used to release software through the environments, using CI and CD, and various deployment strategies such as blue-green, canary, A/B testing, and rolling deployment, describing how and when to use the most appropriate technique.

In the next chapter, we will see how we can monitor a platform running cloud native microservices, using metrics showing the status of the cluster. Of course, the monitoring section will be leveraged by open source tools such as Prometheus and Grafana.

10 Monitoring

Monitoring is a key point of any microservice architecture and, in particular, for any cloud-based architecture. No matter what, your architecture needs to have a monitoring platform so that it can constantly observe the performance of the system, its reliability, its resource availability and consumption, its security and storage, and so on.

However, choosing the correct platform can be difficult, because there are a lot of components that come into play. The tasks that are used to properly implement a monitoring solution platform are as follows:

- **Use one platform**: A platform that's capable of discovering and grasping information of the running systems, and aggregate the result in a comprehensive way using charts.
- **Identify metrics and events**: An application is responsible for exposing these metrics, and the platform should take only the ones that are the most relevant.
- **Split data**: Store application-monitoring data separately from infrastructure-monitoring data, but centralize the monitoring view.
- **Alert**: Provide alerts when limits are met, both for application and infrastructure. For example; when an application is performing slowly, and when the storage is running out of space.
- **Observe user experience**: Response times, throughput, latency, and errors.

In this chapter, we will cover the following topics:

- Prometheus
- Node-exporter
- Grafana

Prometheus

There are lots of different tools for different purposes, some of which provide some of the monitoring features that we described previously. New Relic, Dynatrace, and SolarWinds (just to mention a few) provide powerful SaaS-based monitoring and performance management for cloud environments. However, the most-used open source solution nowadays is called **Prometheus**.

Prometheus is 100% open source and community driven. All of the components are available under the Apache License, version 2.0, on GitHub. Prometheus is also a Cloud Native Computing Foundation member project.

Here are the features of Prometheus, taken directly from the Prometheus website (`https://prometheus.io/`):

- **Dimensional data**: Prometheus implements a highly dimensional data model. Time series are identified by a metric name and a set of key-value pairs.
- **Powerful queries**: PromQL allows for the slicing and dicing of collected time series data to generate ad hoc graphs, tables, and alerts.
- **Great visualization**: Prometheus has multiple modes for visualizing data built-in expression browser, Grafana integration, and a console template language.
- **Efficient storage**: Prometheus stores time series in-memory and on to a local disk in an efficient custom format. Scaling is achieved by functional sharding and federation.
- **Simple operation**: Each server is independent for reliability, relying only on local storage. Written in Go, all binaries are statically linked and easy to deploy.
- **Precise alerting**: Alerts are defined based on Prometheus's flexible PromQL and maintain dimensional information. An alert manager handles notifications and silencing.
- **Many client libraries**: Client libraries allow for the easy instrumentation of services. Over ten languages are supported already and custom libraries are easy to implement.
- **Many integrations**: Existing exporters allow for the bridging of third-party data into Prometheus. Examples include system statistics, as well as Docker, HAProxy, StatsD, and JMX metrics.

Installing Prometheus

1. Before installing Prometheus, make sure that your OpenShift cluster is up and running by issuing the following command:

```
./oc cluster status
Web console URL: https://127.0.0.1:8443/console/
Config is at host directory
Volumes are at host directory
Persistent volumes are at host directory
/opt/rh/okd/3.11/openshift.local.clusterup/openshift.local.pv
Data will be discarded when cluster is destroyed
```

2. Use the following code in case of failure:

```
Error: OpenShift cluster is not running
```

3. Start the cluster as follows:

```
./oc cluster up --server-loglevel=9
Getting a Docker client ...
Checking if image openshift/origin-control-plane:v3.11 is available
...
Checking type of volume mount ...
Determining server IP ...
Checking if OpenShift is already running ...
Checking for supported Docker version (=>1.22) ...
Checking if insecured registry is configured properly in Docker ...
Checking if required ports are available ...
Checking if OpenShift client is configured properly ...
Checking if image openshift/origin-control-plane:v3.11 is available
...
Starting OpenShift using openshift/origin-control-plane:v3.11 ...
...
Server Information ...
OpenShift server started.
The server is accessible via web console at:
https://127.0.0.1:8443
```

4. Once the cluster is available, login as developer, as follows:

```
./oc login -u developer -p developer
```

5. Create a project called `monitoring`:

```
./oc new-project monitoring
```

6. Now use project monitoring on the `https://127.0.0.1:8443` server. You can add applications to this project with the `new-app` command. For example, try the following:

```
oc new-app centos/ruby-25-
centos7~https://github.com/sclorg/ruby-ex.git
```

This will build a new example application in Ruby.

7. Now deploy the Prometheus platform, which is already available as a Docker image from the `Docker.io` repository, as follows:

```
./oc new-app prom/prometheus

--> Found Docker image 5517f70 (45 hours old) from Docker Hub for
"prom/prometheus"
```

An image stream tag will be created as `prometheus:latest`, which will track this image. This image will be deployed in the deployment config called `prometheus`. Port `9090/tcp` will be load-balanced by the `prometheus` service. Other containers can access this service through the `prometheus` host name. This image declares volumes and will default to use non-persistent, host-local storage.

8. You can add persistent volumes later by running `volume dc/prometheus --add ...`:

```
--> Creating resources ...
imagestream.image.openshift.io "prometheus" created
deploymentconfig.apps.openshift.io "prometheus" created
service "prometheus" created
--> Success
```

9. Expose the service by executing the following commands:

```
'oc expose svc/prometheus'
```

10. Run `oc status` to view your app.

11. Let's point the browser on the Web console and check the overview of the Prometheus deployment.

The Web console should look as follows:

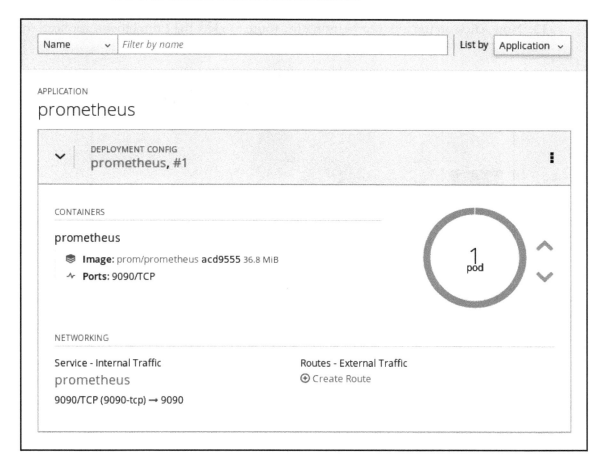

12. The Prometheus platform is still not available, so its service needs to be exported as `route`, as follows:

```
./oc expose service prometheus

route.route.openshift.io/prometheus exposed
```

13. Now, click on the link representing the route to view the Prometheus application. The page should be similar to the following:

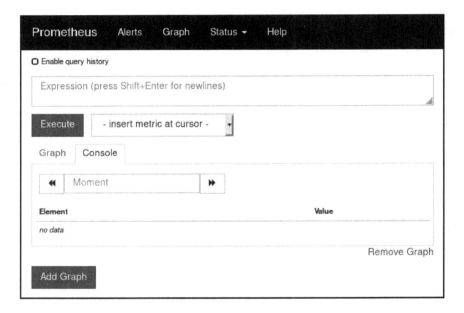

14. To see where Prometheus is grasping the metrics from, select the voice **Targets** from the **Status** menu item, as follows:

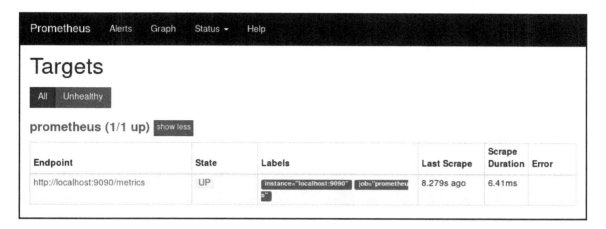

As you can see, Prometheus is grasping metrics from itself.

15. To see all of the available metrics, set the context path of the Prometheus application to `metrics`, and you should see a long list of metrics, along with their values.

> A full reference of the metrics can be found at `https://github.com/PacktPublishing/Hands-On-Cloud-Native-Microservices-with-Jakarta-EE/tree/master/ch10/metrics`

16. If you try to execute the PromQL `process_cpu_seconds_total`, which corresponds to the total user and system CPU time spent in seconds, you should see the **Graph**, as depicted in the following screenshot:

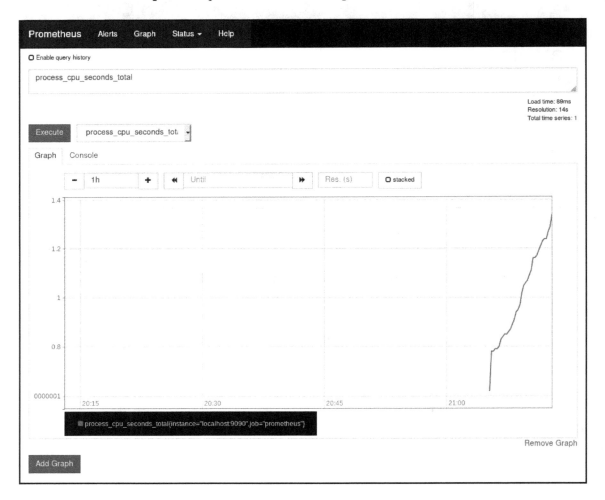

As you can see, the look and feel of the Prometheus interface is not the best that you will desire—that's why most the monitoring dashboard relies on Grafana. We will talk about Grafana later in this chapter.

Before installing Grafana, it is worth mentioning that the metrics provided by Prometheus are not enough for a containers-based cloud solution such as OpenShift. Metrics regarding hosts, containers, and pods are mandatory. For this purpose, the Node-exporter comes into play.

Node-exporter

Node-exporter is a tool that exposes metrics regarding the Linux kernel server. These metrics are about CPU utilization and memory processes, and can be imported into Prometheus in a time series fashion so that they can be represented graphically.

Installing Node-exporter

Installing Node-exporter is very easy, as we can use its Docker image directly, which is available in the Docker.io referencing it on the OpenShift command:

1. To install Node-exporter, issue the following commands:

```
./oc new-app prom/node-exporter
--> Found Docker image b3e7f67 (7 weeks old) from Docker Hub for
"prom/node-exporter"
```

An image stream tag will be created called node-exporter:latest, which will track this image. This image will be deployed in the deployment config file node-exporter. Port 9100/tcp/ will be load-balanced by the node-exporter service.

2. Other containers can access this service through the node-exporter host name:

```
--> Creating resources ...
imagestream.image.openshift.io "node-exporter" created
deploymentconfig.apps.openshift.io "node-exporter" created
service "node-exporter" created
--> Success
```

3. You can expose the service by executing the following commands:

```
'oc expose svc/node-exporter'
```

4. Run `oc status` to view your app. To expose the `node-exporter`, use the following code:

```
./oc expose service node-exporter

route.route.openshift.io/node-exporter exposed
```

Exposing the `node-exporter` via route is just for testing purposes. What we really need is to have Prometheus grasp the metrics provided by Node-exporter.

To achieve such a configuration, the configuration file of Prometheus needs to be updated.

5. If you access the Prometheus pod, you will be able to see the current configuration, as follows:

```
./oc get pods

NAME READY STATUS RESTARTS AGE

node-exporter-1-lgpz2 1/1 Running 0 6m

prometheus-1-qgggp 1/1 Running 0 6h

./oc rsh prometheus-1-qgggp

$ ls -la

total 16

drwxr-xr-x 1 nobody nogroup 4096 Jan 15 20:13 .

drwxr-xr-x 1 root root 4096 Jan 19 14:36 ..

lrwxrwxrwx 1 nobody nogroup 39 Jan 15 20:13 console_libraries ->
/usr/share/prometheus/console_libraries

lrwxrwxrwx 1 nobody nogroup 31 Jan 15 20:13 consoles ->
/usr/share/prometheus/consoles/

lrwxrwxrwx 1 root root 11 Jan 15 20:13 data -> /prometheus

-rw-r--r-- 1 nobody nogroup 926 Jan 15 20:09 prometheus.yml

$ cat prometheus.yml
# my global config
```

```
global:

scrape_interval: 15s
evaluation_interval: 15s

# Alertmanager configuration
alerting:
alertmanagers:
- static_configs:
- targets:

rule_files:
# - "first_rules.yml"
# - "second_rules.yml"

scrape_configs:
- job_name: 'prometheus'
# metrics_path defaults to '/metrics'
# scheme defaults to 'http'.
static_configs:
- targets: ['localhost:9090']
```

Prometheus's configuration needs the following settings to be loaded:

```
- job_name: 'node-exporter'
  static_configs:
    - targets: ['node-exporter:9100']
```

6. These new settings can be placed into a `ConfigMap` and mounted as a volume.

7. Create a `prometheus.yaml` file with the following content:

```
global:
scrape_interval: 15s
evaluation_interval: 15s

alerting:
alertmanagers:
- static_configs:
- targets:

rule_files:
# - "first_rules.yml"
# - "second_rules.yml"

scrape_configs:
- job_name: 'prometheus'
  static_configs:
    - targets: ['localhost:9090']
```

```
- job_name: 'node-exporter'
  static_configs:
    - targets: ['node-exporter:9100']
```

8. Save the file and issue the following command:

```
./oc create configmap prometheus-config-map --from-
file=prometheus.yaml
configmap/prometheus-config-map created
```

Now we need to set the `ConfigMap` in the Prometheus deployment.

9. To do that, select the **Prometheus deployment** from the Web console and edit the YAML configuration. This will add the reference of the `ConfigMap` and set the updated configuration file. You can look at the code of the YAML file at this URL: `https://github.com/PacktPublishing/Hands-On-Cloud-Native-Microservices-with-Jakarta-EE/blob/master/ch10/prometheus-dc.yaml`.

These new settings allows Prometheus to load the new configuration file coming from `ConfigMap`.

10. Now a new Prometheus deployment should be triggered automatically, as follows:

The new Prometheus deployment after loading the new configuration file

11. Going back to the Prometheus application, we should see the `node-exporter` available on Prometheus, as depicted in the following screenshot:

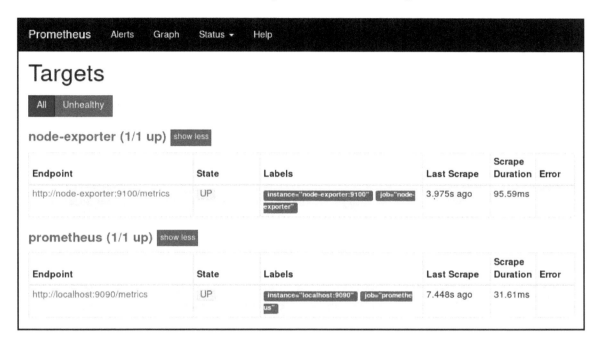

Now it's time to import everything using Grafana.

Grafana

Prometheus's best friend is Grafana. Grafana is open source, and so it provides a great interface for creating and exposing dashboards. It is mainly used for visualizing time series data with charts, pie charts, plots, bars, and gauges.

Grafana supports querying Prometheus. The Grafana data source for Prometheus has been included since Grafana 2.5.0, which was published on October 28, 2015.

Nonetheless, in a cloud container environment, infrastructure metrics are a must, so keeping an eye on the host running the containers must be a key point of the monitoring view.

There is an exporter of such metrics called Node-exporter, which exposes machine-level metrics from the system's kernel, CPU, memory, disk space, disk I/O, network bandwidth, and motherboard temperature.

Installing Grafana

Installing Grafana is very easy, as we can directly use its Docker image, which is available in the Docker.io referencing it on the OpenShift command given in the following steps:

1. First of all, we need to deploy Grafana on OpenShift by issuing the following commands:

   ```
   ./oc new-app grafana/grafana

   --> Found Docker image d0454da (3 days old) from Docker Hub for
   "grafana/grafana"
   ```

   An image stream tag will be created called grafana:latest, which will track this image. This image will be deployed in the deployment config grafana. Port 3000/tcp will be load-balanced by the grafana service.

2. Other containers can access this service through the grafana host name:

   ```
   --> Creating resources ...

   imagestream.image.openshift.io "grafana" created

   deploymentconfig.apps.openshift.io "grafana" created

   service "grafana" created

   --> Success
   ```

3. You can expose this service by executing the following command:

   ```
   'oc expose svc/grafana'
   ```

4. Run oc status to view your app. This will expose it, as follows:

   ```
   ./oc expose service grafana

   route.route.openshift.io/grafana exposed
   ```

5. Now open your browser and point it to the route that's displayed in the Web console.

   By default, Grafana is secured, and you can log in by providing the username and password for `admin`.

6. Next, you will be prompted to change the default password. Set it to be anything of your choice.

7. Next, Grafana asks you to set a data source, as depicted in the following screenshot:

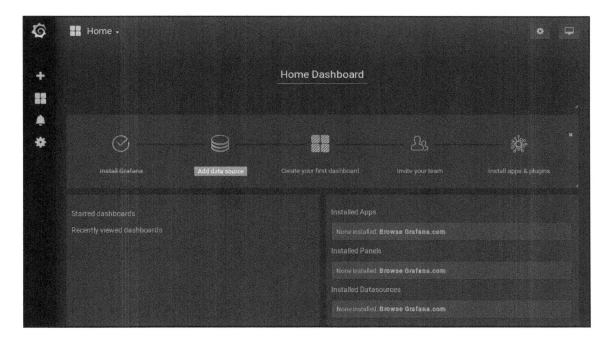

8. Select the Prometheus **Data Sources**:

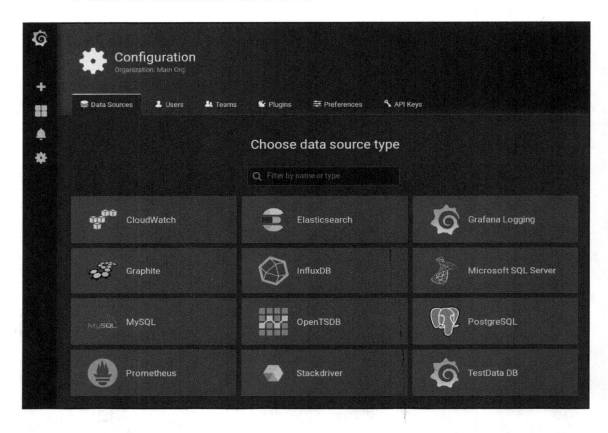

9. Add the following settings:

10. For the **URL**, you should set the Prometheus service name, not the route. **Save & Test** the settings, and then click **Back**.

11. Select the **Prometheus** box and then select the **Dashboards** tab, as shown in the following screenshot:

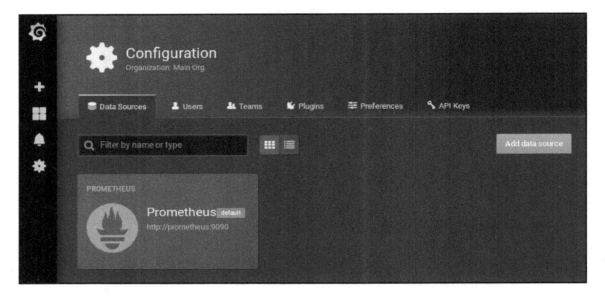

12. Import all the available statistics:

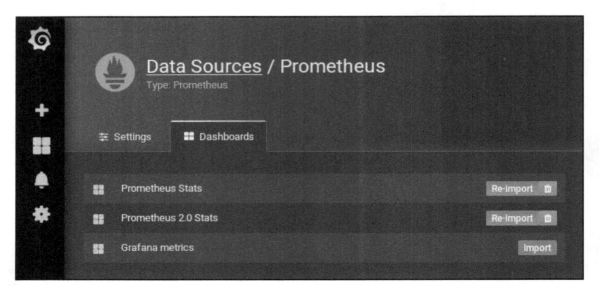

13. By clicking on **Prometheus 2.0 Stats**, you should now see a better monitoring interface:

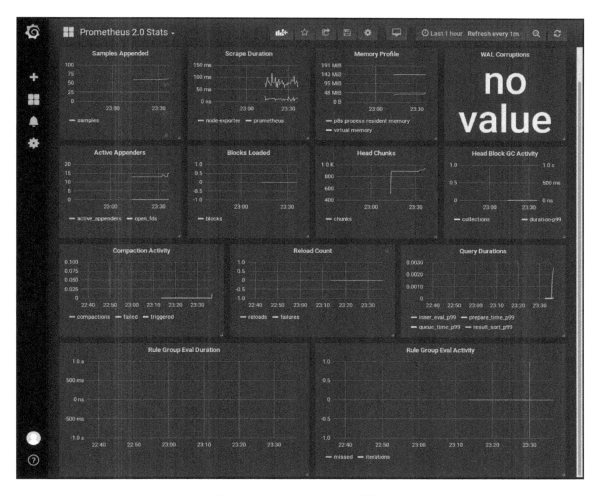

The monitoring interface data on Prometheus 2.0 Stat

This is definitely a better look and feel than the one that's provided by Prometheus. In addition, Grafana provides a series of plugins that you can use for your graphs through its website.

Summary

This was the final chapter of this book. You learned how to deploy and configure a monitoring platform for containers, like Prometheus. You also learned how to extend Prometheus's capabilities by integrating with the `node-exporter` extension. Finally, you learned how to deploy and configure Grafana to graphically display all of the metrics that were collected and stored by Prometheus.

Here comes the end of our long journey. I hope you enjoyed reading this book!

11
Building Microservices Using Spring Boot 2

During the journey that we have made together in this book, we have seen how Java, Jakarta EE, and MicroProfile.io are rapidly evolving to enable those who have built their software architectures using Java EE to build cloud-ready applications.

Our purpose was not to indicate that one development platform is better than another. Our intent was to try to remove many pre-judgments of Jakarta EE and MicroProfile.io, based on feedback related to obsolete versions of Java EE and its monolithic architecture model.

For that reason, in this appendix, we will look at how to create, through Spring Boot, the same microservices that were developed in the previous chapters.

You can find the code for this chapter in the GitHub repository, at `https://github.com/PacktPublishing/Hands-On-Cloud-Native-Microservices-with-Jakarta-EE/tree/master/appendix-A`

Spring Boot

Spring Boot is a great framework that can help developers easily build and run microservices and cloud-native applications.

Historically, it represented the first alternative to Java EE, and, in my opinion, it usually implements new architectural design patterns in a production-ready way.

Over the years, it has evolved to overcome the main critical issues advanced by the project's open source community, which are as follows:

- There are too many XML configuration files needed to implement it
- It is a difficult way to manage the interdependencies between Spring modules

As it was described for Thorntail, Spring Boot can be executed by using the following methods:

- Using an executable JAR file, via the `$ java -jar` command, with the following embedded servlet containers:
    - Tomcat 8.5
    - Jetty 9.4
    - Undertow 1.4
- Via traditional WAR deployments into any application servers or servlet containers that implement the Servlet 3.1+ specifications

The latest release (which, at the time of writing, is v2.0.5) provides build support using Maven or Gradle; it requires Java 8 or higher to run, and it is also based on the Spring 5.0.9 release representing the main core.

Maven settings

Apache Maven is probably the most common build management system: we can consider it the de facto build and package operation for Java applications. In this section, we will use it to build and package our application.

Spring Boot is compatible with Apache Maven 3.2 or higher, and, in order to easily manage all of the Spring Boot dependencies (in particular, the right versions), you can set your Maven POM file to inherit from the `spring-boot-starter-parent` project.

The following is an example of a `pom.xml` file that you can use in your Spring Boot application:

```
<?xml version="1.0" encoding="UTF-8"?>
<project xmlns="http://maven.apache.org/POM/4.0.0"
xmlns:xsi="http://www.w3.org/2001/XMLSchema-instance"
xsi:schemaLocation="http://maven.apache.org/POM/4.0.0 http://maven.apache.
org/xsd/maven-4.0.0.xsd">

    <modelVersion>4.0.0</modelVersion>
    <groupId>com.example</groupId>
    <artifactId>myproject</artifactId>
    <version>0.0.1-SNAPSHOT</version>

    <!-- Inherit defaults from Spring Boot -->
    <parent>
        <groupId>org.springframework.boot</groupId>
        <artifactId>spring-boot-starter-parent</artifactId>
```

```
            <version>2.0.5.RELEASE</version>
    </parent>

    <!-- Add typical dependencies for a web application -->
    <dependencies>
        <dependency>
            <groupId>org.springframework.boot</groupId>
            <artifactId>spring-boot-starter-web</artifactId>
        </dependency>
    </dependencies>

    <!-- Package as an executable jar -->
    <build>
        <plugins>
            <plugin>
                <groupId>org.springframework.boot</groupId>
                <artifactId>spring-boot-maven-plugin</artifactId>
            </plugin>
        </plugins>
    </build>
</project>
```

As usual, you will be able to build and package your application with the following command:

```
$ mvn clean package
```

Gradle settings

Gradle is an open source build automation tool that uses scripts written in Groovy or Kotlin DSL. It's supported by the major IDEs, and you can run it using command-line interfaces, or through a continuous integration server.

Once it has been installed, you can create a new project (or automatically convert an existing Maven project into a Gradle one) by launching the following command from your project's root:

```
$ gradle init
```

In order to use Spring Boot in a Gradle project, you can create a Gradle file such as the following:

```
plugins {
    id 'org.springframework.boot' version '2.0.5.RELEASE'
    id 'java'
}

jar {
    baseName = 'myproject'
    version = '0.0.1-SNAPSHOT'
}

repositories {
    jcenter()
}

dependencies {
    implementation 'org.springframework.boot:spring-boot-
dependencies:2.0.5.RELEASE'
    implementation 'org.springframework.boot:spring-boot-starter-web'
    testImplementation 'org.springframework.boot:spring-boot-starter-test'
}
```

In this XML file, I added the `Spring Boot BOM` file as the first dependency, with the specified Spring Boot version, in order to use the right versions of all Spring Boot modules.

To build the executable JAR file, you can execute the following command:

```
$ ./gradlew mySpringBootJar
```

After that, you can run it by executing the following command:

```
$ java -jar build/libs/gradle-my-spring-boot-project.jar
```

Or you can execute the following Gradle command:

```
$ ./gradlew bootRun
```

Upgrading from an earlier version of Spring Boot

Spring Boot implements a features that enable the developers to analyze the application's environment and print the results at application start up. It can also do an automatic migration of the application properties, using `properties migrator starter`.

To activate the environment, you should add the following Maven dependency to your project:

```
<dependency>
    <groupId>org.springframework.boot</groupId>
    <artifactId>spring-boot-properties-migrator</artifactId>
    <scope>runtime</scope>
</dependency>
```

Once you have completed the analysis and the migration, make sure you remove this module from your project's dependencies.

Building Spring Boot microservices

In this section, we will implement the same football player microservice that we built in `Chapter 4`, *Building Microservices Using Thorntail*. We will analyze the details of the server-side layer of the application, (since the client layer remains the same, implemented using Angular 6).

The result will be a simple football player microservice that handles the football player domain; it will expose CRUD APIs, and it will store and retrieve information using a PostgreSQL database.

You can complete the entire application that was built in `Chapter 4`, *Building Microservices Using Thorntail,* using the approach that we will implement in this chapter.

To build our application, we will use the following tools, and for each one, we will specify the information needed to install it:

- **Apache Maven 3.5.4**: (`https://maven.apache.org/install.html`).
- **JDK 1.8.0_171** (`http://openjdk.java.net/install/`): you are free to use Oracle JDK or OpenJDK, but we recommend OpenJDK.
- **Spring Boot 2.0.5**: We will describe the instructions to install this later on.
- **Docker Community Edition 18.06.1**(`https://docs.docker.com/install/`): this is used to easily install and use the different databases needed for our application.

Project details

In this section, we will build the source code for our microservice. In order to do so, in addition to the prerequisites described previously, you will need PostgreSQL installed on your system. As I mentioned earlier, we will use Docker to install and handle PostgreSQL. I'm using a macOS High Sierra as my working environment. If you have implemented the same project using Thorntail (as described in Chapter 4, *Building Microservices Using Thorntail*, feel free to skip this section; otherwise, follow the instructions that describe how to install and run PostgreSQL in a Docker container.

Database installation and configuration

After installing Docker on your machine, it will be time to run the containerized version of PostgreSQL. In order to do so, open a new Terminal window and launch the following command:

```
$ docker run --name postgres_springboot -e POSTGRES_PASSWORD=postgresPwd -e
POSTGRES_DB=football_players_registry -d -p 5532:5432 postgres
```

This command triggers a pull from Docker's public registry for the PostgreSQL version labelled as the latest, downloading all of the layers that it needs to run the container on, as shown in the following code snippet:

```
Unable to find image 'postgres:latest' locally
latest: Pulling from library/postgres
683abbb4ea60: Pull complete
c5856e38168a: Pull complete
c3e6f1ceebb0: Pull complete
3303bcd00128: Pull complete
ea95ff44bf6e: Pull complete
ea3f31f1e620: Pull complete
234873881fb2: Pull complete
f020aa822d21: Pull complete
27bad92d09a5: Pull complete
6849f0681f5a: Pull complete
a112faac8662: Pull complete
bc92d0ab9365: Pull complete
9e87959714b8: Pull complete
ac7c29b2bea7: Pull complete
Digest:
sha256:d99f15cb8d0f47f0a66274afe30102b5bb7a95464d1e25acb66ccf7bd7bd8479
Status: Downloaded newer image for postgres:latest
83812c6e76656f6abab5bf1f00f07dca7105d5227df3b3b66382659fa55b5077
```

After that, the PostgreSQL image will be launched as a container. To verify this, you can launch the $ docker ps -a command, giving you a list of the created containers and their relative statuses:

```
CONTAINER ID IMAGE COMMAND CREATED
073daeefc52 postgres "docker-entrypoint.s..." Less than a second ago
STATUS PORTS NAMES
Up 4 seconds 0.0.0.0:5532->5432/tcp postgres_springboot
```

I had to split the command result into two lines, in order to make it readable.

You can also check the container logs, in order to retrieve information about the PostgreSQL status. Launch the following command:

```
$ docker logs -f 1073daeefc52
```

1073daeefc52 is the container ID. You should see the following information:

```
PostgreSQL init process complete; ready for start up.

2018-07-13 22:53:36.465 UTC [1] LOG: listening on IPv4 address "0.0.0.0",
port 5432
 2018-07-13 22:53:36.466 UTC [1] LOG: listening on IPv6 address "::", port
5432
 2018-07-13 22:53:36.469 UTC [1] LOG: listening on Unix socket
"/var/run/postgresql/.s.PGSQL.5432"
```

Now it's time to connect to the container, in order to manage it. Launch the following command:

```
$ docker exec -it 1073daeefc52 bash
```

1073daeefc52 is the container ID. Now log in to PostgreSQL with the following command:

```
$ psql -U postgres
```

Now you will be able to interact with the database server, as follows:

```
psql (10.4 (Debian 10.4-2.pgdg90+1))
Type "help" for help.
postgres=#
```

You should be able to see the `football_players_registry` database that we created when we created the container. Run the `\l` command to verify the list of databases:

```
postgres=# \l
                                    List of databases
             Name             |  Owner   | Encoding |  Collate   |
Ctype |   Access privileges
------------------------------+----------+----------+------------+---------
---+-----------------------
 football_players_registry | postgres | UTF8     | en_US.utf8 | en_US.utf8
|
 postgres                     | postgres | UTF8     | en_US.utf8 | en_US.utf8
|
 template0                    | postgres | UTF8     | en_US.utf8 | en_US.utf8
| =c/postgres                 +
                              |          |          |            |
postgres=CTc/postgres
 template1                    | postgres | UTF8     | en_US.utf8 | en_US.utf8
| =c/postgres                 +
                              |          |          |            |
postgres=CTc/postgres
(4 rows)
```

OK; it's time to create a simple table that will host the football players' data. Connect to the `football_players` database with the following command:

$ \connect football_players_registry

Create the table with the following command:

```
CREATE TABLE FOOTBALL_PLAYER(
ID SERIAL PRIMARY KEY NOT NULL,
NAME VARCHAR(50) NOT NULL,
SURNAME VARCHAR(50) NOT NULL,
AGE INT NOT NULL,
TEAM VARCHAR(50) NOT NULL,

POSITION VARCHAR(50) NOT NULL,
PRICE NUMERIC
);
```

Check the table's structure with the following command:

$ \d+ football_player

You should see the following result:

```
football_players_registry=# \d+ football_player
                        Table "public.football_player"
  Column  | Type | Collation | Nullable | Default | Storage  | Stats target |
Description
----------+----------------------+----------+----------+---------+-----------------------
------------------------+----------+---------------+-------------
 id   | integer |   | not null | nextval('football_player_id_seq'::regclass) |
plain |     |     |
 name  | character varying(50) | | not null | | extended |           |
 surname  | character varying(50) | | not null | | extended |           |
 age   | integer | | not null | | plain | |
 team  | character varying(50) | | not null | | extended | |
 position | character varying(50) | | not null | | extended |     |
 price | numeric | | | | main | |
Indexes:
      "football_player_pkey" PRIMARY KEY, btree (id)
```

Creating the source code

We have installed and configured everything that's necessary to create our microservice to manage the registry of players. Now it's time to write the code that's needed to expose our microservice APIs.

We will use the Spring Initializr project generator utility (`https://start.spring.io/`) in order to get a project skeleton to work on. Our microservice, as we described previously, will have to display the APIs that allow us to perform CRUD operations.

To implement our microservice, we will use the following components:

- **Web**: This contains all the modules needed for full web development with a Tomcat servlet container and Spring MVC.
- **Actuator**: This provides production-ready features, to help you monitor and manage your application.
- **DevTools**: These are Spring Boot development tools.
- **JPA**: This is the Java Persistence API, including `spring-data-jpa`, `spring-orm`, and Hibernate.
- **PostgreSQL**: This is the PostgreSQL JDBC driver.

We will use `com.packtpub.springboot` as the Maven **Group** name of the project, and `football-player-microservice` as the **Artifact**. Set these values in the project form generator, as depicted in the following screenshot:

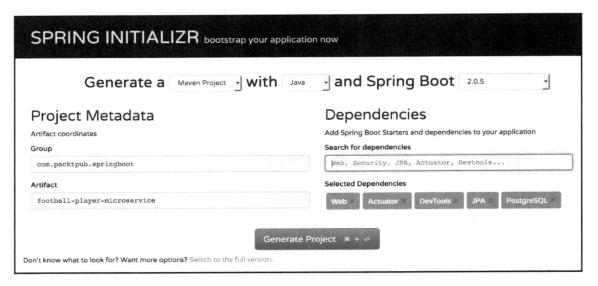

Click on **Generate Project** to create and download the ZIP file with the project skeleton.

Unzip the file to a directory of your choice, and open the Maven project with your favorite IDE (Eclipse, NetBeans, IntelliJ, and so on).

The core element of the project is the Maven `pom.xml` file, which contains all of the dependencies needed to implement our microservice.

The project uses `spring-boot-starter-parent` to correctly manage dependency management, as follows:

```
<parent>
    <groupId>org.springframework.boot</groupId>
    <artifactId>spring-boot-starter-parent</artifactId>
    <version>2.0.5.RELEASE</version>
    <relativePath/> <!-- lookup parent from repository -->
</parent>
```

We will also change the value of the project name from `football-player-microservice` to `Spring Boot Football player microservice`:

```
<modelVersion>4.0.0</modelVersion>
<groupId>com.packtpub.springboot</groupId>
<artifactId>football-player-microservice</artifactId>
<version>0.0.1-SNAPSHOT</version>
<packaging>jar</packaging>

<name>Spring Boot Football player microservice</name>
<description>Demo project for Spring Boot</description>
```

Before launching our first build, we need to set the database settings, in order to disable the default behaviour of Spring Boot to instantiate an in-memory database.

So, let's go into the `src/main/resources` directory and set this value inside the `application.properties` file, as follows:

```
## Spring DATASOURCE (DataSourceAutoConfiguration & DataSourceProperties)

spring.datasource.driver-class-name=org.postgresql.Driver

spring.datasource.url=jdbc:postgresql://localhost:5532/football_players_reg
istry

spring.datasource.username= postgres

spring.datasource.password=postgresPwd

# This property always initialize the database using sql scripts set under
resources directory

spring.datasource.initialization-mode=always

# The SQL dialect makes Hibernate generate better SQL for the chosen
database

spring.jpa.properties.hibernate.dialect=org.hibernate.dialect.PostgreSQLDia
lect

spring.jpa.properties.hibernate.jdbc.lob.non_contextual_creation=true

spring.jpa.hibernate.ddl-auto=none
```

Now it's time to launch the first build, with the following command:

```
$ mvn clean package
```

In this way, we will download all of the dependencies and create the Uber JAR **Artifact,** named `football-player-microservice-0.0.1-SNAPSHOT.jar`.

To check that the project is ready to be used, we can run it by using the following command:

```
$ java -jar target/football-player-microservice-0.0.1-SNAPSHOT.jar
```

We can see that Spring Boot is running, and that the application is deployed:

We have not yet implemented a RESTful API; for that reason, we will use the actuator health check to verify that the application has started correctly.

Invoke `http://localhost:8080/actuator/health`, and check that the result is **STATUS: "UP"**, as shown in the following screenshot:

Now let's stop the Tomcat that was created by Spring Boot, using the *Ctrl + C* command, and start to update our project.

Entity class – JPA

We need a domain model object to map the records inserted into our database. To do this, we will use the JPA specification; so, we will create an entity class for this purpose.

Let's create a new Java package to store the domain model object, and name it `model`. The fully qualified package name will be
`com.packtpub.springboot.footballplayermicroservice.model`.

Next, we will build the domain class, named `FootballPlayer`:

```java
...

import java.io.Serializable;
import java.math.BigInteger;
import javax.persistence.Basic;
import javax.persistence.Column;
import javax.persistence.Entity;
import javax.persistence.GeneratedValue;
import javax.persistence.GenerationType;
import javax.persistence.Id;
import javax.persistence.NamedQueries;
import javax.persistence.NamedQuery;
import javax.persistence.Table;
import javax.validation.constraints.NotNull;
import javax.validation.constraints.Size;
import javax.xml.bind.annotation.XmlRootElement;

/**
 * Domain model class that maps the data stored into football_player table
 * inside database.
 *
 * @author Mauro Vocale
 * @version 1.0.0 29/09/2018
 */
@Entity
@Table(name = "football_player")
@XmlRootElement
@NamedQueries({
@NamedQuery(name = "FootballPlayer.findAll", query
= "SELECT f FROM FootballPlayer f")
})
public class FootballPlayer implements Serializable {

    private static final long serialVersionUID = -92346781936044228L;

    @Id
    @GeneratedValue(strategy = GenerationType.IDENTITY)
    @Basic(optional = false)
    @Column(name = "id")
    private Integer id;

    @Basic(optional = false)
```

```java
@NotNull
@Size(min = 1, max = 50)
@Column(name = "name")
private String name;

@Basic(optional = false)
@NotNull
@Size(min = 1, max = 50)
@Column(name = "surname")
private String surname;

@Basic(optional = false)
@NotNull
@Column(name = "age")
private int age;

@Basic(optional = false)
@NotNull
@Size(min = 1, max = 50)
@Column(name = "team")
private String team;

@Basic(optional = false)
@NotNull
@Size(min = 1, max = 50)
@Column(name = "position")
private String position;

@Column(name = "price")
private BigInteger price;

public FootballPlayer() {
}

public FootballPlayer(String name, String surname, int age,
    String team, String position, BigInteger price) {
    this.name = name;
    this.surname = surname;
    this.age = age;
    this.team = team;
    this.position = position;
    this.price = price;
}

...
```

As you can see, this code is same as the code created in `Chapter 4`, *Building Microservices Using Thorntail*. This means that you can use JPA specifications not only in Java EE/Jakarta EE projects, but also with the Spring framework. The specifications are always portable.

Repository – JPA

Spring Data JPA has a compelling feature: the ability to create repository implementations from a repository interface automatically at runtime.

If you create a custom repository that extends the `org.springframework.data.repository.CrudRepository` interface, you can inherit several methods to work with your entity persistence, including methods for saving, deleting, and finding your entities.

So, let's start to create our custom repository implementation.

Build a new repository interface, named `FootballPlayerRepository`, under the `com.packtpub.springboot.footballplayermicroservice.repository` package, and remember to extend the `org.springframework.data.repository.CrudRepository` interface:

```
import org.springframework.data.repository.CrudRepository;

/**
 * FootballPlayerRepository extends the CrudRepository interface.

 * The type of entity and ID that it works with, FootballPlayer and Integer,
 are

 * specified in the generic parameters on CrudRepository.
 * By extending CrudRepository, FootballPlayerRepository inherits several

 * methods for working with FootballPlayer persistence, including methods
 for

 * saving, deleting, and finding FootballPlayer entities.
 *
 * @author Mauro Vocale
 * @version 30/09/2018
 */
public interface FootballPlayerRepository extends
CrudRepository<FootballPlayer, Integer> {

}
```

To complete managing the database access operations, we need to create the files that are needed to build the database schema and to populate the tables. We will use the Spring Boot database initialization naming convention to do it; thus, we will create the following files under the `src/main/resources` directory:

- `schema.sql`: The file with the table creation SQL commands
- `data.sql`: The file with the SQL insert data commands

In this case, we will not configure the `persistence.xml` file, like we did for the Java EE/Jakarta EE project, since all of the required information is inside the `application.properties` and `*.sql` files.

Now run the application again, using the following command:

```
$ mvn spring-boot:run
```

You will notice that the SQL creation schema and load data scripts were performed by the embedded Tomcat run by Spring Boot, as shown in the following code snippet:

```
2018-09-30 00:20:46.424 INFO 7148 --- [ost-startStop-1]
o.s.jdbc.datasource.init.ScriptUtils : Executing SQL script from URL
[file:/Users/mvocale/Progetti/Hands_on_Cloud_Native_Microservices_with_Java
_EE/appendix-A/football-player-microservice/target/classes/schema.sql]
2018-09-30 00:20:46.433 INFO 7148 --- [ost-startStop-1]
o.s.jdbc.datasource.init.ScriptUtils : Executed SQL script from URL
[file:/Users/mvocale/Progetti/Hands_on_Cloud_Native_Microservices_with_Java
_EE/appendix-A/football-player-microservice/target/classes/schema.sql] in 9
ms.
2018-09-30 00:20:46.437 INFO 7148 --- [ost-startStop-1]
o.s.jdbc.datasource.init.ScriptUtils : Executing SQL script from URL
[file:/Users/mvocale/Progetti/Hands_on_Cloud_Native_Microservices_with_Java
_EE/appendix-A/football-player-microservice/target/classes/data.sql]
2018-09-30 00:20:46.467 INFO 7148 --- [ost-startStop-1]
o.s.jdbc.datasource.init.ScriptUtils : Executed SQL script from URL
[file:/Users/mvocale/Progetti/Hands_on_Cloud_Native_Microservices_with_Java
_EE/appendix-A/football-player-microservice/target/classes/data.sql] in 30
ms.
```

You can also verify the database status with a simple query—for example, SELECT * FROM football_player, which must return all of the values preloaded with the data.sql file.

The RESTful web service

The Spring framework offers an intuitive and easy-to-use model to expose your data, using the RESTful web service, which is the de facto standard for API communication between microservices.

The version that we will use in this section, the 2.0.5 release, automatically exposes CRUD operations as a RESTful API.

As we described in the *Repository – JPA* section, our `FootballPlayerRepository` interface extends the `org.springframework.data.repository.CrudRepository`, from which it inherits the following methods:

```
    ...

    public <S extends T> S save(S s);

    public <S extends T> Iterable<S> saveAll(Iterable<S> itrbl);

    public Optional<T> findById(ID id);

    public boolean existsById(ID id);

    public Iterable<T> findAll();

    public Iterable<T> findAllById(Iterable<ID> itrbl);

    public long count();

    public void deleteById(ID id);

    public void delete(T t);

    public void deleteAll(Iterable<? extends T> itrbl);

    public void deleteAll();
```

Using the `Spring Data Rest` module, as I mentioned previously, you can automatically expose those methods. In order to do so, you should insert the `spring-boot-starter-data-rest` dependency into your Maven `pom.xml` file, as follows:

```
<dependency>
    <groupId>org.springframework.boot</groupId>
    <artifactId>spring-boot-starter-data-rest</artifactId>
</dependency>
```

Then compile and run your project, as follows:

```
$ mvn clean package && mvn spring-boot:run
```

You will be able to obtain the links for the APIs available in your application. If you open a browser and call `http://localhost:8080/`, you will obtain the links to `http://localhost:8080/footballPlayers`, as shown in the following screenshot:

By invoking `http://localhost:8080/footballPlayers`, you will obtain a list of the football players stored in the application, as follows:

```
{
    "_embedded" : {
      "footballPlayers" : [ {
      "name" : "Gianluigi",
      "surname" : "Buffon",
      "age" : 40,
      "team" : "Paris Saint Germain",
      "position" : "goalkeeper",
      "price" : 2,
      "_links" : {
      "self" : {
        "href" : "http://localhost:8080/footballPlayers/1"
      },
      "footballPlayer" : {
        "href" : "http://localhost:8080/footballPlayers/1"
      }
    }
  },
  {
    "name" : "Manuel",
    "surname" : "Neuer",
    "age" : 32,
    "team" : "Bayern Munchen",
    "position" : "goalkeeper",
```

```
    "price" : 35,
    "_links" : {
      "self" : {
        "href" : "http://localhost:8080/footballPlayers/2"
        },
      "footballPlayer" : {
        "href" : "http://localhost:8080/footballPlayers/2"
      }
    }
  },
  ...
}
```

Otherwise, in this section we will define the old-style approach: I will create a service and controller class, in order to invoke the JPA layer (the repository) and expose the API. Due to a bug present in the SpringFox framework, it is impossible to document the API using Swagger, one of the key features of a good microservice. I will therefore follow the scenario that was described earlier, while waiting for the bug to be resolved.

First of all, I will create a service class that is used to decouple the business logic between the REST API controller and the data access layer. I will only implement the basic CRUD method, and not all collections made available by the CRUD repository interface.

Its implementation, in our case, is very easy, and it seems like only a pass-through; in a real production use case, you can use the business logic operation, in order to adhere to the separation of duties pattern:

```
@Service
public class FootballPlayerService {

    @Autowired
    private FootballPlayerRepository repository;

    public Iterable<FootballPlayer> findAll() {
        return repository.findAll();
    }

    public FootballPlayer save(FootballPlayer entity) {
        return repository.save(entity);
    }

    public void deleteById(Integer id) {
        repository.deleteById(id);
    }

    public Optional<FootballPlayer> findById(Integer id) {
```

```
    return repository.findById(id);
    }

}
```

Now we will expose our services method by using a RESTful web service, as follows:

```
@RestController
@RequestMapping("/footballplayer")
public class FootballPlayerRESTController {

    @Autowired
    private FootballPlayerService service;

    @RequestMapping(method = RequestMethod.GET, produces =
"application/json")
    public Iterable<FootballPlayer> findAll() {
        return service.findAll();
    }

    @RequestMapping(value = "/save", method = RequestMethod.POST, produces
= "application/json")
    public FootballPlayer save(@RequestBody FootballPlayer entity) {
        return service.save(entity);
    }

    @RequestMapping(value = "/update/{id}", method = RequestMethod.PUT,
produces = "application/json")
    public FootballPlayer edit(@PathVariable Integer id, @RequestBody
FootballPlayer entity) {
        return service.save(entity);
    }

    @RequestMapping(value = "/delete/{id}", method = RequestMethod.DELETE,
produces = "application/json")
    public void delete(@PathVariable Integer id) {
        service.deleteById(id);
    }

    @RequestMapping(value = "/show/{id}", method = RequestMethod.GET,
produces = "application/json")
    public Optional<FootballPlayer> findById(@PathVariable Integer id) {
        return service.findById(id);
    }
}
```

As you can see, we have defined the following:

- The API paths
- The API parameters
- The producers and consumers payload types

Now we can invoke the API that retrieves the list of football players, as follows:

```
$ curl http://localhost:8080/footballplayer | json_pp
```

The output should be similar to the following (for convenience, we have only shown a portion of the code):

```
[
{
   "id":1,
   "name":"Gianluigi",
   "surname":"Buffon",
   "age":40,
   "team":"Paris Saint Germain",
   "position":"goalkeeper",
   "price":2
},
{
   "id":2,
   "name":"Manuel",
   "surname":"Neuer",
   "age":32,
   "team":"Bayern Munchen",
   "position":"goalkeeper",
   "price":35
},
{
   "id":3,
   "name":"Keylor",
   "surname":"Navas",
   "age":31,
   "team":"Real Madrid",
   "position":"goalkeeper",
   "price":18
},
...
]
```

Finally, we will create the JUnit test, in order to ensure that our APIs work properly.

Let's add the Maven dependencies, as follows:

```
<dependency>
    <groupId>org.springframework.boot</groupId>
    <artifactId>spring-boot-starter-test</artifactId>
    <scope>test</scope>
</dependency>
<dependency>
    <groupId>com.jayway.jsonpath</groupId>
    <artifactId>json-path</artifactId>
    <scope>test</scope>
</dependency>
```

As usual, I didn't specify the version, because it is automatically handled by the `spring-boot-starter-parent` BOM.

Next, I will build the test methods inside the class `com.packtpub.springboot.footballplayermicroservice.FootballPlayerMicroserviceApplicationTests`, which was created by the Spring Initializr utility.

The `test` class will look as follows:

```
@RunWith(SpringRunner.class)
@SpringBootTest(classes = FootballPlayerMicroserviceApplication.class,
webEnvironment = SpringBootTest.WebEnvironment.RANDOM_PORT)
@FixMethodOrder(MethodSorters.NAME_ASCENDING)
public class FootballPlayerMicroserviceApplicationTests {
    private final HttpHeaders headers = new HttpHeaders();

    private final TestRestTemplate restTemplate = new TestRestTemplate();

    @LocalServerPort
    private int port;

    @Test
    public void test_1_FindAll() throws IOException {
        System.out.println("findAll");
        HttpEntity<String> entity = new HttpEntity<>(null, headers);
        ResponseEntity<String> response =
            restTemplate.exchange(createURLWithPort("/footballplayer"),
                HttpMethod.GET, entity, String.class);

        assertThat(response.getStatusCode()).isEqualTo(HttpStatus.OK);

        JSONArray jsonArray = JsonPath.read(response.getBody(), "$.[*]");
        assertThat(23).isEqualTo(jsonArray.size());
```

```
    }

    @Test
    public void test_2_Create() {
        System.out.println("create");
        FootballPlayer player = new FootballPlayer("Mauro", "Vocale", 38,
"Juventus", "central
            midfielder", new BigInteger("100"));

        HttpEntity<FootballPlayer> entity = new HttpEntity<>(player,
headers);
        ResponseEntity<String> response = restTemplate.exchange(
            createURLWithPort("/footballplayer/save"),
                HttpMethod.POST, entity, String.class);

        assertThat(response.getStatusCode()).isEqualTo(HttpStatus.OK);
        assertThat(response.getBody()).isEqualTo(
"{\"id\":24,\"name\":\"Mauro\",\"surname\":\"Vocale\",\"age\":38,\"team\":\
"Juventus\",\"position\":\"central midfielder\",\"price\":100}");
    }
    ....
```

Let's analyze the most important sections of the class.

I will run the test suite using the `SpringRunner` class, as defined inside the `@RunWith` annotation. `SpringRunner` is an alias for the `SpringJUnit4ClassRunner` class, and it has the utilities needed to create the Spring context and perform the test.

I decided to implement an integration test, so I didn't mock anything; instead I called the real methods.

In order to do this, I needed to create a real Spring execution environment. Using the `@SpringBootTest` annotation, I set the class to launch (in our case `FootballPlayerMicroserviceApplication.class`), and a random port where the embedded servlet containers were executed.

Finally, I had to execute the test in a well-defined order, to avoid failures related to the absence of my test records. In order to do this, I set the `FixMethodOrder(MethodSorters.NAME_ASCENDING)`. This way, Spring executed the test based on the method's name. This is the reason for using an ascending number in the method's name.

Swagger documentation and OpenAPI

The microservice architecture will drive the enterprise architecture ecosystem to build a huge number of APIs, through which data can be exposed and communication can be implemented between the various microservices.

For this reason, it is essential to document the API, in order to facilitate its proper use by users. To standardize how REST APIs are described, a consortium of forward-looking industry experts created the **OpenAPI Initiative (OAI)**.

The OAI purpose is to create and evolve a vendor-neutral / standard description format.

SmartBear company donated the Swagger specification to the OAI in order to set it as the starting point of this open specification. For that reason, Swagger can be considered the de facto standard for API documentation.

Spring does not have a built-in mechanism to generate API documentation, but, as usual, the open source community, through frameworks such as SpringFox, makes this operation very easy.

SpringFox enable developers to create, automatically, a readable specifications for JSON APIs that there written using the Spring framework.

As I mentioned earlier, SpringFox is not a component of the Spring framework—for this reason it's not approved by the Spring framework contributors.

We will configure our simple microservice implementation, in order to document our APIs and build an easy portal that not only shows the API documentation, but will also make it available to users for testing.

The first operation that's needed to integrate Swagger and SpringFox is setting the relative dependencies in the Maven `pom.xml` file, as follows:

```xml
<dependency>
    <groupId>io.springfox</groupId>
    <artifactId>springfox-swagger2</artifactId>
    <version>2.9.2</version>
</dependency>
<dependency>
    <groupId>io.springfox</groupId>
    <artifactId>springfox-swagger-ui</artifactId>
    <version>2.9.2</version>
</dependency>
```

Then we will create a Docket bean in a Spring Boot configuration, to integrate Swagger 2 inside our application.

This way, SpringFox provides primary API configurations, with sensible defaults and convenient methods for configuration.

The following code shows the implementation of the bean:

```
@Configuration
@EnableSwagger2
public class SwaggerConfig extends WebMvcConfigurationSupport {
    @Bean
    public Docket api() {
        return new Docket(DocumentationType.SWAGGER_2).select()
            .apis(RequestHandlerSelectors.basePackage(
"com.packtpub.springboot.footballplayermicroservice.controller"))
            .paths(PathSelectors.any())
            .build();
    }
    @Override
    protected void addResourceHandlers(ResourceHandlerRegistry registry) {
        registry.addResourceHandler("swagger-ui.html")
            .addResourceLocations("classpath:/META-INF/resources/");
        registry.addResourceHandler("/webjars/**")
            .addResourceLocations("classpath:/META-
INF/resources/webjars/");
    }
}
```

We used the `@EnableSwagger2` annotation to enable Swagger support in the class. The key point of the class is the `api` method, which filters the controllers and methods being documented, using string predicates.

The `RequestHandlerSelectors.basePackage` predicate matches the `com.packtpub.springboot.footballplayermicroservice.controller` base package, to filter the API that will be documented. For the API path, I didn't set a filter, so I decided to expose all APIs.

Now you can run the application with the following command:

```
$ mvn spring-boot:run
```

You should be able to test the configuration by starting the app and pointing your browser to `http://localhost:8080/v2/api-docs`.

This way, you can retrieve the JSON representations of the documentation of your APIs.

The following code snippet shows a portion of what you will see in your browser:

```json
{
    "swagger":"2.0",
        "info":{
            "description":"Api Documentation",
            "version":"1.0",
            "title":"Api Documentation",
            "termsOfService":"urn:tos",
            "contact":{
            },
            "license":{
                "name":"Apache 2.0",
                "url":"http://www.apache.org/licenses/LICENSE-2.0"
            }
        },
        "host":"localhost:8080",
        "basePath":"/",
        "tags":[
        {
            "name":"football-player-rest-controller",
            "description":"Football Player REST Controller"
        }
        ],
        "paths":{
            "/footballplayer":{
                "get":{
                    "tags":[
                        "football-player-rest-controller"
                    ],
                    "summary":"findAll",
                    "operationId":"findAllUsingGET",
                    "produces":[
                        "application/json"
                    ],
                    "responses":{
                        "200":{
                            "description":"OK",
                            "schema":{
    "$ref":"#/definitions/Iterable«FootballPlayer»"
                            }
                        },
                        "401":{
                            "description":"Unauthorized"
                        },
                        "403":{
```

```
                            "description":"Forbidden"
                },
                "404":{
                    "description":"Not Found"
                }
            },
            "deprecated":false
        }
    },
    "/footballplayer/delete/{id}":{
    "delete":{
        "tags":[
            "football-player-rest-controller"
        ],
        "summary":"delete",
        "operationId":"deleteUsingDELETE",
        "produces":[
            "application/json"
        ],
        "parameters":[
        {
            "name":"id",
            "in":"path",
            "description":"id",
            "required":true,
            "type":"integer",
            "format":"int32"
        }
        ],
        "responses":{
            "200":{
                "description":"OK"
            },
            "204":{
                "description":"No Content"
            },
            "401":{
                "description":"Unauthorized"
            },
            "403":{
                "description":"Forbidden"
            }
        },
        "deprecated":false
    }
    },
    ....
```

In order to get readable, structured documentation, we will use the Swagger UI, a portal in which the users can see the full documentation for our APIs, and also test them.

If you invoke the `http://localhost:8080/swagger-ui.html` URL, you will see the generated documentation rendered by the Swagger UI, as follows:

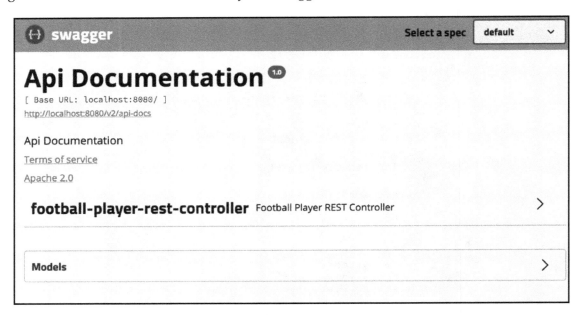

As you can see, Swagger 2 generated documentation related to the **football-player-rest-controller**, using the camel-case naming convention, to retrieve the words used in our class, and to get the **Models** used by our controller.

Before we start to use the newly constructed microservice, we will customize the header part of the console, in order to explain to our users what type of API documentation is described in the UI.

We will add the `metadata` API info to the `SwaggerConfig` class, as follows:

```
private ApiInfo metaData() {
    return new ApiInfoBuilder()
        .title("Spring Boot REST API")
        .description("\"Spring Boot REST API for Football Player
Microservice\"")
        .version("1.0.0")
        .license("Apache License Version 2.0")
        .licenseUrl("https://www.apache.org/licenses/LICENSE-2.0\"")
        .contact(new Contact("Mauro Vocale",
```

```
        "https://github.com/Hands-on-MSA-JakartaEE",
        "mauro.vocale@gmail.com"))
    .build();
}
```

Remember to also add the invocation of the `metaData` method to the pipeline builder, inside the `api` method of the `SwaggerConfig` class.

Now run the application again, as follows:

```
$ mvn spring-boot:run
```

You will now see more detailed information related to the organization that built and exposed the APIs:

Now it's time to customize our controller class. The goal is to describe the purpose of our operation endpoint. We will use the `@ApiOperation` annotation to describe the endpoint and its response type, as follows:

```
...
@ApiOperation(value = "View all available football players", response
= Iterable.class)
@ApiResponses(value = {
@ApiResponse(code = 200, message = "Successfully retrieved list"),
@ApiResponse(code = 404, message = "The resource you were trying to reach
is not found")
```

```java
    }
)
@RequestMapping(method = RequestMethod.GET, produces = "application/json")
public Iterable<FootballPlayer> findAll() {
    return service.findAll();
}

@ApiOperation(value = "Add a football player")
@RequestMapping(value = "/save", method = RequestMethod.POST, produces =
"application/json")
public FootballPlayer save(@RequestBody FootballPlayer entity) {
    return service.save(entity);
}

@ApiOperation(value = "Update a football player")
@RequestMapping(value = "/update/{id}", method = RequestMethod.PUT,
produces = "application/json")
public FootballPlayer edit(@PathVariable Integer id, @RequestBody
FootballPlayer entity) {
    return service.save(entity);
}

@ApiOperation(value = "Delete a football player")
@RequestMapping(value = "/delete/{id}", method = RequestMethod.DELETE,
produces = "application/json")
public void delete(@PathVariable Integer id) {
    service.deleteById(id);
}

@ApiOperation(value = "Search a football player with an ID", response =
FootballPlayer.class)
@RequestMapping(value = "/show/{id}", method = RequestMethod.GET, produces
= "application/json")
public Optional<FootballPlayer> findById(@PathVariable Integer id) {
    return service.findById(id);
}
...
```

In the browser, the output of the operation endpoints will look as follows:

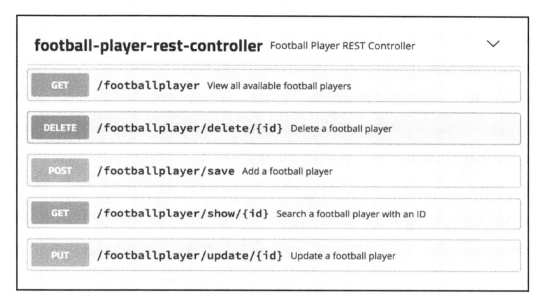

Now the user has a good idea of which APIs are exposed by our microservice application, as well as the target of each one.

Now let's start to test one of these. We will expand the **Search a football player with an ID** API, which has the following path—/footballplayer/show/{id}:

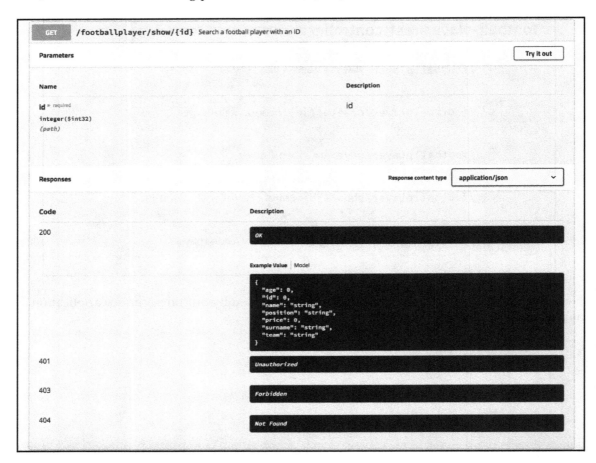

As you can see, Swagger shows you the following:

- The HTTP verb of the API, which is **GET.**
- A brief description of the API.
- The parameter needed to invoke the API (in our case, **Id**).
- The different types of response:
  - A JSON object representation
  - HTTP error codes

Any user who would like to use our API will be able to start to develop the code to interact with it, since they have all of the elements needed to do so.

To test the API, the user only needs to do the following:

1. Click on the **Try it out** button, as follows:

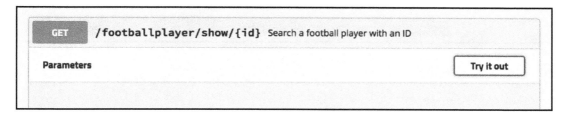

2. Insert the ID parameter and click on the **Execute** button:

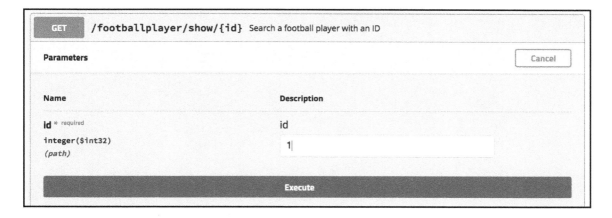

3. Finally, the user will see the response of the API call:

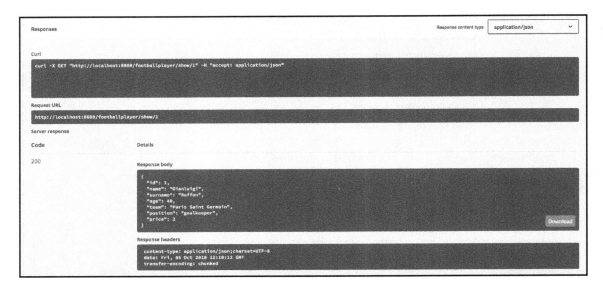

END

12
Building Microservices Using Vert.X

In Chapter 2, *Microservices and Reactive Architecture*, we spoke about reactive systems and reactive architectures, and how this approach differs from the traditional Java EE/Jakarta EE development model.

One of the main differences is that the reactive development model is event-driven and asynchronous by default. So, there is no way to implement I/O blocking code, and the usage of the kernel thread is very low.

In order to compare the different development choices made by the two architectural platforms, we will try to analyze how to realize, through Eclipse Vert.x, the same microservices developed in the previous chapters.

You will find the code described in this chapter in this GitHub repository https://github.com/PacktPublishing/Hands-On-Cloud-Native-Microservices-with-Jakarta-EE/tree/master/appendix-B.

Vert.x

Vert.x is an open source Eclipse toolkit used to build distributed and reactive systems that provides a flexible way to write applications that are lightweight and responsive through its implementations of Reactive Stream principles.

It is designed to be cloud-native: it allows many processes to run with very few resources (threads, CPU, and so on). In this way, Vert.x applications can use their CPU quotas more effectively in cloud environments. There is not unnecessary overhead caused by the creation of a great number of new threads.

It defines an asynchronous and non-blocking development model based on an event loop that handles requests, and avoids long waitings, on the client side, while the server side is stressed by a high number of invocations.

Since it's a toolkit and not a framework, Vert.x can be used as a typical third-party library, and you are free to choose the component needed for your target.

You can use Vert.x with multiple languages including Java, JavaScript, Groovy, Ruby, Ceylon, Scala, and Kotlin. In our example, we will use the Java language.

Maven settings

Apache Maven is probably the most common build management system used—we can consider this the de facto standard for build and package operations for Java applications. In this section, we will use it to build and package our application.

Vert.x is compatible with Apache Maven 3.2 or above and, in order to easily manage all Vert.x dependencies, in particular the right versions, you can set your Maven POM file to inherit from the `vertx-stack-depchain` BOM.

The following is an example of a `pom.xml` that you can use in your Vert.x application:

```xml
<?xml version="1.0" encoding="UTF-8"?>
<project xmlns="http://maven.apache.org/POM/4.0.0"
xmlns:xsi="http://www.w3.org/2001/XMLSchema-instance"
xsi:schemaLocation="http://maven.apache.org/POM/4.0.0
http://maven.apache.org/xsd/maven-4.0.0.xsd">
<modelVersion>4.0.0</modelVersion>

...

<properties>
   <java.version>1.8</java.version>
    <maven-compiler-plugin.version>3.5.1</maven-compiler-plugin.version>
    <maven-shade-plugin.version>2.4.3</maven-shade-plugin.version>
    <maven-surefire-plugin.version>2.21.0</maven-surefire-plugin.version>
    <exec-maven-plugin.version>1.5.0</exec-maven-plugin.version>
    <vertx.version>3.5.4</vertx.version>
    ...
</properties>

<dependencyManagement>
    <dependencies>
        <dependency>
            <groupId>io.vertx</groupId>
```

```xml
                <artifactId>vertx-stack-depchain</artifactId>
                <version>${vertx.version}</version>
                <type>pom</type>
                <scope>import</scope>
            </dependency>
        </dependencies>
    </dependencyManagement>

    <dependencies>
        ...
    </dependencies>

    <build>
        <pluginManagement>
            <plugins>
                <plugin>
                    <artifactId>maven-compiler-plugin</artifactId>
                    <version>3.5.1</version>
                    <configuration>
                        <source>1.8</source>
                        <target>1.8</target>
                    </configuration>
                </plugin>
            </plugins>
        </pluginManagement>
        <plugins>
            <plugin>
                <groupId>org.apache.maven.plugins</groupId>
                <artifactId>maven-shade-plugin</artifactId>
                <version>${maven-shade-plugin.version}</version>
                <executions>
                    <execution>
                        <phase>package</phase>
                        <goals>
                            <goal>shade</goal>
                        </goals>
                        <configuration>
                            <transformers>
                                <transformer
implementation="org.apache.maven.plugins.shade.resource.ManifestResourceTra
nsformer">
                                    <manifestEntries>
                                        <Main-Class>io.vertx.core.Launcher</Main-
Class>
                                        <Main-Verticle>${main.verticle}</Main-
Verticle>
                                    </manifestEntries>
                                </transformer>
```

```
                        <transformer
implementation="org.apache.maven.plugins.shade.resource.AppendingTransforme
r">
                            <resource>
                            META-
INF/services/io.vertx.core.spi.VerticleFactory
                            </resource>
                        </transformer>
                    </transformers>
                    <outputFile>
                    ${project.build.directory}/${project.artifactId}-
${project.version}-fat.jar
                    </outputFile>
                </configuration>
            </execution>
        </executions>
    </plugin>
    ...
    </plugins>
</build>
</project>
```

After that, as usual, you will be able to build and package your application with the following command:

```
$ mvn clean package
```

Gradle settings

Gradle is an open source build automation tool that uses scripts written in Groovy or Kotlin DSL. It is supported by the major IDEs, and you can run it using command-line interfaces or through a continuous integration server.

Once installed, you can create a new project or automatically convert an existing Maven project into a Gradle one, by launching the following command from your project's root:

```
$ gradle init
```

In order to use Vert.x in a Gradle project, you can create a Gradle file, such as the following one:

```
plugins {
    id 'java'
    id 'application'
    id 'com.github.johnrengelman.shadow' version '2.0.4'
}
```

```
ext {
    vertxVersion = '3.5.4'
    junitJupiterEngineVersion = '5.2.0'
}

repositories {
    mavenLocal()
    jcenter()
}

group = 'com.packtpub.vertx'
version = '1.0.0-SNAPSHOT'

sourceCompatibility = '1.8'
mainClassName = 'io.vertx.core.Launcher'

def mainVerticleName = 'com.packtpub.vertx.football-player-
microservice.MainVerticle'
def watchForChange = 'src/**/*'
def doOnChange = './gradlew classes'

dependencies {
    implementation "io.vertx:vertx-core:$vertxVersion"
    implementation "io.vertx:vertx-config:$vertxVersion"
...
}

shadowJar {
    classifier = 'fat'
    manifest {
        attributes 'Main-Verticle': mainVerticleName
    }
    mergeServiceFiles {
        include 'META-INF/services/io.vertx.core.spi.VerticleFactory'
    }
}
...
run {
    args = ['run', mainVerticleName, "--redeploy=$watchForChange", "--
launcher-
        class=$mainClassName", "--on-redeploy=$doOnChange"]
}

...
```

This snippet will add a declaration of the Vert.x version as an external dependency—in this way, you don't need to have a specific version as these are implicitly defined in the BOM file.

To build the executable JAR, you can execute the following command:

```
$ ./gradlew shadowJar
```

After that, you can run it by executing the following command:

```
$ java -jar build/libs/gradle-my-vertx-project.jar
```

Alternatively, you can execute the following Gradle command instead:

```
$ ./gradlew run
```

Building a football player microservice

In this section, I will implement the same football player microservice build that we saw in Chapter 4, *Building Microservices Using Thorntail*. I will analyze the details of the server-side layer of the application, (since the client layer remains the same, implemented using Angular 6).

The results will be a simple football player microservice that handles the football players' domain: it will expose CRUD APIs and will store and retrieve information using a PostgreSQL database.

You can complete the entire application build that we saw in Chapter 4, *Building Microservices Using Thorntail,* using the same approach that we will implement here.

To build the application, I will use the following tools, and for each one I will specify the information needed to install it:

- **Apache Maven 3.5.4**: https://maven.apache.org/install.html
- **JDK 1.8.0_171**: You are free to use Oracle JDK or OpenJDK, but we recommend OpenJDK (http://openjdk.java.net/install/)
- **Vert.x version 3.5.4**: We will describe the instructions to use this later
- **Docker Community Edition 18.06.1**: In order to easily install and use the different databases needed for our application (https://docs.docker.com/install/)

Project details

In this section, I will build the source code for our microservice. In order to do it, aside from the prerequisites described previously, I need PostgreSQL installed on the system. As I said previously, I use Docker to install and handle PostgreSQL. I'm using a macOS High Sierra as my working environment; if you have implemented the same project using Thorntail, as described in `Chapter 4`, *Building Microservices Using Thorntail*, feel free to skip this section. Otherwise, follow the instructions that describe how to install and run PostgreSQL in a Docker container.

Database installation and configuration

After installing Docker on your machine, it's time to run the containerized version of PostgreSQL. In order to do so, open a new terminal window and launch the following command:

```
$ docker run --name postgres_vertx -e POSTGRES_PASSWORD=postgresPwd -e
POSTGRES_DB=football_players_registry -d -p 5532:5432 postgres
```

This command triggers a pull from Docker's public registry for the PostgreSQL version labelled as the latest, downloading all the layers it needs to run the container on, as follows:

```
Unable to find image 'postgres:latest' locally
latest: Pulling from library/postgres
683abbb4ea60: Pull complete
c5856e38168a: Pull complete
c3e6f1ceebb0: Pull complete
3303bcd00128: Pull complete
ea95ff44bf6e: Pull complete
ea3f31f1e620: Pull complete
234873881fb2: Pull complete
f020aa822d21: Pull complete
27bad92d09a5: Pull complete
6849f0681f5a: Pull complete
a112faac8662: Pull complete
bc92d0ab9365: Pull complete
9e87959714b8: Pull complete
ac7c29b2bea7: Pull complete
Digest:
sha256:d99f15cb8d0f47f0a66274afe30102b5bb7a95464d1e25acb66ccf7bd7bd8479
Status: Downloaded newer image for postgres:latest
83812c6e76656f6abab5bf1f00f07dca7105d5227df3b3b66382659fa55b5077
```

After that, the PostgreSQL image is launched as a container. To verify it, you can launch the `$ docker ps -a` command, which gives you a list of the created containers and the relative status:

```
CONTAINER ID IMAGE COMMAND CREATED

1073daeefc52 postgres "docker-entrypoint.s..." Less than a second ago

STATUS PORTS NAMES

Up 4 seconds 0.0.0.0:5532->5432/tcp postgres_vertx
```

I had to split the command result over two lines in order to make it readable.

You can also check the container logs in order to retrieve information about the PostgreSQL status. Launch the following command:

```
$ docker logs -f 1073daeefc52
```

Here, `1073daeefc52` is the container ID. You should find the following information:

```
PostgreSQL init process complete; ready for start up.

2018-07-13 22:53:36.465 UTC [1] LOG: listening on IPv4 address "0.0.0.0",
port 5432
2018-07-13 22:53:36.466 UTC [1] LOG: listening on IPv6 address "::", port
5432
2018-07-13 22:53:36.469 UTC [1] LOG: listening on Unix socket
"/var/run/postgresql/.s.PGSQL.5432"
```

Now it's time to connect to the container in order to manage it. Launch the following command:

```
$ docker exec -it 1073daeefc52 bash
```

Here, `1073daeefc52` is the container ID. Now log in to the PostgreSQL with the following command:

```
$ psql -U postgres
```

Now you can interact with the database server:

```
psql (10.4 (Debian 10.4-2.pgdg90+1))
Type "help" for help.
postgres=#
```

You should be able to see the `football_players_registry` database that we created when creating the container. Run the `\l` command and verify the list of databases:

```
postgres=# \l
                                         List of databases
            Name                 |  Owner   | Encoding |  Collate    |
Ctype |   Access privileges
---------------------------------+----------+----------+-------------+---------
---+-----------------------
 football_players_registry | postgres | UTF8     | en_US.utf8 | en_US.utf8
|
 postgres                        | postgres | UTF8     | en_US.utf8 | en_US.utf8
|
 template0                       | postgres | UTF8     | en_US.utf8 | en_US.utf8
 | =c/postgres                   +
                                 |          |          |            |           |
postgres=CTc/postgres
 template1                       | postgres | UTF8     | en_US.utf8 | en_US.utf8
 | =c/postgres                   +
                                 |          |          |            |           |
postgres=CTc/postgres
(4 rows)
```

OK, it's time to create our simple table to host the football players' data. Connect to the `football_players` database with this command:

```
$ \connect football_players_registry
```

And create the table with the following command:

```
CREATE TABLE FOOTBALL_PLAYER(
ID SERIAL PRIMARY KEY NOT NULL,
NAME VARCHAR(50) NOT NULL,
SURNAME VARCHAR(50) NOT NULL,
AGE INT NOT NULL,
TEAM VARCHAR(50) NOT NULL,

POSITION VARCHAR(50) NOT NULL,
PRICE NUMERIC
);
```

Check the table structure with the following command:

```
$ \d+ football_player
```

You should see the following result:

```
football_players_registry=# \d+ football_player
                        Table "public.football_player"
  Column  | Type | Collation | Nullable | Default | Storage  | Stats target |
Description
----------+---------------------+----------+---------+---------+--------------------
-----------------------+----------+-------------+------------
 id       | integer |  | not null | nextval('football_player_id_seq'::regclass) |
plain    |            |
 name     | character varying(50) |  | not null |  | extended |            |
 surname  | character varying(50) |  | not null |  | extended |            |
 age      | integer |  | not null |  | plain |  |
 team     | character varying(50) |  | not null |  | extended |  |
 position | character varying(50) |  | not null |  | extended |    |
 price    | numeric |  |  |  | main |  |
Indexes:
        "football_player_pkey" PRIMARY KEY, btree (id)
```

Creating the source code

I have installed and configured everything necessary to create the microservice to manage the registry of players. Now it's time to write the code needed to expose our microservice APIs.

I use the Vert.x project generator utility, http://start.vertx.io/ , in order to get the project skeleton to work on. The microservice, as described earlier, will have to display APIs that allow us to perform CRUD operations.

To implement the microservice, I will use the following components:

- **Core**: As the name suggested it contains the core functionalities as the support for HTTP
- **Config**: Provides an extensible way to configure Vert.x applications
- **Web**: Toolkit that contains utilities required to build web applications and HTTP microservices
- **JDBC client**: This component enables developers to communicate with any JDBC-compliant database but with a different approach, the asynchronous API

We will use `com.packtpub.vertx` as the Maven **Group** name of the project, and `footballplayermicroservice` as the **Artifact**. Set these values in the project form generator as depicted in the following screenshot:

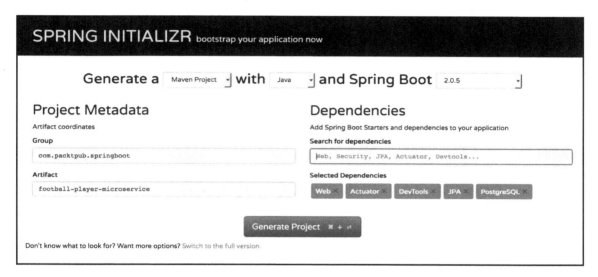

Click **Generate Project** to create and download a ZIP file with the project skeleton.

Unzip the file into a directory of your choice and open the Maven project with your favorite IDE (Eclipse, NetBeans, IntelliJ, and so on).

The core element of the project is the Maven `pom.xml` file, which contains all the dependencies needed to implement our microservice.

The project uses `vertx-stack-depchain` to correctly manage `dependencyManagement`:

```
<dependencyManagement>
    <dependencies>
        <dependency>
            <groupId>io.vertx</groupId>
            <artifactId>vertx-stack-depchain</artifactId>
            <version>${vertx.version}</version>
            <type>pom</type>
            <scope>import</scope>
        </dependency>
    </dependencies>
</dependencyManagement>
```

We also need to add the PostgreSQL JDBC driver dependency in the Maven `pom.xml` file in order to connect to the database used to store the football player information:

```
<dependency>
    <groupId>org.postgresql</groupId>
    <artifactId>postgresql</artifactId>
    <version>9.4.1212</version>
</dependency>
```

Now it's time to launch the first build with this command:

```
$ mvn clean package
```

After that, you can test that your application is up and running with the following command:

```
$ java -jar
$PROJECT_HOME/footballplayermicroservice/target/footballplayermicroservice-
1.0.0-SNAPSHOT-fat.jar
```

Here, the `$PROJECT_HOME` variable is the path where you have to unzip the project generated by the Vert.x project generator utility. You will visualize an output like this:

```
HTTP server started on http://localhost:8080
Oct 11, 2018 10:41:06 AM
io.vertx.core.impl.launcher.commands.VertxIsolatedDeployer
INFO: Succeeded in deploying verticle
```

Put the `http://localhost:8080` URL into your browser, and you will see this message: **Hello from Vert.x!**

Now let's stop our application using the *Ctrl + C* command, and start to update our project.

The data access layer

Vert.x doesn't have a module to use JPA specifications, so we will not create an entity.

Instead, we need to have an object that transfers the attributes of a football player from and to a database. For this reason, we create a data transfer object, named `FootballPlayer`, in order to do this:

```
package com.packtpub.vertx.footballplayermicroservice.model;

import java.io.Serializable;

import java.math.BigInteger;
```

```java
public class FootballPlayer implements Serializable {

    private static final long serialVersionUID = -92346781936044228L;

    private Integer id;

    private String name;

    private String surname;

    private int age;

    private String team;

    private String position;

    private BigInteger price;

    public FootballPlayer() {
    }

    public FootballPlayer(Integer id, String name, String surname, int age,
        String team, String position, BigInteger price) {
        this.id = id;
        this.name = name;
        this.surname = surname;
        this.age = age;
        this.team = team;
        this.position = position;
        this.price = price;
    }

    // Getters and Setters
    ...
}
```

The second step is to create a configuration file with the parameters needed to establish a JDBC connection with the database. In the `src/main/conf` directory, put a file named `my-application-conf.json` with the following parameters:

- `url`: The JDBC URL to connect to the database
- `driver_class`: The JDBC driver needed to use JDBC API
- `user`: The username used to connect to the database
- `password`: The password used to connect to the database

This is a simple scenario—in a production environment, you must mask the JDBC credentials.

The following is the snapshot of the file:

```
{
    "url": "jdbc:postgresql://localhost:5532/football_players_registry",
    "driver_class": "org.postgresql.Driver",
    "user": "postgres",
    "password": "postgresPwd"
}
```

Then we will create, in the `src/main/resources` folder, two files, `schema.sql` and `data.sql`, in order to create the required table structure and preload data into our database.

You will find the code in the GitHub repository.

The final step is to build a class responsible for interacting with the database in order to perform the following operations:

- Create database tables
- Preload a set of data
- CRUD operations plus the `findAll` method

The following snippet shows our class:

```
public class FootballPlayerDAO {

    public Future<FootballPlayer> insert(SQLConnection connection,
        FootballPlayer footballPlayer, boolean closeConnection) {
        Future<FootballPlayer> future = Future.future();
        String sql = "INSERT INTO football_player (name, surname, age,
team,
            position, price) VALUES (?, ?, ?, ?, ?, ?)";

        connection.updateWithParams(sql, new
JsonArray().add(footballPlayer.getName())
            .add(footballPlayer.getSurname())
            .add(footballPlayer.getAge()).add(footballPlayer.getTeam())
            .add(footballPlayer.getPosition())
            .add(footballPlayer.getPrice().intValue()),
            ar -> {
                if (closeConnection) {
                    connection.close();
                }
```

```
                future.handle(ar.map(res -> new
FootballPlayer(res.getKeys().getInteger(0),
                    footballPlayer.getName(), footballPlayer.getSurname(),
                    footballPlayer.getAge(), footballPlayer.getTeam(),
                    footballPlayer.getPosition(),
footballPlayer.getPrice()))));
            });
        return future;
    }

    public Future<SQLConnection> connect(JDBCClient jdbc) {
        Future<SQLConnection> future = Future.future();
        jdbc.getConnection(ar -> future.handle(ar.map(c -> c.setOptions(
            new SQLOptions().setAutoGeneratedKeys(true))))
        );
        return future;
    }

...

}
```

As you can see, Vert.x uses a different approach for database interaction. The schema is different from the traditional one that you usually use with the Java JDBC API.

The following is globally the traditional approach:

```
String sql = "SELECT * FROM MY_TABLE";
ResultSet rs = stmt.executeQuery(sql);
```

This then becomes as follows:

```
connection.query("SELECT * FROM Products", result -> {
// do something with the result
});
```

In Vert.x, but also in general in all reactive architectures, all operations are asynchronous and they are handled by the Future class.

The RESTful web service

In this section, we will explore how to expose the RESTful API.

The main unit in Vert.x is the verticle—using this class, we will be able to handle, always in an asynchronous way, requests for our data.

We will create two classes: a `helper` needed to build the responses associated with specific HTTP verbs, and the `verticle` class, which exposes the API.

The `ActionHelper` class is an easy utility class that helps us build responses:

```java
public class ActionHelper {
    /**
     * Returns a handler writing the received {@link AsyncResult} to the routing
     * context and setting the HTTP status to the given status.
     *
     * @param context the routing context
     * @param status the status
     * @return the handler
     */
    private static <T> Handler<AsyncResult<T>>
writeJsonResponse(RoutingContext context, int
        status) {
        return ar -> {
            if (ar.failed()) {
                if (ar.cause() instanceof NoSuchElementException) {
context.response().setStatusCode(404).end(ar.cause().getMessage());
                } else {
                    context.fail(ar.cause());
                }
            } else {
context.response().setStatusCode(status).putHeader("content-type",
                    "application/json;charset=utf-8")
                    .end(Json.encodePrettily(ar.result()));
            }
        };
    }

    public static <T> Handler<AsyncResult<T>> ok(RoutingContext rc) {
        return writeJsonResponse(rc, 200);
    }

    public static <T> Handler<AsyncResult<T>> created(RoutingContext rc) {
        return writeJsonResponse(rc, 201);
    }

    public static Handler<AsyncResult<Void>> noContent(RoutingContext rc)
{
        return ar -> {
            if (ar.failed()) {
                if (ar.cause() instanceof NoSuchElementException) {
rc.response().setStatusCode(404).end(ar.cause().getMessage());
                } else {
```

```
                            rc.fail(ar.cause());
                        }
                } else {
                    rc.response().setStatusCode(204).end();
                }
            };
        }

        private ActionHelper() {
        }
    }
```

This class uses an instance of RoutingContext to handle requests and build a response, with HTTP return code and an object representation, based on the HTTP verb used by the request.

This helper class will be used by the verticle class, in our case FootballPlayerVerticle, which implements routes and exposes APIs.

Let's start analyzing it. In the first part of code, we will perform the following:

1. Create an HTTP server that listens to the 8080 port.

2. Make it available to handle requests to the path to our APIs.

3. Also, define a way to create our database tables, and preload data:

```
public class FootballPlayerVerticle extends AbstractVerticle {

    private JDBCClient jdbc;

    @Override
    public void start(Future<Void> fut) {
        // Create a router object.
        Router router = Router.router(vertx);

        // Point 2
        router.route("/").handler(routingContext -> {
            HttpServerResponse response = routingContext.response();
            response.putHeader("content-type", "text/html")
            .end("<h1>Football Player Vert.x 3 microservice
application</h1>");
        });

        router.get("/footballplayer").handler(this::getAll);
        router.get("/footballplayer/show/:id").handler(this::getOne);
        router.route("/footballplayer*").handler(BodyHandler.create());
```

```
        router.post("/footballplayer/save").handler(this::addOne);
router.delete("/footballplayer/delete/:id").handler(this::deleteOne);
        router.put("/footballplayer/update/:id").handler(this::updateOne);

        // Point 3
        ConfigStoreOptions fileStore = new
ConfigStoreOptions().setType("file")
            .setFormat("json").setConfig(new JsonObject().put("path",
                "src/main/conf/my-application-conf.json"));

        ConfigRetrieverOptions options = new
ConfigRetrieverOptions().addStore(fileStore);
        ConfigRetriever retriever = ConfigRetriever.create(vertx, options);

        // Start sequence:
        // 1 - Retrieve the configuration
        // |- 2 - Create the JDBC client
        // |- 3 - Connect to the database (retrieve a connection)
        // |- 4 - Create table if needed
        // |- 5 - Add some data if needed
        // |- 6 - Close connection when done
        // |- 7 - Start HTTP server
        // |- 8 - we are done!
        ConfigRetriever.getConfigAsFuture(retriever).compose(config -> {
            jdbc = JDBCClient.createShared(vertx, config, "Players-List");
            FootballPlayerDAO dao = new FootballPlayerDAO();
            return dao.connect(jdbc).compose(connection -> {
                Future<Void> future = Future.future();
createTableIfNeeded(connection).compose(this::createSomeDataIfNone)
                    .setHandler(x -> {
                    connection.close();
                    future.handle(x.mapEmpty());
                });
                return future;
            })

            // Point 1
            .compose(v -> createHttpServer(config, router));
            })
        .setHandler(fut);
    }

    // Point 1
    private Future<Void> createHttpServer(JsonObject config, Router router)
{
        Future<Void> future = Future.future();
        vertx.createHttpServer().requestHandler(router::accept)
            .listen(config.getInteger("HTTP_PORT", 8080),
```

```
                 res -> future.handle(res.mapEmpty()));
        return future;
    }

    // Point 3
    private Future<SQLConnection> createTableIfNeeded(SQLConnection
connection) {
        FootballPlayerDAO dao = new FootballPlayerDAO();
        return dao.createTableIfNeeded(vertx.fileSystem(), connection);
    }

    // Point 3
    private Future<SQLConnection> createSomeDataIfNone(SQLConnection
connection) {
        FootballPlayerDAO dao = new FootballPlayerDAO();
        return dao.createSomeDataIfNone(vertx.fileSystem(), connection);
    }


    ...

}
```

In the code described previously, I have set the `// Point X` comment to highlight where we have implemented the points described in the preceding list. As usual, all operations are asynchronous and return a `Future` type.

For all paths handled by the HTTP server, there is a method that is responsible for intercepting the request, contacting the database, performing the operation, and returning a response.

For example: the invocation to the `/footballplayer/show/:id` path is mapped in this way:

```
router.get("/footballplayer/show/:id").handler(this::getOne);
```

That means that there is a method, `getOne`, which will handle the request and return a response:

```
private void getOne(RoutingContext rc) {
    String id = rc.pathParam("id");
    FootballPlayerDAO dao = new FootballPlayerDAO();
    dao.connect(jdbc).compose(connection -> dao.queryOne(connection,
id)).setHandler(ok(rc));
}
```

The behaviour is simple: the DAO class will query the database, using the queryOne method, and, using the ok method of our utility helper class, will build a response with the 200 HTTP code and the JSON representation of our football player.

Let's try to do it—start the application using this command:

```
$ java -jar $PROJECT_HOME/target/footballplayermicroservice-1.0.0-SNAPSHOT-fat.jar
```

And then invoke the API:

```
$ curl http://localhost:8080/footballplayer/show/1 | json_pp
```

You will retrieve your football player:

```
{
    "team" : "Paris Saint Germain",
    "id" : 1,
    "name" : "Gianluigi",
    "age" : 40,
    "price" : 2,
    "surname" : "Buffon",
    "position" : "goalkeeper"
}
```

Creating the test code

We have implemented our microservice, but it is extremely important to test it in order to improve its quality and make future code evolution easier.

Vert.x gives developers the opportunity to easily integrate JUnit in order to implement a strong test suite. In our example, we will implement an integration test in order to verify the good behaviour of our code, and to see it in action.

To use JUnit, you need to have these dependencies in your Maven pom.xml:

```
<dependency>
    <groupId>io.vertx</groupId>
    <artifactId>vertx-unit</artifactId>
    <scope>test</scope>
</dependency>
<dependency>
    <groupId>io.vertx</groupId>
    <artifactId>vertx-junit5</artifactId>
    <scope>test</scope>
</dependency>
```

```
<dependency>
    <groupId>org.junit.platform</groupId>
    <artifactId>junit-platform-launcher</artifactId>
    <version>${junit-platform-launcher.version}</version>
    <scope>test</scope>
</dependency>
```

Then we should be ready to create our `test` class to verify the results of our APIs:

```
@ExtendWith(VertxExtension.class)
public class TestFootballPlayerVerticle {

    @BeforeEach
    void deploy_verticle(Vertx vertx, VertxTestContext testContext) {
        vertx.deployVerticle(new FootballPlayerVerticle(), testContext.
        succeeding(id -> testContext.completeNow()));
    }

    @Test
    @DisplayName("Should start a Web Server on port 8080 and the GET all
API"
        + "returns an array of 24 elements")
    @Timeout(value = 10, timeUnit = TimeUnit.SECONDS)
    void findAll(Vertx vertx, VertxTestContext testContext) throws
Throwable {
        System.out.println("FIND ALL ****************");
        vertx.createHttpClient().getNow(8080, "localhost",
"/footballplayer",
        response -> testContext.verify(() -> {
        assertTrue(response.statusCode() == 200);
        response.bodyHandler(body -> {
            JsonArray array = new JsonArray(body);
            assertTrue(23 == array.size());
            testContext.completeNow();
            });
        }));
    }

    @Test
    @DisplayName(
        "Should start a Web Server on port 8080 and, using the POST API,"
        + "insert a new football player")
    @Timeout(value = 10, timeUnit = TimeUnit.SECONDS)
    public void create(Vertx vertx, VertxTestContext context) {
        System.out.println("CREATE ****************");
        final String json = Json.encodePrettily(new FootballPlayer(null,
"Mauro", "Vocale", 38,
                "Juventus", "central midfielder", new BigInteger("100")));
```

```
        final String length = Integer.toString(json.length());

        vertx.createHttpClient().post(8080, "localhost",
"/footballplayer/save")
            .putHeader("content-type", "application/json")
            .putHeader("content-length", length)
            .handler(response -> {
                assertTrue(response.statusCode() == 201);
                assertTrue(response.headers().get("content-
type").contains("application/json"));
                response.bodyHandler(body -> {
                    final FootballPlayer footballPlayer =
Json.decodeValue(
                        body.toString(), FootballPlayer.class);
assertTrue(footballPlayer.getName().equalsIgnoreCase("Mauro"));
                    assertTrue(footballPlayer.getAge() == 38);
                    assertTrue(footballPlayer.getId() != null);
                    context.completeNow();
                });
            }).write(json).end();
    }
    ...

}
```

To run our test, we used the `VertxExtension` class, which allows the injection of Vert.x and `VertxTestContext` parameters, as well as an automatic life cycle on the `VertxTestContext` instance.

With the `@BeforeEach` annotation, we set our routine to execute deployment of the `verticle` class before the execution on every single test, in order to have the data needed for their execution.

Then, in every method, we created an HTTP client, using the `vertx.createHttpClient()` method, against which we perform the HTTP verb operation (GET, POST, PUT, or DELETE).

We set the parameter needed for the invocation and verified the assertion.

Now you are ready to launch the test with this command:

```
$ mvn test
```

You will see that all tests have passed:

```
[INFO] Tests run: 5, Failures: 0, Errors: 0, Skipped: 0, Time elapsed:
1.677 s - in
com.packtpub.vertx.footballplayermicroservice.TestFootballPlayerVerticle
[INFO]
[INFO] Results:
[INFO]
[INFO] Tests run: 5, Failures: 0, Errors: 0, Skipped: 0
[INFO]
[INFO] -----------------------------------------------------------------
----
[INFO] BUILD SUCCESS
[INFO] -----------------------------------------------------------------
----
```

The football player microservice – Vert.x + RxJava

We have implemented our football player microservice in order to make it asynchronous and non-I/O-blocking. But we can obtain something more if we use Vert.x and RxJava together.

RxJava is a great implementation of Rx for the Java programming language, and gives you some features that combine the power of Vert.x `Future` with the benefits of Rx operators.

In order to use RxJava, you must set the following dependency in your Maven `pom.xml`:

```
<dependency>
    <groupId>io.vertx</groupId>
    <artifactId>vertx-rx-java2</artifactId>
</dependency>
```

Let's start with an easy example.

We can create three new classes that implement the same methods described earlier, but in a reactive manner:

- `FootballPlayerReactiveVerticle`
- `ActionHelperReactive`
- `FootballPlayerReactiveDAO`

In the `FootballPlayerVerticle` class, we have created the method needed to build the HTTP server that handles requests to our APIs:

```
private Future<Void> createHttpServer(JsonObject config, Router router) {
    Future<Void> future = Future.future();
vertx.createHttpServer().requestHandler(router::accept).listen(config.getIn
teger("HTTP_PORT",
        8080),res -> future.handle(res.mapEmpty()));
    return future;
}
```

We modify the `FootballPlayerReactiveVerticle` class in order to return an Rx `Completable` class, which is a stream that indicates its completion:

```
private Completable createHttpServerReactive(JsonObject config, Router
router) {
    return vertx.createHttpServer().requestHandler(router::accept)
        .rxListen(config.getInteger("HTTP_PORT", 8080)).toCompletable();
}
```

Another important element is the way we connect to the database.

In our DAO, we have created the following method to do this:

```
public Future<SQLConnection> connect(JDBCClient jdbc) {
    Future<SQLConnection> future = Future.future();
    jdbc.getConnection(ar -> future.handle(ar.map(c -> c.setOptions(
        new SQLOptions().setAutoGeneratedKeys(true))))
    );
    return future;
}
```

In the `FootballPlayerReactiveDAO` class, we can change the method to return an Rx `Single` instead of a `Future`. A `Single` is like an object of `Observable`, but instead of emitting a series of values, it emits one value or an error notification. The following is the revisited method:

```
public Single<SQLConnection> connectReactive(JDBCClient jdbc) {
    return jdbc.rxGetConnection().map(c -> c.setOptions(new
        SQLOptions().setAutoGeneratedKeys(true)));
}
```

All interactions will be done in a reactive manner: for example, to read the file that contains the instructions for creating database tables and populate them, we can use `rxReadFile` from the `FileSystem` class:

```
public Single<SQLConnection> createTableIfNeeded(FileSystem fileSystem,
SQLConnection connection) {
    return fileSystem.rxReadFile("schema.sql").map(Buffer::toString)
.flatMapCompletable(connection::rxExecute).toSingleDefault(connection);
}

public Single<SQLConnection> createSomeDataIfNone(FileSystem fileSystem,
SQLConnection
    connection) {
    return connection.rxQuery("SELECT * FROM football_player").flatMap(rs
-> {
        if (rs.getResults().isEmpty()) {
            return fileSystem.rxReadFile("data.sql")
                .map(Buffer::toString)
                .flatMapCompletable(connection::rxExecute)
                .toSingleDefault(connection);
        } else {
            return Single.just(connection);
        }
    });
}
```

All the classes used in the reactive version of our implementation belong to the `io.vertx.reactivex` package.

Also, the method needed to perform CRUD operations can be revisited in a reactive manner. For example, the `update` method can be rewritten in this way:

```
public Single<FootballPlayer> update(SQLConnection connection, String id,
FootballPlayer
    footballPlayer) {
    String sql = "UPDATE football_player SET name = ?, surname = ?, age =
?, team = ?, position =
        ?, price = ? WHERE id = ?";
    return connection.rxUpdateWithParams(sql, new JsonArray().add(
        footballPlayer.getName()).add(footballPlayer.getSurname())
            .add(footballPlayer.getAge()).add(footballPlayer.getTeam())
            .add(footballPlayer.getPosition()).add(footballPlayer.
                getPrice().intValue()).add(Integer.valueOf(id)))
            .map(res -> new FootballPlayer(res.getKeys().getInteger(0),
                footballPlayer.getName(), footballPlayer.getSurname(),
                footballPlayer.getAge(), footballPlayer.getTeam(),
                footballPlayer.getPosition(), footballPlayer.getPrice()))
```

```
                    .doFinally(() -> {
                        connection.close();
        });
    }
```

The main difference from the version implemented in `FootballPlayerDAO` is the use of
`rxUpdateWithParams`, which will execute the SQL `UPDATE` operation and return a `Single`
object instead of a `Future`, closing the JDBC connection at the end of the method.

The final pipeline to build the HTTP server, using the configurations defined in the `Config`
files, which must be able to handle our APIs, is as follows:

```
retriever.rxGetConfig().doOnSuccess(config -> jdbc =
JDBCClient.createShared(vertx,
    config, "My-Reading-List"))
    .flatMap(config -> dao.connect(jdbc)
    .flatMap(connection -> this.createTableIfNeeded(connection)
    .flatMap(this::createSomeDataIfNone)
    .doAfterTerminate(connection::close))
    .map(x -> config))
    .flatMapCompletable(config -> createHttpServer(config, router))
    .subscribe(CompletableHelper.toObserver(fut));
```

I used the `flatMap` method to concatenate the operations, and the `doOnSuccess` method to
receive the item from the observed stream and implement logic related to them.

The key part of the pipeline is the `subscribe` method: if it's not invoked, nothing will
happen since streams are lazy.

Other Books You May Enjoy

If you enjoyed this book, you may be interested in these other books by Packt:

Java EE 8 Microservices
Kamalmeet Singh et al.

ISBN: 978-1-78847-514-3

- Build microservices from the ground up with Java EE 8
- Implement and deploy microservices with Spring Boot
- Develop reactive pipelines for asynchronous communication
- Use caching mechanisms and JSON Web Token (JWT) to create scalable and secure microservices
- Empower microservices with the Micro Profile effort and implement health checks, fault tolerance, and monitoring mechanisms
- Use containers to build and deploy microservices
- Create contract-first documentation with Swagger and API Blueprint

Spring 5.0 Microservices - Second Edition
Rajesh R V

ISBN: 978-1-78712-768-5

- Familiarize yourself with the microservices architecture and its benefits
- Find out how to avoid common challenges and pitfalls while developing microservices
- Use Spring Boot and Spring Cloud to develop microservices
- Handle logging and monitoring microservices
- Leverage Reactive Programming in Spring 5.0 to build modern cloud native applications
- Manage internet-scale microservices using Docker, Mesos, and Marathon
- Gain insights into the latest inclusion of Reactive Streams in Spring and make applications more resilient and scalable

Leave a review - let other readers know what you think

Please share your thoughts on this book with others by leaving a review on the site that you bought it from. If you purchased the book from Amazon, please leave us an honest review on this book's Amazon page. This is vital so that other potential readers can see and use your unbiased opinion to make purchasing decisions, we can understand what our customers think about our products, and our authors can see your feedback on the title that they have worked with Packt to create. It will only take a few minutes of your time, but is valuable to other potential customers, our authors, and Packt. Thank you!

Index

www.ingramcontent.com/pod-product-compliance
Lightning Source LLC
Chambersburg PA
CBHW080617060326
40690CB00021B/4725